The Underground Railroad
in Illinois

To the Students at Meridian
Middle School,

Here, at last, is the
book you've been wait-
ing for. I enjoyed
being at your school
and know you will
enjoy this book.

Jennette Tilley Turner

3-16-01

Other titles by Glennette Tilley Turner

Follow in their Footsteps
(Dutton/Cobblehill)

Take a Walk in Their Shoes
(Dutton/Cobblehill)

Lewis Howard Latimer
(Silver Burdett Press)

Running for Our Lives
(Holiday House)

The Underground Railroad in DuPage County Illinois
(Newman)

Surprise for Mrs. Burns
(Albert Whitman)

The Underground Railroad in Illinois

BY

Glennette Tilley Turner

INTRODUCTION BY

Dr. Juliet E.K. Walker

NEWMAN EDUCATIONAL PUBLISHING
GLEN ELLYN, ILLINOIS

In memory of my mother
PHYLLIS JONES TILLEY
a courageous, dynamic role model who inspired
and supported me through the writing of this book.

Dedicated To:
BLANCHE AND BRENDA ELLIOTT

ALBERT HARRIS

DARWIN WALTON

IDA CRESS

INEZ GLEAVES

JIM SMITH

JOYCE BREISETH

SADIE WARREN

PHEBE JACOBSEN

VINCENT DEFOREST

RACHEL JEAN MEEHAN

MADELINE STRATTON-MORRIS

"You work and toil and earn bread and I'll eat it. No matter in what shape it comes, whether from the mouth of a king who seeks to bestride his people of his own nation and live by the fruit of their labor, or from one race of men as an apology for enslaving another race, it is the same tyrannical principle."

Abraham Lincoln describing slavery during
the Lincoln-Douglas Debate in Alton, Illinois, October 15, 1858.

Credits

EDITING:	Darwin Walton and Barbie Campbell
CONTENT CONSULTANTS:	James Terry Ransom, Sr. and Charlotte Johnson
RESOURCE CONSULTANTS:	Michael Flug and Addie Harris
DESIGN:	Joeffrey Trimmingham
TYPESETTING:	Valerie Govan, Nevin Govan and Paitra Russell
PROOFREADING:	Amy Martin, Nancy Wolff, Jackie McQueen and David Davenport
PHOTOGRAPHY:	Lynard M. Jones
COVER ART:	Jean Kuhn and Mark Schram
LINE DRAWINGS:	Dorothy Kennard and Parker Linehart
WOODCUT:	Dr. Margaret Burroughs
INDEXING:	Sadie Flucas and Dorletta Esjean Payton

OWEN LOVEJOY

Courtesy of the DuSable Museum of African American History

Contents

GRAUE MILL

Acknowledgements

Special thanks and acknowledgements to those who provided encouragement, information, leads, transportation, or materials. AAUW, Abraham Lincoln Bookstore, Mr. Robert Henry Adams, Mrs. R. Adams, Mr. E. C. Alft, Mrs. Yvonne Luckett Almo, Members of Alpha Kappa Alpha, Alpha Kappa Delta, Mr. Fred Anderson, Ms. J. A. Anderson, Mr. Jerry Anderson, ASALH, Miss Mehret Asgedom,Ms. Marita Axley, Mr. James Ayars, Mr. Warren Ballard, Mr. Everett Barlow, Miss Elma Barnes, Mrs. Ruby Barnett, Mrs. Shirley Beal, Mr. and Mrs. Bill Beebe, Mr. John Bennett, Mr. Gunnar Benson, Mrs. P. Bickhaus, Mr. Glenn Biertitz, Big Woods Congregational Church, Ms. Alice Biggers, Black Student Union of MacMurray College, Mrs. Estelle Black, The Black Literary Umbrella, Mrs. Jane Blakely, Mr. and Mrs. Talkeaus Blank, Dr. Charles L. Blockson, Ms. Amy Blue, Mrs. Cleo Boger, Mrs. Mable Bradshaw, Mr. and Mrs. Jerry Bradshaw, Mrs. Helen Branch, Dr. and Mrs. Chris Breiseth, Mrs. Joyce Breiseth, Mrs. Bright, Mr. Ron Brinkman, Mr. Joe Eddie Brown, Mrs. Alice Browning, Mrs. Jerry Brunton, Mr. DennisBuck, Mrs. Janet Buckner, Mrs. Larman Buckner, Major Edgar Bundy, Dr. Margaret Burroughs, Dr. Tony Burroughs, Ms. Eleanor H. Bussell, Cairo Public Library, Mrs. Calacci, Mrs. Vivian Caldwell, Mr. and Mrs. Carney, Miss D. Carver, Mrs. Cheryl Chapman, Mr. Jim Charleton, Mrs. Cherry, Mr. Mark Cherry, Chicago Area School Librarians, Mrs. Oliver Chitty, Ms. Theresa Christopher, Dr. Walter Coffey, Levi Coffin House, Mr. Andrew Coiley, Mrs. Rebecca Coiley, College of DuPage Library, Mrs. Jean Condon, Mr. Alden Congrave, Congregational Church of Batavia, Mrs. Laura Conley, Mrs. Ruth Cording, Ms. Rosalin Cornelia, Mr. John Costerisan, Mr. Richard Crabb, Mr. and Mrs. Charles Crutcher, The D. A. R., Mr. Robert Dalton, Ms. Sharon Darling, Mr. Abraham Davis, Mrs. Doris Davis, Dr. Nancy Dawson, Delta Kappa Gamma, Mrs. Ruth Deter, Ms. Lois Dixon, Dr. James Dorsey, Mrs. Charles Dugan, DuPage Historical Museum, DuPage Writers Club, Mrs. Margaret Dutton, Mrs. Carolyn Eastwood, Mrs. Sherwood Eddy, Mrs. Jessie Edell, Mrs. Mary Edmond, Ms. Joan Edwards, Mr. Sherwood Edwards, Mrs. Marge Edwards, Mrs. Blanche Elliot, Mr. and Mrs. H. Erickson, Mrs. Pauline Ericson, Ms.Linda Evans, Mr. Eugene Feldman, Mrs. Connie Fetzer, Miss Grace Finch, Mr. Herman Fischer, Mr. Robert Fitzgerald, Mr. Michael Flug, Mr. and Mrs. Bill Fontville, Ms. Elizabeth Fuller, Ms. Jane Gallegos, Mayor Gamon, Mrs. Lucia Gates, Ms. Marie Gecik, Mrs. Gerndt, Mrs. Martha Gettinger, Mr. James Getz, Mrs. Evelyn Goetz, Mrs. Liza Goldwasser, Mr. George Goodrich, Mrs. Jane Grassman, The Greater Alton Convention and Tourism Bureau, Graue Mill and Museum, Ms. Elaine Graybill, Mrs. Dora Griffin, Dr. Lucille Gufstason, Judge William Guild, Mr. John Gunser, Bart Halleman, Mrs. H. V. B. Halliburton, Mr. Fidepe H. Hammurabi, The Horace Hardy Family, Vivian G. Harsh Room of Carter G. Woodson Regional Library, Mrs. Hart, Mrs. Jean Hastings, Mrs. Pat Haughton, Mrs. Jane Heckman, Mrs. C. Hedgley, Ms. Mabel Heins, Mr. W. Helms, Mr. and Mrs. Hendrickson, Ms. Rosa Hernandez, Mr. John Hesterman, the Reverends Higgenbotton, Mrs. Louise Hines, Mrs. Hipple, Mrs. Betty Hollingsworth, Ms. Pat Holm,

Mrs. Ann M. Holstrom, Mrs. Barbara Howard, Mrs. Shirley Howard, Mrs. Betty Hurst, International Black Writers Conference, Ms. Nalo Jackson, Mrs. Queen Esther Jackson, Mrs, Phebe Jacobsen, Ms. Erica James, Mr. David Janes, Mr. Vernon Jarrett, Mrs. Charlotte Johnson, Mrs. Jean Jones, Mr. Bob Jordan, Mr. Donald Joyce, Mrs. Percy Julian, Ms. Sharyn Kane, Mrs. Phyllis Kelley, Mrs. Marion G. Kelliher, Mrs. M. Kennan, Mr. Lawrence Kiner, Ms. L. Kreyminski, Mrs. Jean Kuhn, Ms. Judy Kuzel, Mr. Carl Landrum, Mrs. Richard Larson, Dr. Hugo Leaming, Ms. Elizabeth Leech, Mrs. L. Lehman, Mr. Keith Letsche, Attorney George Lewis, The Lincoln Museum, Mrs. R. Lincoln, Ms. C. A. Lofton, Longfellow School Faculty, Ms. Marlene Lu, Mr. and. Mrs. Lutter, Mr. Ricky Lyda, Ms. Peg Martin, Ms. Marianna Mason, Dr. and Mrs. Mark Mayeau, Ms. Patricia McAllister, Mrs. Leana McCain, Mrs. Sara McCormack, Ms. Doris J. McKay, Mrs. Lucille McGregor, McHenry County Historical Society, Dr. Larry A. McClellan, Mrs. Jean Meehan and family, Ms. June Meece, Mrs. Sarah Meisels, Mrs. A. L. Mertz, Milburn Congregational Church, Dr. Arthur Miller, Mrs. Dollie Millinder, Ms. Naomi Millinder, Milton House, Mr. Homer Moffat, Mrs. Jean Moore, Mrs. Lucille Mooreland, Mrs. Maria Mootry, Mr. Robert Morgan, Mr. Herb Morphew, Ms. Vera Naretty, National Park Service, Mrs. Nelson, Ms. Ellen Neupert, Newberry Library, Mr. Edward Newsome, Mrs. Maenell Newsome, Mr. and Mrs. Glenn Nicholads, Mrs. Edith Nowack, Mr. Rex Nyautat, Mrs. Betty Obendorf, Onarga Public Library, Mr. Thomas Orlando, Mr. Simeon Osby, Mr. Ott, Mrs. Jean Parker, Mrs. Elsie Paxon, Mrs. H. Pearsall, Mrs. Mary Peccarelli, Mr. Leo Pelje, Ms. Marianne Peroni, Mrs. Peters, Miss Bonnie Peterson, Mr. Ed D. Petrik, Mr. Bill Pihos, Mr. Reid Pombaugh, Mrs. Helen Pottiger, Mr. Ramon Price, Margaret and Robert Pruter, Dr. Benjamin Quarels, Quincy Historical Society, Quincy Public Library, Mr. James T. Ransom Sr., Mr. Terry Ransom, Ms. Sharilyn Ratch, Professor Christopher Reed, Ms. Judy Reinert, Mrs. Reinhardt, Mr. R. Curtin Rice, Ms. Louise Rich, Mr. Fred Rich, Rev. Ben Richardson, Mrs. Katherine Robertson, Mr. David Ross, Mrs. Nell Santos, Ms. Cookie Santucci, Mr. Bill Scales, Mrs. P. Schrage, Mr. and Mrs. Carl Schultz, Ms. G. B. Shaner, Mrs. Lillian Shaw, Mrs. Lois Sicher, Rev. Willie Simmons, Mrs. August Sindt, Mr. Brian Sitler, Ms. Dorita Smith, Ms. Monica Smith, Dr. and Mrs. Smith, Mr. Weldon Smith, Ms. Leo Sparks, Mr. Keith Speckman, Mr. Albert Cornelius Spurlock, Mr. Sonny Stancyzk, Mrs. Madeline Stratton, Ms. Debbie Steffes, Mr. Curtis Strode, Mr. Raleigh Sutton, Miss Arlene Swanson, Miss Stefany Tanda, Ms. Norma Terran, Rev. R. Thompson, Mrs. Thompson, Mr. Charlie Thurston, Mrs. Phyllis Tilley, Mr. John Tilley, Mrs. Margaret Tobias, Mrs. Nina Triplett, The Turner family, Mr. Albert Turner, Mr. John Turner, Ms. Cathy Tutor, Mrs. Gloria Urch, Ms. Cindy Van Horn, Dr. and Mrs. James Vercoe, Mr. and Mrs. Fred Walddusser, Mrs. Debbi Welch, Mr. Jim West, Mrs. Anna Westlake, Drs. Don and Helen Westlake, Wheaton College Library, Wheaton Public Library, Mr. John Whiteside, Willard Library, Mr. and Mrs. Alice Wilson, Ms. Pam Wilson, Mrs. Lina Witherspoon, Dr. and Mrs. John Wittich, Rev. Barbara Wolf, Ms. Ruthmay Wood, Yorkville Congregational Church, and many others.

About this Book

This book could have been called "What You Always Wanted To Know About the Underground Railroad In Illinois—And Didn't Know Who or Where To Ask".

In it you'll find answers and sources of further information. It is written for you if you are just learning that the Underground Railroad operated in Illinois, if or you already knew that and want to learn more details.

With this in mind, the book is intended to be a tool which you can use as you wish.

You may want to read it page by page, skim through it from time to time and read pages that are of special interest to you, or use it as a reference book

Since the book is designed for all these different uses, you will find that some stories are cross referenced several times because they are examples of more than one aspect of the Underground Railroad. Also since the questions are all interconnected they are arranged in one of many possible sequences and can be read in any order.

*   *   *

This book contains much of the information Glennette Tilley Turner has collected since the late 1960's. Even after many years of research, she is still discovering "new" information. There is more remaining to be discovered.

It is difficult to positively authenticate many aspects of the Underground Railroad. It is sometimes necessary to go with the preponderance of the evidence since it's impossible to question anyone who took part in it. Finding records is a challenge since the Underground Railroad was illegal and participants were subject to fines or imprisonment. However there are some remaining documents, accounts and locations which provide insight into this fascinating, little known chapter of Illinois history. Although it was impossible to include all of the stories in this book, you will find many of them on the following pages. See the "Dear Reader" letter for more details on this extensive study.

Introduction

The Underground Railroad was an escape route traveled by numerous slaves who were fleeing bondage and seeking to make new lives for themselves and their families. They faced an ever-present danger of being recaptured, severely punished, and "sold South."

Anti-slavery people and abolitionists both white and black aided slaves by providing lodging, food and transportation. They risked large fines, ostracism and imprisonment.

"Free" Frank McWorter was a former slave who came to Illinois during that turbulent period. He came to this state on his own rather than by way of the Underground Railroad, yet his farm and New Philadelphia, the town he founded in Pike County in 1836, were used as stations on the Underground Railroad. Here "Free" Frank lived some twenty miles from the Mississippi River. Directly across the river was the town of Hannibal in the slave state of Missouri. "Free" Frank's farm and town were strategically located on the roads that ran to Quincy. These roads ran north and across the Illinois River to Jacksonville and Springfield to the east, three other places where fugitive slaves could find shelter.

Courtesy the DuSable Museum of African American History

For those slaves, who perhaps wanted additional security and guidance in their trek north to freedom, "Free" Frank's sons risked their own freedom by taking many of the fugitive slaves to Canada. During this time "Free" Frank and his sons also risked their freedom as they repeatedly went back to the South to buy family members from slavery. "Free" Frank, by his actions, is symbolic of man's quest for freedom.

In this book Glennette Turner transports you back to those eventful days and acquaints you with the rich legacy that we share.

Dr. Juliet E.K. Walker
Great-great granddaughter of "Free" Frank McWorter
Professor of History, University of Illinois

PREVIOUS PAGE: BUST FREE FRANK MCWORTER, 1995, SHIRLEY MOSS
Courtesy of the DuSable Museum of African American History

Source of Overview illustrations: The National Park Service

Overview

ILLINOIS: THE MISSING CHAPTER IN THE UNDERGROUND RAILROAD

Imagine the intrigue, daring and trust demonstrated when the Underground Railroad (UGRR) operated on roads, rivers and overland routes that we still travel along today. As you know, before and during the U.S. Civil War many men, women, and children who were held in bondage made daring escapes. Many were assisted by people known as abolitionists—who worked to end, or abolish, slavery.

Enslaved people had been escaping ever since the institution of slavery began hundreds of years ago. At first, bondage in the United States was neither lifelong nor limited to people of African descent. In early colonial days both white Europeans and black Africans were brought to the Virginia colonies as indentured servants. They worked without pay from four to seven years to repay any debts they had. After this time, they were assigned land and were free to go on with their lives. There were also unsuccessful attempts to enslave Native Americans.

By the early 1770s, however, it became increasingly common to enslave black servants for life. For example, in 1640, one black and two white indentured servants escaped together. When they were recaptured, a Virginia court ordered the white servants to serve only one additional year and the black servant to serve for his entire lifetime. Virginia landowners adopted the idea of "perpetual servitude" from Caribbean landowners and enacted laws that allowed it. Africans were abducted from their homeland and brought to North America chained together in stench-filled slave ships. Naturally, they tried every possible means to keep from being enslaved. If they were unable to avoid capture, they attempted escape in spite of severe consequences.

Enslaved Africans had to determine the best time and method of escape and rely heavily on their own decisions and actions. They had to know how to evade bloodhound dogs, and find and recognize edible plants. They had to travel through all kinds of weather conditions and treacherous terrain, often crossing rivers before getting to states in which slavery was not legal.

CROSS SECTION OF A DENSELY-PACKED SLAVE SHIP WITH HUMAN CARGO.
"Now that the whole ship's cargo were confined together, it became absolutely pestilential. The closeness of the place and the heat of the climate...almost suffocated us... The shrieks of the women and the groans of the dying rendered it a scene of horror almost inconceivable...I began to hope that death would soon put an end to my miseries" ~ *Olaudah Equiano, sold from Africa into New World Slavery at age 12*

In many instances abolitionists helped by providing hiding places, or transporting and guiding fugitive slaves on their journey to freedom. Some abolitionists risked their lives and livelihoods in this humanitarian effort, but not all abolitionists believed that helping slaves escape was the most effective way to end slavery, and while there were very dedicated cooperative efforts among some abolitionists, many fleeing slaves did not have any way of knowing this assistance was available.

In some cases the slaves learned of black, white, or Native American sympathizers by word of mouth. Sometimes slaves were aided by strangers they happened to meet along the way. Still others escaped without assistance though the odds against success were formidable. If unsuccessful, all of their resistance had life-threatening consequences.

Slaveholders held the power of life or death over the people they enslaved. They had weapons. They had supportive laws and the ability to sell or separate enslaved Africans from others who spoke the same language.

Rebelling slaves often denied their would-be enslavers of free labor in many ways. Some fought to free themselves, starved themselves, sabotaged farm equipment and some escaped.

Freedom meant many things. Most of all, it meant being able to keep families together. While living in slavery, members of a family might be sold to different slaveholders, and moved to wherever the slaveholder wished to take them. Freedom meant that parents and children could live together without fear of being separated. It also meant being paid for their work and having the right to vote, get an education, and own land. Many freedom seekers set out against overwhelming odds.

The Underground Railroad was most active about the time that actual railroads were being built. (When the excitement of traveling by train captured the imagination of the public.)

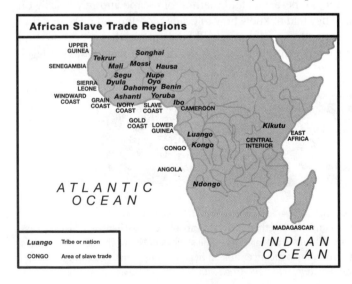

AFRICAN HOMELANDS
Enslaved Africans represented many different peoples each with distinct cultures, religions, and languages. Most originated from the coast or the interior of West Africa, between present-day Senegal and Angola. Other enslaved peoples originally came from Madagascar and Tanzania in East Africa.

Until that time the fastest way to travel was by horseback. The "Iron Horse", as early steam powered trains were sometimes called, could travel longer and faster than any real horse, and the railroad terms "passenger", "conductor", "agent", and "station" all lent themselves to coded, double meanings.

In 1831, a Kentucky slaveholder was pursuing an enslaved African by the name of Tice Davids. The slaveholder lost track of Davids on the banks of the Ohio River near Ripley, Ohio. The slaveholder tried to explain the slave's sudden disappearance by saying, "He must have gone on some kind of underground railroad."

The word "underground" was perfect. After all, whatever is done underground can't be seen by people above ground therefore it's done in secrecy, and secrecy was essential to a successful escape.

For that reason, this book may speak of any escaped slave as having used the Underground Railroad, whether or not he or she was assisted by abolitionists.

The most concentrated Underground Railroad activity took place along the East Coast of the United States. There were a number of reasons for this. Among them, the thirteen original states were on the East Coast; at one time slavery was legal in all of those states. Slavery continued in the agricultural states in the South after it was abolished in the industrial states of the North. Although the northern states came to be known as "free states," the two sections of the country remained interdependent. Many of the slave states produced farm products like cotton, sugar cane, and tobacco which were shipped to northern manufacturing centers. Products manufactured in the north such as woven cloth and rum were sold in the United States and abroad.

Not everyone in the South supported slavery, nor was support for slavery limited to the South.

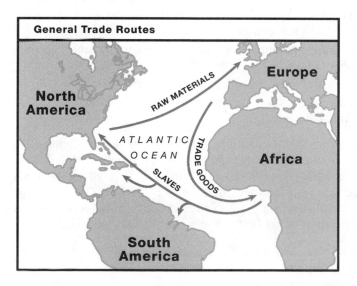

General Trade Routes

THE TRIANGLE TRADE
The demands of European consumers for New World crops and goods helped fuel the slave trade. Following a triangular route between Africa, the Caribbean and North America, slave traders from Holland, Portugal, France and England delivered Africans in exchange for products such as rum, sugar and tobacco that European consumers wanted. Eventually the trading route also distributed Virginia Tobacco, New England rum, and indigo and rice from South Carolina and Georgia.

In such northern cities as Philadelphia, Boston and New York there were people who supported slavery and others who were indifferent to it.

People who were against slavery had different reasons for opposing it. Some were motivated by religious beliefs, political reasons, economic considerations, a sense of fairness, or other personal reasons. Fugitive slaves or freedmen, for example, could not fully enjoy their freedom if some of their family members were enslaved.

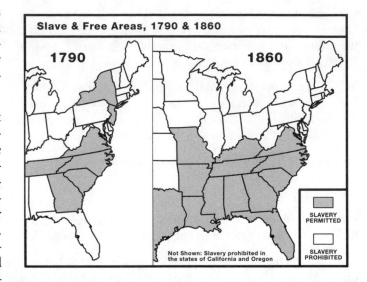

Although fewer passengers journeyed through Illinois than through some eastern states, the people and events in Illinois played a key role in the abolition of slavery. Examples include:

- ~ The Lincoln-Douglas debates
- ~ Abraham Lincoln's election as President of the U.S.;
- ~ Senator Stephen A. Douglas' role in passing the omnibus bill that contained the Fugitive Slave Law of 1850;
- ~ The Dred Scott decision in which the U.S. Supreme Court ruled that a slave taken into free states and territories did not become free (a slaveholder had transported Dred Scott into free states, one of which was Illinois);
- ~ Elijah Lovejoy's death defending his antislavery press, which later became a powerful symbol for Freedom of Press;
- ~ The anti-slavery work of Elijah Lovejoy's brother, Congressman Owen Lovejoy;
- ~ Senator Lyman Trumbull's authorship of the Thirteenth Amendment to the Constitution of the United States.

In 1793, Congress passed a Fugitive Slave Act signed by President George Washington. This law stated that enslaved Africans could be returned to slavery, but it was not strictly enforced. It was the 1850 Fugitive Slave Law that caused the greatest upheaval. This law applied to all areas within the United States, slaves who had settled in the North went to Canada. While Canada was the most frequent destination, slaves who fled from southern states often found sanctuary in Florida, the western parts of the United States, and in the Caribbean, Mexico, Africa and Europe.

The critical role of black abolitionists has been largely overlooked in traditional accounts of Underground Railroad operations. Because every Underground Railroad operator took great personal risks, the black abolitionists risked all the consequences that their white counterparts risked, plus probable enslavement. Many were escaped slaves, and their former slave masters would have found great satisfaction in re-enslaving and punishing them severely as a warning to other slaves. Free black abolitionists were only half free if they had settled in states where laws known as Black Codes denied them full citizenship, and Illinois was one such state.

In spite of this, black men and women, like wealthy tailor John Jones and his wife Mary Richardson Jones, fought the institution of slavery. They worked with Rev. Richard DeBaptiste, their fellow members of Olivet Baptist Church and with these organizations established at Quinn Chapel African Methodist Episcopal Church: the Vigilance Committee, the Liberty Association, and "The Big Four" (whose membership consisted of Emma Atkinson and the three other women). They worked with white abolitionists including Dr. C.V. Dyer; newspaper editor Zebina Eastman; Judge Harvey Hurd; pharmacist and church leader Philo Carpenter; detective Allan Pinkerton; Rev. Flavel Bascome of the First Presbyterian Church; and attorneys Calvin DeWolf, Lemuel C.P. Freerer, and George Manierre. They worked with black abolitionists including Rev. Abram Hall of Quinn Chapel; newspaper man and mill operator Henry O. Wagoner; Joseph and Anna Hudlun whose home was one of the first built by black Chicagoans, tailor William Styles; barbers Louis Isbell, William Johnson, and Joseph Barquet. The Joneses also entertained the nationally known John Brown and Frederick Douglass.

Some black abolitionists felt safer working alone, figuring, the fewer people involved the better.

Efforts of black abolitionists on behalf of the battle against slavery were not limited to helping fellow black people. For example, in Alton, a black man by the name of William "Scotty" Johnston, a skilled stone mason by trade, buried the body of white abolitionist Elijah Lovejoy in a secret place to protect it from Lovejoy's enemies. According to Alton historian Charlotte Johnson, "Scotty" Johnston prepared Lovejoy's body and coffin. He followed an old custom,

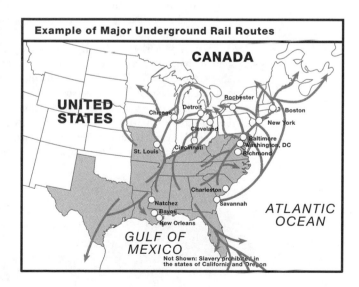

Example of Major Underground Rail Routes

CANADA

UNITED STATES

Rochester
Chicago   Detroit   Boston
                          New York
          Cleveland
St. Louis   Cincinnati   Baltimore
                         Washington, DC
                         Richmond

Charleston
Natchez   Savannah   ATLANTIC
Bayou   OCEAN
New Orleans

GULF OF MEXICO

Not Shown: Slavery prohibited in the states of California and Oregon

SELLING SOUTH

To meet the growing demands of sugar and cotton, slaveholders developed an active domestic slave trade to move surplus workers to the Deep South. New Orleans, Louisiana, became the largest slave mart, followed by Richmond, Virginia; Natchez, Mississippi; and Charleston, South Carolina. Between 1820 and 1860 more than 60 percent of the Upper South's enslaved population was "sold South." Covering 25 to 30 miles a day on foot, men, women and children marched south in large groups called coffles. Former bondsman Charles Ball remembered that slave traders bound the women together with rope. They fastened the men first with chains around their necks then handcuffed them in pairs. The traders removed the restraints when the coffle neared the market.

that of collecting poke berries and staining the coffin with their juice. He refused to accept payment for his efforts, but shared some details with his son and two other people— a black man named Anderson who had been a clerk in Lovejoy's newspaper office, and black UGRR operator Issac Kelley who was the head deacon at Union Baptist Church. For many years Lovejoy's grave was marked with a pine board with the letters E. P. L. carved into it. Eventually that marker was lost.

Some time later a white minister named Thomas Dimmock, located the spot where Johnston had buried Lovejoy. Finding that a road in the Alton Cemetery had been built over the grave, Dimmock had Lovejoy's body reburied at the new site and marked with a small marble gravestone on which these words were engraved in Latin, "Here lies Lovejoy. Spare him now that he is buried." Dimmock then sought the support of the citizens of Alton to erect a more fitting monument. He established a monument committee on which UGRR operator Issac Kelley served. Dimmock believed it was appropriate that the Lovejoy Monument be watched over by the black citizens of Alton and he named Kelley as the first trustee responsible for conducting an annual observance in Lovejoy's memory. This tradition continues in the fall of each year.

Dear Reader

Soon after our family moved to Wheaton in 1968, a new neighbor's chance remark, "I hear the Underground Railroad operated around here," altered the course of my life. On the one hand, I couldn't imagine that there was truth to what I heard; on the other, I couldn't dismiss it. I kept wondering: might there have been Underground Railroad activity in Illinois? If so, where? And why? I could not picture anyone who escaped from slavery in the South taking the "scenic route" to Canada.

As a grade school student, I had learned of the Underground Railroad and was intrigued by accounts of daring escapes and rescues by Harriet Tubman and other conductors. I thought, however, that the Underground Railroad had operated only in states east of Illinois.

To satisfy my curiosity, I went to the DuPage County Museum expecting to find that there was no historical basis to my neighbor's remark. To my surprise I found some reference to the Underground Railroad in a line here or a footnote there.

While these items provided only partial answers, they stirred my curiosity and generated more questions. My study broadened. I found that Vera Cooley had written an article for the *Illinois Historical Journal*, Larry Gara had written the <u>Liberty Line</u>, and there were references to the Underground Railroad in the Illinois Federal Writers Project materials. Prior to that, Wilbur Siebert of Ohio had attempted to identify Underground Railroad routes in many states, and Rufus Blanchard had written about some Chicago abolitionists. In more recent years Dr. Charles L. Blockson did extensive writing on the multi-state Underground Railroad operations.

While these writings were very helpful, they left me with many unanswered questions about the Underground Railroad in this state. So I delved further.

Piecing together these clues with others, I learned that some of the Underground Railroad "passengers" who came through Illinois escaped from bondage in Kentucky or Tennessee. Most passengers had been enslaved in Missouri; and those persons entered Illinois at Mississippi River towns such as Quincy,

Illinois Senator Carol Moseley-Braun, chief sponsor of the Underground Railroad Network to Freedom Act; sponsors of the House bill, Congressmen Portman and Stokes; and Senate co-sponsor Senator DeVine hold a press conference following the signing of this historic legislation.

Alton and Chester. Many of them followed the Illinois River system and Indian trails. They traveled independently or with the aid of both black and white Underground Railroad "station operators" and "conductors".

The more I delved into the study, the more I could discern patterns, so I continued to study, visiting libraries and museums. I checked primary sources and visited sites identified with the Underground Railroad. Next, I began compiling and analyzing the information I had found.

Professor Wilbur Siebert, pioneering Underground Railroad researcher. *Courtesy of Ohio Historical Society.*

In the first half of the nineteenth century most passengers went in the direction of Chicago which was the terminus of the Illinois Underground Railroad. Chicago had a sizable enough black community to assume some degree of "safety," so some passengers stopped there. Others continued their journey, often walking along the lower portion of Lake Michigan, through Indiana and on through the state of Michigan, crossing the Detroit River to Canada.

Abolitionists sometimes arranged for passengers to travel essentially the same route by wagons, trains and sailing ships. Passengers, who entered Illinois at Rock Island, passed through Iowa before crossing the Mississippi River into Illinois. Some passengers traveled toward Chicago and Lake Michigan while others followed an alternate route northward along the Rock River into Wisconsin.

Galesburg was not near the banks of the Illinois River, however it was a frequent stop for UGRR passengers because many of the townspeople were known to have strong abolitionist sentiments. Typically, passengers from Illinois and other northern states went to Canada with the expectation they would be free under British rule. Passengers from states in closer proximity to Mexico or the Caribbean fled to those locations rather than Canada.

Although Illinois had restrictive Black Codes prior to the Fugitive Slave Act of 1850, many persons fleeing bondage chose to settle in

Dr. Charles L. Blockson based the UGRR cover story in the July 1984 *National Geographic* Magazine on his many years of research. *Courtesy of Charles L. Blockson*

Illinois. Many people were experienced farmers or skilled artisans; who, once free, happily applied their talents toward earning a living. When the Fugitive Slave Act of 1850 permitted slave catchers to follow slaves into free states and return them to bondage, large numbers of former slaves pulled up stakes and moved to Canada.

Conducting research on the topic of the Underground Railroad led to the study of related topics (e.g. organizations such as the Illinois Anti-slavery Society, the African Methodist Episcopal [A.M.E.] and Congregational churches; newspapers such as the *Genius of Universal Emancipation,* and of individual abolitionists and passengers).

As my search broadened, I found that Illinois had a significant impact on the Underground Railroad, larger issues related to slavery, and ultimately on the Civil War. (See the "Overview" of this book for examples of this). Although numerically fewer enslaved Africans passed through Illinois than through Pennsylvania or Ohio, the Illinois Underground Railroad was a very important part of a multi-state network.

My early findings were published in <u>The Underground Railroad in DuPage County Illinois</u>, in 1981 and revised in 1984, in games and a booklet of interdisciplinary classroom activities. Later I explored other ways of conveying the information, including a juvenile historical novel entitled <u>Running For Our Lives</u>, and a collective biography <u>Take a Walk in Their Shoes</u>, which contains a short skit about Underground Railroad operator Frederick Douglass. I also was fortunate enough to conduct a videotape interview with the 93-year-old great niece of Harriet Tubman.

I hope this essay has whetted your curiosity and that you will read books, visit museums, libraries, and sites such as Owen Lovejoy's home in Princeton, Illinois, and Graue Mill in Oakbrook. Also talk with historians and descendants of people who participated in the anti-slavery movement, and check to see if your own family might have had some involvement in the Underground Railroad in Illinois.

Have Fun!!

James T. Ransom, convenor of the Illinois Underground Railroad Association and the designer of the Illinois Underground Railroad map.
Courtesy of James T. Ransom

Glennette Tilley Turner served on the nine member National Park Service Underground Railroad Advisory Committee. She has been a consultant on many Underground Railroad projects including the Chicago Tribune Sunday Magazine's *Underground Railroad cover story, Naper Settlement, Graue Mill and Museum, and the Wheaton History Center. She has written articles on the subject for publications of the National Parks and Conservation Association, the Illinois State Library, and the Illinois Bureau of Tourism; and been interviewed on C-SPAN and other cable and network television programs. She was an advisor for a film produced for the Illinois Bureau of Tourism and one of the authors featured in a film produced for the Illinois State Library. She serves on the board of the Graue Mill and Museum, the DuPage Historical Society, and Lake Forest College National Alumni Association and is an Illinois Humanities Council Road Scholar. She is a recipient of the Margaret Landon Award of the Wheaton Historic Preservation Council, the Studs Terkel Humanities Award and the Irma Kingsley Johnson Award of the Friends of Amistad. She was named Outstanding Woman Educator in DuPage County by the YWCA and received a commendation from the Illinois State Legislature. Mrs. Turner is a supervisor of student teachers at National Louis University.*

THE AUTHOR AT THE WHITE HOUSE TO WITNESS THE SIGNING OF THE UNDERGROUND RAILROAD NETWORK TO FREEDOM ACT.

DID YOU KNOW THAT ...
YOU LIVE NEAR
A SECRET RAILROAD?

Few things on television are as exciting as the real life drama of the Underground Railroad. Even though its time has passed, there are many intriguing local links with the events that surrounded the Underground Railroad.

If you live in Illinois, you live within 100 miles of a place that played a role in the daring and courage of the UGRR. You may have heard stories of this "secret railroad" in other states, but did you realize that places all around here were part of it?

1. What was the Underground Railroad?

Since everyone desires to be free, enslaved people had been escaping for as long as slavery existed. The greatest Underground Railroad activity was between 1835 and 1861, the year the Civil War began.

It was not a subway or any other type of train that ran underground. It was a cooperative effort of enslaved Africans* who wanted freedom more than anything else in the world and of many courageous black, white and Native American people who although free themselves, believed slavery was wrong.

Sometimes individuals and groups coordinated their efforts. Sometimes they worked alone. Sometimes enslaved people escaped without assistance from anyone else. The common denominator was that every effort was made to keep the escape or whereabouts of the person who was escaping, a secret from would-be captors.

The National Park Service Handbook defines the Underground Railroad as "the name given to the many ways that blacks took to escape slavery in the southern United States before the Civil War."

Actually the Underground Railroad continued to operate throughout the Civil War. (It is a little known fact that there was also an Underground Railroad in reverse. In the South enslaved Africans fed, hid and guided black and white Union soldiers who had been separated from their units.) The Underground Railroad transcended race. It was people working together for a common goal, and although humane, it was risky business for everyone involved. It became a model for other freedom movements in the United States and around the world.

$200 Reward.

RANAWAY from the subscriber, on the night of Thursday, the 30th of September.

FIVE NEGRO SLAVES,

To-wit: one Negro man, his wife, and three children.

The man is a black negro, full height, very erect, his face a little thin. He is about forty years of age, and calls himself *Washington Reed*, and is known by the name of Washington. He is probably well dressed, possibly takes with him an ivory headed cane, and is of good address. Several of his teeth are gone.

Mary, his wife, is about thirty years of age, a bright mulatto woman, and quite stout and strong.

The oldest of the children is a boy, of the name of FIELDING, twelve years of age, a dark mulatto, with heavy eyelids. He probably wore a new cloth cap.

MATILDA, the second child, is a girl, six years of age, rather a dark mulatto, but a bright and smart looking child.

MALGOLM, the youngest, is a boy, four years old, a lighter mulatto than the last, and about equally as bright. He probably also wore a cloth cap. If examined, he will be found to have a swelling at the navel.

It is supposed that they are making their way to Chicago, and that a white man accompanies them, that they will travel chiefly at night, and most probably in a covered wagon.

A reward of $150 will be paid for their apprehension, so that I can get them, if taken within one hundred miles of St. Louis, and $200 if taken beyond that, and secured so that I can get them, and other reasonable additional charges, if delivered to the subscriber, or to THOMAS ALLEN, Esq., at St. Louis, Mo. The above negroes, for the last few years, have been in possession of Thomas Allen, Esq., of St. Louis.

WM. RUSSELL.

ST. LOUIS, Oct 1, 1847.

Courtesy of The Library of Congress

---

* The words "enslaved African" is preferable to the word "slave" because they accurately describe the condition of persons held in bondage. However, for the sake of brevity the shorter term "slave" is sometimes used in this book. The term "freedom seeker" is self explanatory.

2. Why was it called an "Underground Railroad?"

Enslaved people had always escaped on their own and sometimes with the help of others. The term "Underground Railroad" (or "Railway") became popular when, in the mid-1800s, real railroads with powerful steam engines were being built. They captured the public imagination, and the trains were nicknamed "iron horses" because they were so much stronger and faster than horses. Prior to that, a horse was the fastest way of traveling.

It was during these years that the Underground Railroad (or UGRR) was most active. This is the most common explanation of how the Underground Railroad was first called "underground":

> A slave was being pursued. He seemed to disappear right before the pursuer's very eyes. The pursuer said that the slave seemed to "go underground."

The two ideas were linked, thus the term "Underground Railroad" resulted.

ILLINOIS CENTRAL RAILROAD

The Illinois Central during construction. This is the line on which porter George Burroughs hid slaves on the Cairo to Chicago run, and for which Abraham Lincoln was a lawyer and Allan Pinkerton, a detective. *Courtesy of Illinois Gulf Railroad*

HARRIET TUBMAN

Harriet Tubman's name is probably the best known of the many Underground Railroad agents. Harriet Tubman was often called "Moses" because, after escaping from slavery, she returned to the South at least 15 times to personally lead 300 men, women, and children out of bondage.

She was born in Bucktown on the Eastern Shore of Maryland, where her parents were enslaved on the plantation of Edward Brodas.

From early childhood, she experienced harsh cruelties of slavery. She was hired out to work in a household some distance from the Brodas plantation. (She was to babysit for a woman whom she called "Miss Susan." The slaveholder, Brodas, was to be paid for Harriet's work.)

One of her jobs was to stay awake and rock the baby's cradle all night long. If she dozed off or did anything displeasing, Miss Susan whipped her severely.

Harriet escaped from this situation and hid in a pig-pen for four days. Although she competed with the piglets for slop, by the fourth day she was so hungry she went back to Miss Susan's. She was punished and returned to the Brodas plantation.

Later, her head was injured when she was struck by a metal weight that was thrown at another slave by a would-be slave catcher. She was near death for many months, but her mother eventually nursed her back to health.

From then on the slaveholder believed Harriet Tubman was dull-witted. Harriet realized this and sometimes acted the part.

She proved to be a genius when it came to making repeated trips in and out of slave territory in spite of a $40,000 reward for her capture. She had made her own escape in 1849. At first she went to the home of a white Underground Railroad operator who transported her to the next town. From there she traveled through dense forests, swamps, and crossed the Delaware River before reaching Philadelphia. In Philadelphia she met William Still and other Vigilance Committee members.

She wasn't content to be free knowing that her family and many other people were still enslaved. She took jobs as a domestic worker and had help from William Still in Philadelphia; Thomas Garrett in Wilmington, Delaware; and other abolitionists to make return trips to rescue her parents and hundreds of other people. After the Fugitive Slave Act was passed in 1850, she no longer felt safe when she reached northern states. She took the people she rescued on to St. Catherine's, Ontario, Canada, where they were protected under British law.

Although Harriet Tubman followed routes east of Illinois, no discussion of the Underground Railroad is complete without the story of this legendary Underground Railroad conductor.

HARRIET TUBMAN

3.   Why were railroad terms (words) used?

Railroads were new and so were the railroad terms. Since saying something like, "I'm going to meet the train" wouldn't arouse any suspicion, abolitionists involved in the UGRR simply added new coded meanings to these words.

A "passenger" was an escaping slave.

Stopping places were called "stations" (or "depots" as early train stations were called).

A "coach" or "train" was the code name for any wagon, bobsled or other mode of transportation.

A "conductor" was a person who took passengers from one station to another.

This classic political cartoon features the work of Reverend John Cross and Benjamin Lundy who were noted for Illinois UGRR work. Cross was active in Knox, Lee and DuPage counties. Lundy's publication from the Lowell-Hennepin area became the Chicago based *Western Citizen,* which published this cartoon.

4. Were real railroads ever used in escapes?

Yes. If fleeing slaves traveled as coach passengers, they usually disguised themselves so they would not be recognized by slavecatchers. They used such methods of disguise as wearing heavy veils and gloves, darkening their skin, or knocking out front teeth to avoid fitting the slaveholder's description. Often fleeing passengers traveled out of view in boxcars.

In Illinois the Illinois Central (or I.C.) was the most heavily used railroad since it linked southern and northern parts of the state. UGRR passengers and conductors utilized actual railroads in many ways. For example:

~ Near Tamaroa, B. G. Root, a surveyor for the I.C., had tracks and a depot placed on his property. Runaway slaves waited in empty freight cars. When Chicago-bound trains arrived B. G. Root hitched these freight cars to the trains.

~ George L. Burroughs was a free black man recruited in Canada as an UGRR agent. He came to Illinois to work as a porter on the I.C. This job gave him an opportunity to smuggle Underground Railroad passengers between Cairo and Chicago. These passengers had probably escaped from slavery in Kentucky or Tennessee, crossing the Ohio River into Illinois.

~ According to tradition, a pre Civil War homestead in Amboy known as the "Old Pankhurst Farm" was an Underground Railroad stop. The regional headquarters of the I. C. were located in Amboy.

~ James Wilson continued his UGRR work when he moved from Sparta to Centralia. After the I.C. was built in 1854, he and George McGee and several I.C. employees used the railroad to "do the work of the UGRR." An I.C. freight conductor, Larry Wiggins, would unlock the boxcars at night and hide UGRR passengers with enough food to last until the train reached Chicago. One or two coach conductors also cooperated by "forgetting" to collect tickets from any UGRR passengers.

~ Lewis Thomas was probably the person responsible for the I.C. being routed through Springfield. There was a special stop on his property about six miles east of Virden. Rumor has it that his house was an UGRR stop with tunnels leading to the barn and to a man-made lake near the house.

~ Allan Pinkerton, the detective from Dundee who later headed President Lincoln's secret service, attended a secret meeting at Henry Wagoner's mill, raised $300 or $400, and arranged for a train coach on the Michigan Central Railroad to transport the slaves John Brown freed from Missouri. John Brown and his party had been hotly pursued across all the states they traveled through before reaching Chicago on the Rock Island Railroad.

ELLEN AND WILLIAM CRAFT

~ In 1914, long after the UGRR had stopped operating, J.G. Koester of Carlinville recalled that he had seen Harmon Griggs, who was the first Chicago and Alton Railroad agent, conceal two UGRR passengers at the depot.

~ On one occasion, two people thought to be UGRR passengers got off the Chicago and Alton train in Lexington, Illinois, where they were transported by a member of the Mahan family to a home south of Pontiac.

~ Dr. C.V. Dyer, president of the Chicago, Burlington & Quincy Railroad, made that railroad line available to UGRR passengers.

~ The home of Deacon Birges in Farmington, Illinois, was reportedly connected by an underground tunnel to the railroad.

~ Some Chicago-bound passengers were able to make a portion of their journey on the Chicago, Galena & Union Railroad.

The most widely publicized use of real trains took place on the East Coast. Ellen and William Craft made a daring escape by train. Ellen, who appeared to be white, pretended to be a young slaveholder going North for medical care. She could not write, so she put her arm in a sling to keep from being asked to sign any papers. William pretended to be "his master's" manservant. They traveled on several steamboats to Washington, DC from Macon, Georgia and took a train from Washington to Baltimore, Maryland. In the Baltimore station, the station agent refused to sell William a ticket without a bond. William's fast thinking and talking is the only thing that saved them. William asserted, "My master must not be delayed." The station agent let them proceed. They reached Philadelphia and went on to Boston where they found refuge in the home of black abolitionists Lewis and Harriet Hayden. Further details of their daring escape can be read in the book, <u>Running a Thousand Miles to Freedom</u> .

On the grounds surrounding this historic house B.G. Roots placed railroad tracks. The house was also reportedly an UGRR station.
Courtesy of Jean and Calvin Ibendahl.

5.   What other ways did passengers travel?

More people traveled all or most of their trip on foot than any other way. Sometimes they had to swim rivers, cross icy waterways, and trudge through snake infested swamps.

Other means of traveling were riding on horseback, hiding in various types of carriers such as farm wagons, stagecoaches, springboards or democratic buggies and covered (Conestoga) wagons. They traveled as passengers, workmen, stowaways or hoboes on canal boats, steamers, riverboats, ferryboats, flatboats and trains.

ESCAPING ON TOP OF A TRAIN

6. Where did the Underground Railroad operate?

The UGRR operations in Pennsylvania, Ohio, New York, Delaware, and other north-eastern states are generally known. Operations in Illinois and neighboring Midwestern states are less well known.

According to the survey conducted by National Park Service historians, there was UGRR activity in at least twenty-nine states and the District of Columbia. The least well known are the operations in Southern states.

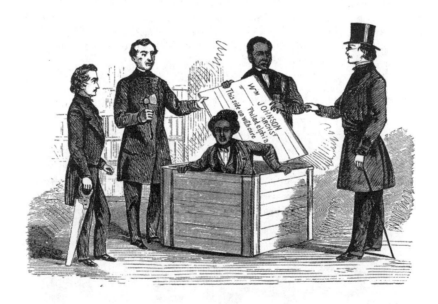

The Resurrection of Henry "Box" Brown.

According to oral histories, when a slave hunter rode to the Israel Blodgett home asking for water, Avis Blodgett took a pail and a cup to the spring near the cabin and served the captured slaves. The slave hunter was said to have cursed her asking, "Why in the devil are you giving water to them?" She replied that the slaves could not get the water for themselves. They were bound, but he was perfectly able to help himself. Les Schrader's painting records that moment. *Courtesy of Naper Settlement Heritage Society with original painting on exhibit at Naper Settlement, Naperville, IL.*

In 1833, Alexander Howard built his frame home to serve as the local stop and postal station on the Templeton Stage coach route between Chicago and Ottawa. Named for the grove of Paw Paw trees growing around this building once located at 143 Jefferson Avenue, the house has been relocated to Naper Settlement. It and some other stage coach stops are believed to have been Underground Railroad stations. *Courtesy of Naper Settlement Heritage Society with original painting on exhibit at Naper Settlement, Naperville, IL.*

Before the automobile came into use, travelers between Aurora and Naperville espe-cially welcomed the sight of the "Halfway House," knowing that their two-hour trip was half over. It is rumored that the home was also an Underground Railroad station. Imagine what a happy sight it was to "passengers" who had traveled all the way from Missouri. *Courtesy of the Naperville Settlement Society with original painting on exhibit at Naper Settlement, Naperville, IL.*

Placing a high value on education, Naperville, by 1832, had a significant center for learn-ing in Naper Academy. The building was the refuge for Stephen A. Douglas during one of his senatorial campaign speeches in Naperville on September 27, 1856. Originally addressing a group gathered at the corner of Jefferson and Eagle streets, an unexpected-ly early snowstorm drove the crowd one block north to the Academy, the present site of the Naper Elementary School. *Courtesy of Naper Settlement Heritage Society with original painting on exhibit at Naper Settlement, Naperville, IL.*

7.   Who were the passengers?

The passengers were African-Americans fleeing bondage. Most had struck out on their own. Some were aided as they traveled, others were not.

They traveled light, frequently with only the clothes they were wearing when they escaped. However, some succeeded in escaping with a cherished object. One UGRR worker observed, "Through all their dangers and trials many of them still hung onto an old banjo or an old fiddle."

Some men and women escaped alone and went back to rescue their families. While others, who had the rare opportunity to receive minimal pay for their labor, tried to purchase the freedom of family members.

One story took place in the Western suburbs of Chicago. It is the experience of a man whose story was recorded but whose name was omitted from the history books.

He and his family were enslaved in Missouri. He was freed, but his family was not, so he remained in the area, hoping to gain his family's freedom. He received 50 cents for a day's work and made regular payments to his former slaveholder toward the purchase of his wife and two children. He did this for two years, then learned that the slaveholder had betrayed him and sold his family to a slaver in Georgia. The man tried in vain to locate his family and finally broken-hearted, set out for Canada alone.

En route he stopped at the home of Deacon William Strong (whose Underground Railroad station stood at the northeast corner of Eola Road and New York Street, Aurora, until recently.) Deacon Strong escorted the man to the home of Avis and Israel Blodgett in Downers Grove. When they reached the Blodgett's, the man learned that his wife and children were asleep inside! They had escaped on the Underground Railroad and arrived that very night. Needless to say, that family was overjoyed to be reunited.

Another family, by the name of Armstrong, was reunited when the mother returned south. The husband, wife and one child escaped to Canada in 1842. The mother could not bear leaving her other five children in bondage, so she returned to Kentucky. Disguising herself, she hid near a spring and whispered instructions to the children as they got water. She and the children all escaped the next night.

Joanna Garner fled from bondage in Virginia and Missouri. She was attempting to make her way to Canada with her twin daughters. The Civil War had ended by the time she reached St. Charles and she decided to remain there. Unlike many former slaves, she received government land on which to establish a life in freedom. Her land was on a linear block near the center of town. She was a skillful business woman and maintained her family by selling off parcels of land, and receiving some of her pay for doing domestic work in the form of three small houses which she joined together. A descendant still lives on the block where she first settled. Hers is one of the oldest families, black or white, living in St. Charles.

The home of William and Carolyn Strong stood at the intersection of Eola Road and Aurora Road (renamed New York Street). Slaves came here by way of Princeton, Somonauk, Plano, Jericho, Little Rock, John Wagner's or Dan Smith's in Aurora and went to Downers Grove or Little Rock. Deacon Strong had originally belonged to the Big Woods Church. He was instrumental in the organization of Congregational churches in Aurora and Batavia.

Not all efforts to gain freedom for oneself or for family members ended so happily. These following accounts indicate that even when people thought they had reached safety or had reason to be hopeful or that they might be reunited with their loved ones, other factors changed the outcome.

Robert Allan was an ex-slave who worked in Peoria for 12 years in an effort to earn enough money to buy his mother, brothers and sister. In 1857, he had his savings in the bank and wrote the slaveholder in Jackson, Mississippi to arrange the purchase of his family members. The slaveholder wrote saying two brothers had drowned crossing the Tennessee River and thought the other family members were satisfied with their situation. In any event, they were not for sale. The slaveholder ended the letter telling Robert Allan never to write his family again.

After the Civil War, the daughter of Elihu Wolcott of Jacksonville told this story of a mother who had escaped from slavery in Missouri with her two daughters. They reached Springfield with the cooperation of black UGRR conductor Ben Henderson and Rev. William Kirby. The mother and daughters were part of a group of six or seven UGRR passengers which included a crippled man who used his crutch to fight off slave catchers. The mother and daughters were captured and sent back to St. Louis. When their enslaver arrived, he only wanted the daughters. The mother could have escaped but refused to go without her children. The mother was sold, and the enslaver refused to pay the slave catchers who prevented the escape of this family.

An elderly black man, who had lived in Chicago for a number of years, was kidnapped and carried off into slavery. He was taken from Chicago to LaSalle and then by steamboat to St. Louis. (LaSalle was at that time the starting point for a line of steamers that ran to St. Louis.) The kidnappers were Chicago men who were arrested but discharged for lack of proof.

The case of Peter Still had both happy and tragic elements. Peter and a younger brother were separated from their family and sold to an Alabama slaveholder. Peter remained enslaved in Alabama 40 years, married, and had eleven children, only three of whom survived. His younger brother also died.

Peter took extra work and entrusted his small earnings to a Jewish man named Joseph Friedman. When Peter had $500 saved he was able to buy his freedom. He went to the offices of the Philadelphia Vigilance Committee. There, an African American man, a Quaker by the name of William Still, interviewed him. In the course of the interview, the two men realized they were long separated blood brothers! William also reunited Peter with their parents who lived nearby.

Peter yearned to free his wife and children, and a white Quaker, Seth Conklin, offered to go to Alabama for them. Before accepting his offer, Peter wanted to make an attempt to rescue his family himself.

PETER STILL

He made a secret visit to Tuscumbia, Alabama, but was unable to spirit his family away, so he returned to Conklin who planned to pose as a slaveholder traveling with his slaves. Conklin reached and rescued Peter's family, but they were recaptured near Vincennes, Indiana. The family was returned to slavery under the Fugitive Slave Law, and their captor received $10 per head for their return.

Meanwhile, Conklin was arrested and a few days later was reported to have drowned accidentally. Peter Still later offered $2500 for his family's freedom, but their slaveholder did not respond.

8. Did all passengers have assistance?

No. Countless slaves escaped by depending only upon their own resourcefulness.

The desire to be free "and belong to oneself" was overwhelming. Many individuals and families had waited patiently for years for their chance to escape.

Some slaves who knew of Underground Railroad workers and stations did not use this help because:

~ They chose not to entrust their lives to anyone else,
~ They had a feeling "making free" was something one ought to do for oneself,
~ Or they were not offered aid.

"Free" Frank McWorter is one man who did not use the help of UGRR workers as a means of gaining his freedom. He was born a slave in South Carolina in 1777. In 1795, he was taken to Kentucky, where after fifteen years he was allowed to hire out on his own time. During the War of 1812, he began to manufacture saltpeter, which was used to make explosives. After being enslaved for almost twenty years, he purchased his freedom at age 42. He had, however, first purchased his wife's freedom. "Free" Frank, his wife and freeborn children arrived to Illinois in 1830. For two years they were the only settlers in Hadley Township, Pike County, Illinois.

"Free" Frank built a successful farm and engaged in the stock raising business. In 1836, he founded a town called New Philadelphia, and during the period from 1835 until his death, he purchased thirteen family members from slavery in Kentucky, including children, grandchildren, and great-grandchildren. He spent about $15,000 to purchase freedom for himself and his family. Provisions in his will provided funds for the purchase of three more family members.

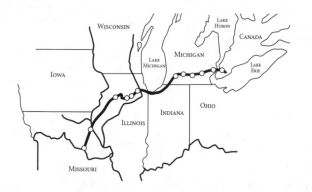

THE JOURNEY FROM MISSOURI TO CANADA BY WAY OF THE QUINCY ROUTE.

The story of the Illinois Anti-Slavery movement is interlocked with that of the work of black and white abolitionists along the Atlantic seacoast. In both parts of the nation, there were many men and women—some well known, others not so well known—who played key roles in this movement and in the operation of the Underground Railroad. These roles were all different and sometimes in conflict, but, combined, they helped shape a pivotal period of American history.

Benjamin Lundy was a Quaker, born in New Jersey. As a young man he went to Wheeling, West Virginia where he saw a coffle of enslaved Africans. Seeing fellow human beings chained together in this way made an indelible impression on Lundy and caused him to dedicate the rest of his life to the abolition of slavery. In 1821, he began publication of the *Genius for Universal Emancipation*, which was probably the first anti-slavery publication.

Lundy influenced many people in many states.One such person was William Lloyd Garrison, who later became one of the most controversial figures in the anti-slavery movement. Garrison served as co-editor while Lundy was publishing *Genius for Universal Emancipation* from Baltimore, Maryland.

Both Lundy and Garrison attended the First Annual Negro Convention in Philadelphia, June 6 through 11, 1831. They were there in support of an idea suggested by Samuel Cornish, a free black man from Delaware. Cornish, who had begun publication of the *Freedom's Journal* newspaper in 1827, urged that a manual labor college be established to train young black men. Plans for the school were defeated by supporters of colonization, but many early backers of the school remained hopeful. The Third Annual Negro Convention gave Garrison the money to go to England to raise funds to establish a school. Garrison went to England but did not bring back money for education.

Lundy and Garrison had parted company in the meantime. They had different opinions on political action, on colonization, the process of emancipation and the use of language.

Garrison had begun publication of his own paper, *Liberator*, on January 1, 1831. This was two years after the publication of <u>David Walker's Appeal</u> in Boston and months before Nat Turner's insurrection in Virginia.

James Forten, a wealthy black sailmaker in Philadelphia, purchased enough subscriptions for Garrison to start the *Liberator*. Forten came to the rescue again in 1834, when he gave Garrison funds to keep the paper from being discontinued.

Reading the *Liberator* inspired eleven Putnam County men to establish the first anti-slavery society in Illinois in February 1833. Their goal was to accomplish equality of rights and privileges among all persons. The women of Putnam County founded Illinois' first women's anti-slavery society in 1842. Members of Esther Lewis Lundy's family played prominent roles in these organizations. These groups later disagreed with Garrison, who discouraged political involvement, as they helped establish the Liberty Party in Illinois.

In 1842, George Latimer, the father of inventor Lewis Howard Latimer, was imprisoned in Boston for escaping from slavery. Frederick Douglass, who had escaped only four years earlier, had written to Garrison about his efforts to raise money to purchase George Latimer's freedom. Garrison printed Douglass' letter in the *Liberator*.

This was the first of Douglass' writings to be published. Douglass went on to write books and edit his own newspaper, the *North Star*.

After splitting up with Garrison, Lundy continued publishing in different cities until he moved to Illinois shortly before his death. Even during that short time, he touched the lives of Hooper Warren and Zebina Eastman whose *Western Citizen* was later acquired by the *Chicago Tribune*.

The American Anti-Slavery Society was an outgrowth of a movement that began with the Quakers and continued with Presbyterians, Congregationalists, and Baptists. The Society, which was as political as it was religious, was organized in December 1833.

It was a letter from the secretary of that Society which prompted newspaper editor Rev. Elijah Lovejoy to ask readers if it was time to form an Illinois Anti-Slavery Society. When Lovejoy was killed defending his press, a black man by the name of Scotty Johnston protected and buried his body.

Elijah Lovejoy's death inspired his brother, Owen to devote the rest of his life to working—as minister, UGRR operator, and Congressman—against slavery.

9. Where did Illinois UGRR passengers begin and end their journey to freedom?

Illinois Underground Railroad passengers came from different slave states.

Most of the people who escaped through Illinois had been in bondage in Missouri, and a large number of the slaves in Missouri had lived on plantations in counties along the Missouri River, where some even worked on riverboats that plied the Missouri and Mississippi Rivers. Others who came through Illinois had traveled from Tennessee, Kentucky, Virginia and other southern states.

Although most UGRR passengers reached Illinois by crossing the Mississippi River, the Tennessee and Cumberland and Ohio Rivers were also important "water highways" as were many creeks, streams and the Illinois & Michigan Canal . UGRR passengers made long dangerous journeys to reach Illinois. No one knows how many drowned or became victims of the bitter cold, quicksand, disease, snakebite, hunger, or angry slaveholders.

Before starting their journey they had:
  ~ Calculated the best time to escape
  ~ Stashed away whatever rations they could
  ~ Coordinated escape plans with family members.

During their journey they:
  ~ Hid in forests, or caves when possible
  ~ Foraged for food
  ~ Crossed treacherous terrain
  ~ Used medicinal herbs to cure illness
  ~ Endured extreme weather conditions in order to evade slave catchers.

Just as caves and forests provided natural hiding places, rivers provided natural pathways. This was especially true of many Illinois rivers which could be followed to the Chicago area. Most rivers tend to flow southward; so, to go north, a person would walk against the current.

Before the Fugitive Slave Act of 1850, Chicago attracted a large number of UGRR passengers. There were about 378 black people in Chicago at that time, and not all of them had been enslaved. Passengers who settled in the Chicago area, found safety in numbers and the strong anti-slavery sentiment there.

Some passengers settled in rural areas of Illinois, Michigan, or Wisconsin and became self-sufficient farmers. Others settled in small Illinois towns. (Since slaves had done the work of the plantations, many had skills with which to earn a living as blacksmiths, seamstresses, cooks, carpenters, deckhands, teamsters, domestic workers, or health care providers. These skills were needed in communities where they settled.) Still others remained in Illinois briefly. Andrew Jackson, the son of a white plantation owner and an enslaved African woman, escaped from bondage in Mississippi. He reached Deerfield, Illinois, where he spent the winter of 1858 in the home of Lorenz Ott, doing such winter chores as building a white picket fence.

Even in Illinois, passengers were advertised in "runaway notices." In order to limit their mobility, the status of free and indentured black people were kept on file in the counties where they resided.

After the 1850 Fugitive Slave Act, most passengers who had settled in northern states left their homes, jobs, and churches and went to Canada where they would be protected by British law. Some free born black people also went to Canada, believing they were safer moving there than remaining in the United States. Rev. W.M. Mitchell was one such person. He worked with escaped slaves in Canada and his accounts of the UGRR helped build British support for the North during the Civil War.

Canada wasn't the only international destination. Passengers in the southern states sought freedom in the Caribbean or Mexico.

SETTLERS IN WINDSOR, ONTARIO

10. How was life different in Canada?

Being in Canada gave former slaves a chance to live out some of their hopes and dreams. Although they experienced all the challenges of "starting from scratch" and getting used to new surroundings, they could realize their most precious goal: keeping their families together. They could experience what Dr. Martin Luther King, Jr. later called, "a sense of somebodiness."

They could work and be paid for their labor. They could legally marry. They could now learn to read, write and provide education an for their children. (In the Buxton settlement near Chatham, Ontario, former slaves established such an excellent school that white neighbors transferred their children to this school.) After the Civil War, John T. Rapier, who became a U.S. Congressman from Alabama, and a number of other black graduates returned to the United States as leaders. They were free to worship as they wished. In Canada former slaves could move from place to place without fear of being recaptured. They could own land. They found that black men, like white men, could vote, and the men of North Buxton exercised this new freedom with skill. (Neither Canada nor the United States allowed women to vote.) Many years passed before women of any race were allowed to vote in Canada or the United States.

Realizing how many adjustments the newly free men and women faced, Mary Ann Shadd, the editor of the *Provincial Freedman* newspaper, published "Notes of Canada West." It was a short, but very informative, guide to things newcomers would need to know.

WOMEN IN THE ANTI-SLAVERY MOVEMENT

Women played a much more significant role in the anti-slavery movement than is generally known. Women worked in private and in public, and much of their work was both under reported or completely unrecorded.

In households that were Underground Railroad stations, it was the woman who cooked meals, made pallets, and cared for sick or injured passengers. Even if a husband and wife cooperated in their UGRR activities, it was very likely that the husband would be the only family member credited in the history books.

Individual women made contributions that had far reaching consequences. Examples on the East Coast included: the Maryland woman whose home was a refuge when Harriet Tubman escaped. Lucretia Mott, who spoke to the U.S. Congress against slavery, and the slaveholder's wife who taught Frederick Douglass to read. Avis Blodgett, Susan Richardson, Harriet Overton, and the "Big Four" at Quinn Chapel A.M.E. Church are among Illinois UGRR heroines.

Women combined their efforts in anti-slavery organizations. In churches and elsewhere in the antislavery movement there was hostility to women in public roles. Women who lectured or taught were regarded as being "utterly spoiled for domestic life."

Nevertheless, an interdenominational group of black and white women formed the Philadelphia Female Anti-Slavery Society on December 8, 1833, four days after the American Anti-Slavery Society was formed. (Lucretia Mott had been invited to speak to the American Anti-Slavery Society by its president, Beriah Green. However, women were not invited to join. Instead they were encouraged to organize a female society which they promptly did.) Women in Massachusetts, Maine, New Hampshire, Rhode Island and Michigan also formed societies.

Women's societies circulated anti-slavery literature and petitions to Congress to end slavery. In Boston and Philadelphia, the societies held fundraising fairs. They sold fancy pastries and needlework to finance activities such as the printing and distribution of literature and the purchase of shoes for UGRR passengers. A handbill announced a fair held by the "ladies of color"at the house of Mrs. Rilla Harris" is an illustration in Dwight Lowell Dumond's book, Antislavery.

In spite of the hostility toward the public participation of women, black and white women such as Sarah and Angelina Grimke, Abby Kelly, Frances Ellen Watkins Harper, Sallie Holley, and Grace Douglass were not discouraged.

In the Midwest, then called "the West," there was far less opposition to female participation than in the East. Dwight Dumond states in his book, "The difficulty of travel and communication and the common burden shared by men and women in the newer regions led to joint effort in the cause of emancipation. "Women in the West not only carried the burden of the petition campaign, they played an important role, sometimes the dominant one in the underground railroad."

Women in the Midwest were coworkers with men, rather than subordinates. In 1839, the American Anti-Slavery Society considered whether to let women vote, only one delegate from Illinois and Michigan voted to deny the vote to women. Women also were present at the formation of state and local antislavery conventions. By the mid-1850's they assumed leadership positions in these groups. Dedicated women like Sojourner Truth and Laura Haviland worked cooperatively with equally dedicated men as William Lambert and George DeBaptiste in Michigan.

Women teachers like Eliza Chappel Porter and text book writers introduced antislavery teachings into the schools. They used such materials as the "Abolitionist ABC's" and textbooks with antislavery poems. One geography book included pictures of how African people were kidnapped from their homelands.

Many of the women who were active in state and local societies wrote widely distributed antislavery materials. While Harriet Beecher Stowe's name is well known, others such as Margaret Chandler are not. Beginning in 1829 Chandler wrote for Benjamin Lundy's *Genius for Universal Emancipation.* According to Lundy, Chandler was the first woman to make slavery the main topic of her writing. Lundy had such respect for her that when she died, he collected and published her essays and letters.

Jane Grey Swisshelm, Mary Ann Shadd Cary, and Mary Brown Davis were other pioneers in using their writings to speak out against slavery.

The issue of women's participation in the national American Anti-Slavery Society was brought to a head by William Lloyd Garrison. In addition to raising this important human rights issue, Garrison alienated many anti-slavery men by his opposition to the Constitution, the Bible, and political action against slavery. Garrison flooded the 1840 convention with women delegates from Massachusetts. His delegation won on a narrow margin. Lucretia Mott, Lydia Marie Child, and Maria W. Chapman were elected to the executive committee.

The response of those who disagreed with Garrison on one or more issues was to form the American and Foreign Anti-Slavery Society. In the meantime they had found in the Liberty Party, a new outlet for their political expression.

A World Anti-Slavery Convention was held in London, England, in June 1840. It was planned as an international gathering of anti-slavery men.

The Garrison-led American Anti-Slavery Society appointed Lucretia Mott as one of its delegates to this international gathering. The Massachusetts and Pennsylvania societies had appointed other women to serve as delegates.

After learning of this the organizers of the world convention requested a list of the "names of the *gentlemen*" who were to be delegates from America. One American society withdrew its female delegates, but the women from Garrison-influenced societies went to London.

There was immediate discussion about whether to seat delegates, that is, women, who were not on the membership list. American abolitionist, Wendell Phillips, offered a possible solution, but in the debate that followed, Phillips' motion was overwhelmingly defeated.

Garrison had arrived late. Instead of taking his seat in the convention, he sat with the women who had hoped to be delegates.

THE 1840 CONVENTION OF THE WORLD
ANTI-SLAVERY SOCIETY IN LONDON.

11. Who operated the Underground Railroad stations?

All kinds of people helped operate the stations, some white, black, and Native American.

Some station operators had been born in this country. Of those, some were born free; others were born into bondage. Some were from New England or elsewhere in the North. Others were from the South. Some had come from Scotland, Germany, or other countries in Europe. Some were wealthy. Others indigent. Some had come to the United States to flee oppression or religious persecution in their homelands. Some identified themselves as Quakers, Congregationalists, Presbyterians, Jews, Baptists, Covenanters, Wesleyans, Methodists, Lutherans, Unitarians, or as members of the Dutch Reformed Church.

Some would have been happy to assist one slave. Some helped many slaves. They were inspired by religious beliefs, their personal senses of justice, and the words of the Declaration of Independence: "All men are created equal and endowed by their Maker with certain inalienable rights." Some church and town founders who took the Golden Rule so seriously that, although there were civil laws against helping fugitives, they followed a "Higher Law."

People involved in the anti-slavery movement included:

~ Former slaveholder Southerners like Governor Edward Coles, who fought valiantly to keep Illinois from becoming a slave state, or Dr. Silas Hamilton, who had tried to run a model plantation, came to Illinois. Both freed their slaves before settling in Illinois.

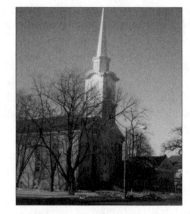

~ Free black people and former slaves, many of whose names are unrecorded in history books. After gaining her own freedom and going to work as a maid in the home of Waukegan grain dealer, James Cory, a black woman named Merina, would escort UGRR passengers to freedom in broad daylight. (Anyone seeing her with a group of black men would assume the men were also working for Cory.)

~ White and black church founders. The home of Thompson Paxton in Eola was the first meeting place of the Big and Little Woods Church and an UGRR station.

Courtesy of Congregational Church of Batavia.

~Emma Jane Atkinson whose work was central to the success of the UGRR in Chicago and of Quinn Chapel.

~ Members of the Liberty political party, who acted on their belief in the natural equality of all persons.

~ The legendary Harriet Tubman, who escaped from slavery then went back South again and again to personally free some three hundred enslaved people.

~ Underground Railroad conductors like John L. Beveridge of Somonauk, who later became better known as Governor of Illinois than for his UGRR activities.

~ Levi Coffin, a white southerner who moved to Richmond, Indiana and helped so many passengers to escape, became known as "President of the UGRR."

~ Henry "Box" Brown who was carefully crated in a box (2 ft. 8 in. deep, 2 ft. wide and 3 ft. long) and shipped to freedom by James Smith, a sympathetic white carpenter.

~ Pioneers in new settlements. North of Chicago, Philo Judson erected a building at Davis Street and Orrington Avenue in Evanston (then called Ridgeville). This building, which housed the town's post office and Colvin's General Store was also the meeting place of the town's first club, and anti-slavery organization formed in protest of the 1850 Fugitive Slave Act.

~ South of Chicago, where Thornton Road (now Indiana Avenue) crossed the Calumet River, the home of a Dutch Reformed family was strategically located near the ferry crossing. This house, known as the Jan Ton House, was reportedly an Underground Railroad station.

~ Native Americans who, prior to being removed from the land in the East and Middle West, befriended black freedom seekers. It is likely that Native Americans who lived in the wetlands around Lake Calumet shared their survival skills and knowledge of the ecology of that region with UGRR passengers who had followed Thornton Road or Vincennes Road to what is now the Riverdale/Dolton area.

~ The Seminole Indians of Florida who took great risks to provide sanctuary to slaves escaping from plantations in South Carolina and Georgia.

~ Abolitionist professors at Transylvannia College in Lexington, Kentucky.

~ Farmers, lawyers, tailors, railroad executives, maids, coopers, artists, millers, journalists, or innkeepers who used their work situations to lend a helping hand. Deacon Jirah Platt used a hollow haystack with a blind entrance as a hiding place for UGRR passengers in Mendon.

~ Two steamboat captains, Walker and Blake, often allowed Underground Railroad passengers to come aboard ship in Chicago and work as firemen in exchange for their passage to Canada.

CHARLES VOLNEY DYER

Charles Volney Dyer became better known for his abolitionist activities than for his medical practice. Born in Clarendon, Vermont, and educated at Middleburg College, he came to Chicago in August 1835. He married Louisa Gifford, the sister of Elgin founder, James T. Gifford.

Both Dr. and Mrs. Dyer were active in the anti-slavery movement. They were friends of Owen Lovejoy, Allan Pinkerton, Philo Carpenter and other prominent abolitionists.

As stated elsewhere in this book, he was president of the Chicago Burlington & Quincy Railroad and often arranged transportation of UGRR passengers on the CB & Q trains. As a result he was sometimes called "President of the Illinois Underground Railroad."

The day after the 1850 Fugitive Slave Act was passed, he was one of a group of black and white abolitionists who chartered enough train coaches to transport early fugitive slaves in the Chicago area to freedom in Canada. The group of abolitionists included Zebina Eastmen, John Jones, Calvin DeWolf, Henry Bradford, L.C.P. Freer, Louis Isbell, H.O. Wagoner and Mr. Bridges.

Some details of Dr. Dyer's anti-slavery activities did not have to do with railroad operations. Probably the most dramatic took place at the Mansion House Hotel; when Dr. Dyer learned that a man who had escaped from bondage in Kentucky had been caught and shackled by the slavecatcher, he cut the man's ropes and said, "You don't belong to anybody. Go about your own business."

A member of the slaveholder's armed posse attacked Dr. Dyer, who responded by breaking his cane over the assailant's head. Following this, some sympathetic friends gave Dr. Dyer a gold-headed cane which is now at the Chicago Historical Society.

Dyer had great respect for the power of the written word. This was consistent with his family and his anti-slavery activities. He was a descendent of the Quaker martyr, Mary Dyer. His wife had written an address to the Women of America. An anti-slavery convention was held in Chicago some years after the death of Alton newspaper editor, Elijah Lovejoy. Dr. Dyer was chairman of the committee to establish a national anti-slavery newspaper in Washington, D.C. The paper was named *National Era*. It's first editor was Gammiel Bailey. Frederick Douglass, Mary Ann Shadd and Richard Greener were later associated with it.

In 1863, President Abraham Lincoln recognized the work of Dr. Dyer who was a personal friend. The President appointed Dr. Dyer judge of the mixed court for the suppression of the slave trade. Sessions of this international tribunal were helped in Sierra Leone, Africa. Dr. Dyer was in Rome when President Lincoln was assassinated. He addressed Americans there on that occasion.

Chas. V. Dyer

12. What the role did churches play in the anti-slavery movement?

The role of churches in the Underground Railroad was very significant. Because many Underground Railroad workers had strong church connections, they often worked within these religious organizations in addition to taking individual actions.

In 1838 the Northern Baptist Association of Illinois met at Community Baptist Church in Warrenville. They met in response to the death of Elijah Lovejoy and passed a resolution condemning slavery. In 1844 there was an anti-slavery mass meeting of all the Baptist churches in Illinois. The delegates called for the establishment of an anti-slavery newspaper. The first edition of the *Western Christian* was published in Elgin in 1845.

A group of Reformed Presbyterians are known as the Covenanters, or Seceders. Their members came to Illinois to establish a series of UGRR stations. These stations were placed along the Rockwood/Chester route that passed through Eden, Coulterville, and Oakdale, down to a point near Nashville.

African Methodist Episcopal churches were built at relatively close distances. In addition to being houses of worship, they were community meeting places, schools, and Underground Railroad stations. Rev. Paul Quinn, for whom Quinn Chapels in Chicago and in Brooklyn, Illinois are named, established many churches throughout the Middle West. Many of the ministers and members had escaped from slavery and worked actively to help others escape. The same was true of the black Baptist churches. The minister of Zion Missionary Baptist Church is a prime example. After making his own escape, then returning to rescue family members, Rev. Thomas Jefferson Houston repeatedly crossed the Mississippi River to transport slaves to free territory. More details of his life and work are described in Question 27.

Some areas of Illinois were settled by people from a center of religious revival in Oneida, New York. This is how Galesburg, Genesco, Lyndon, Princeton, Bailey Grove, and the Libson colonies were formed. Many of the people were Congregationalists and took a strong stand against slavery. In what later became Kendall County, Congregational churches were formed between 1835 and 1858 in Big Grove, Bristol (Yorkville), Libson, Newark, Oswego, Little Rock, and Plano. These churches became centers of abolitionism and UGRR activities. They often expressed their views in statements such as this by the Bristol congregational members in 1846.

"We testify against the whole system of human slavery as practiced in these United States. We consider the chattel principle or holding property in man, as a most heaven forbidding and God-provoking sin. The 'sum of all villainies', as it effects those enslaved. That we cannot hold fellowship with voluntary slaveholders or their ablation. We cannot permit their preachers to occupy our pulpit, or those who justify them in slave holding, to sit at our communion."

HENRY O. WAGONER

Henry O. Wagoner was born in Hagerstown, Maryland, on February 27, 1816. When he was five, his grandmother taught him the alphabet. He had less than a year of formal education, but he had no paper or slate, instead, he wrote on board fences with chalk.

As a young man, he did every kind of farm work. When he as twenty-two, he went to Baltimore, then left for the West within the same week of September 1838 that Frederick Douglass escaped from bondage in Baltimore.

Wagoner stopped in Wheeling, West Virginia, Cincinnati and Dayton, Ohio during the winter term where he taught people with even less schooling. He went on to New Orleans in the spring, then traveled north to St. Louis. From there he went to Galena, Illinois, where he got a job on a Whig party newspaper, *The Northwestern Gazette* and *Galena Advertiser*. During his years there, he learned to set type, and did many jobs on the newspaper including compositing, overlooking circulation and billing.

Wagoner bought real estate which he later sold to the Honorable E.B. Washburne. They became friends.

In 1842, Wagoner went to Chatham, Ontario, Canada then called Canada West. He was employed by the *Chatham Journal* newspaper and later by the County School commissioners as a teacher.

Wagoner later moved to Chicago where he went to work at Zebina Eastman's *Western Citizen*. He invested in real estate and engaged in various kinds of businesses. In the meantime, Frederick Douglass had begun publishing the *North Star*. Wagoner subscribed and occasionally wrote articles for that newspaper.

Wagoner had been involved in the UGRR Railroad and other anti-slavery work throughout his adult life. In 1857, he met John Brown. Two years later when Brown made the daring rescue of eleven Missouri slaves, Wagoner furnished food and lodging for them. Reportedly he hid the slaves in his mill after hanging a "closed for repairs" sign on the front door.

Tailor John Jones housed John Brown and his white assistants. As black men both Wagoner and Jones took great personal risks. They were liable under the Fugitive Slave Act and the Illinois Black Codes. The pressure was eased when detective Allan Pinkerton raised funds to transport Brown and his entire party to Detroit by train.

Wagoner experienced financial hard times in Chicago and went to Denver for a year. At the beginning of the Civil War he worked in support of the Union Army. When black men were allowed to enlist, Wagoner was asked to recruit men for the Twenty-Ninth U.S. Colored Infantry. He was asked by Governor Andrews of Massachusetts to recruit for the Fifth Cavalry and Governor Yates of Illinois commissioned him to go to Mississippi to recruit refugees and contrabands of war.

At the war's end Wagoner received a letter of recommendation from General Ulysses S. Grant.

Wagoner returned to Denver after the Civil War where he resumed business activities. He was appointed deputy sheriff of Arapaho County and served as an election judge. His son, who was also named Henry, was Consul in France.

These are excerpts expressing the sentiments of Congregational Church of Batavia:

~ Resolved, that the system of American slavery finds no place or sanction in the Bible but is entirely opposed to the spirit and letter of the word of God.
~ Resolved, that American slavery is a violation of all the principals of national justice, and an outrage upon humanity, which a civilized and especially a Christian community ought to look upon with detestation and horror.

The resolutions in which the Millburn Congregational Church clearly stated its support of the UGRR is printed in the "Extra! Extra! Read All About It" chapter in this book.

In 1845 black abolitionist and women's rights advocate Sojourner Truth spoke at the Congregationalist Church of Lake County. The following year a large religious antislavery meeting was held in Half Day.

MEETING OF ABOLITIONISTS
Courtesy of The DuSable Museum of African American History

BARNEY FORD

Like Henry O. Wagoner, Barney Ford was a self-taught man from the South. Ford's mother had drowned while trying to find an UGRR agent to help him escape from slavery.

The men met in Chicago and Wagoner soon convinced Ford to join him in his UGRR work. Their families were linked when Ford married Wagoner's sister-in-law, Julia. The Fords set out by ship for the California gold rush. After arriving in Nicaragua, Ford opened a hotel there rather than continuing on to California. He called it the U.S. Hotel and he hosted many dignitaries from the States. Later he returned to Chicago for a while and then moved to Colorado.

In 1865, Colorado prohibited black voting rights.

Wagoner urged Ford to lobby in Washington, DC against this. Ford enlisted the support of Senator Charles Sumner of Massachusetts and the provision was eliminated.

Wagoner, Ford and two other black pioneers established Colorado's first adult education classes. Black people came to Wagoner's house to learn the "3-R's" and the principles of democratic government.

Ford built and operated two huge Inter-Ocean hotels in Denver and Cheyenne, they catered to wealthy patrons and had a reputation for serving "the squarest meal between two oceans." Both Wagoner and Ford overcame repeated business troubles and took their civic responsibilities very seriously.

SYLVESTER LIND

Sylvester Lind was an active conductor on the Underground Railroad and was involved in the founding of Lake Forest. Born in Scotland, he came to Chicago to work as a carpenter. Five years later, he entered the lumber business. Following this, he established the Lind and Dunlap firm. It had lumber mills at Cedar River, Michigan and directly west of Washington Island in Door County.

Lind made and lost several fortunes during the ups and downs of Chicago's economy. He selected Lake Forest for his home in support of the community and the college. Upon pledging $100,000, the college was named for him when it was founded in 1857. However, he was unable to meet his pledge and the name was changed to Lake Forest College in 1865.

Following this, Lind became prosperous again until the Chicago Fire in 1871. He later served as Mayor of Lake Forest. Although he was no longer wealthy he was still highly respected.

In addition to his business and civic interests Lind played an important role in the anti-slavery movement. According to an article written by Lake Forest College student, William Danforth, Lind was an UGRR conductor.

His lumberyard on the Chicago River was a location where Underground Railroad passengers could board ships that plied the Great Lakes. Under the Fugitive Slave Act, a ship captain risked losing his ship if caught transporting former slaves; however Lind and other abolitionists arranged for captains to "look the other way" while the UGRR passengers stowed away. The passengers would get off at a refueling stop between Lind's Michigan lumber mill and Washington Island. There they'd board a ship heading for Detroit. Before these ships reached Detroit, their captains would drift close enough to the Canadian shore in the narrow St. Clair River for the stowaways to leap to freedom in Ontario, Canada.

It is a coincidence that the family who later purchased Lind's home had family ties to the anti-slavery movement. The new owners were Katherine McKim Garrison Norton and Charles Dyer Norton.

Mrs. Norton was the descendant of two abolitionists. According to the 1912 History of Lake County, Illinois one of her grandfathers was William Lloyd Garrison editor of the *Liberator* newspaper. Her other grandfather was abolitionist James Miller McKim. (Mr. and Mrs. McKim accompanied Mrs. John Brown to claim her husband's body at Harper's Ferry.)

There is a probable family relationship between Charles Dyer Norton and abolitionist Charles Volney Dyer. It is known that Dr. Dyer was a supporter of Lake Forest. He came to town and spoke at a rally celebrating the new community in June of 1859. It is possible that some of his descendants decided to settle there.

SYLVESTER LIND
Courtesy of Lake Forest College.

13. How did the UGRR station operators and conductors assist passengers?

Underground Railroad workers assisted passengers in the following ways:

~ By using hay stacks, barns, wells, lofts, basements, attics, and secret enclosures behind fireplaces, under staircases, or in closets as hiding places. Prior to becoming the governor of Illinois, John L. Beveridge of Somonauk used an underground straw stack room as his UGRR station. Two small boys from a neighboring farm discovered it quite by accident. They were playing on top of a straw stack when suddenly the straw gave way and they fell into a hole seven or eight feet deep. Unhurt, they got up, looked around. and realized they were in a circular room that was lined in straw and covered with a straw roof. They got out by climbing a dead tree which stood in the middle of the room. Many years later, after one of the boys returned from serving in the Civil War and secrecy was no longer necessary, a member the Beveridge family told him the purpose of the mystery room.

~ By providing warm food. UGRR passengers had to forage and flee at the same time. They were unable to cook because their pursuers could see firelight. Although many knew how to set traps or hunt with slingshots, these activities would have revealed their whereabouts.

~ By furnishing heavy clothing. As you know, the southern climate is warmer than the northern climate. Many slaves had no shoes or other winter-weight clothing.

~ By making disguises available. In McDonough County the Allison family kept old gowns, hoods and coats in their attics. These disguises helped many UGRR passengers evade slave catcher David Chrisman and reach the Blazer family's station.

~ By providing transportation to the next station, a river, or longer distances. Wagons "going to town" sometimes had human cargo beneath garden produce or false flooring in the wagon. Transportation was also secured on trains, barges, stagecoaches, or clipper ships. Artist Sheldon Peck of Lombard transported UGRR passengers when he returned to the Chicago area from his studio in St. Louis. Only in rare instances did UGRR workers transport passengers all the way to Canada, however, the sons of "Free Frank" McWorter sometimes escorted passengers to Canada from their farm in Pike County.

~ By supplying information about routes to the next station, persons to contact, or a password to use. In his research historian Larry McClellan found that in the 1850s members of small but well established black communities in Joliet worked with white abolitionists in Will County. Undoubtedly, they directed UGRR passengers to stations in Plainfield and in DuPage County.

~ By informing passengers of the best times to travel and places of refuge. Robert

GALESBURG

Galesburg had a reputation for being the headquarters of abolition in Illinois. In 1857 an article in a Bloomington newspaper referred to Galesburg as an "abolition hole," unlike Quincy, Alton, or Chester it wasn't a river town. It was situated near the Old Galena Trail and on the Chicago Burlington, and Quincy Railroad line after the 1850's.

What made it an anti-slavery center were the views of its founders. George Washington Gale, for whom the town was named, was a minister in upstate New York. He was an educator, who, like a number of other people in the East, dreamed of forming colleges and towns on the rich farm lands of what was then called the West. In 1836 he chose to locate in an area between the Illinois and Mississippi Rivers known as the "Military Tract".

The following year the Illinois State Legislature granted a charter for Knox Manual Labor College. H. H. Kellogg, was the first president of the college. He was also pastor of the Old First Church which stood at the corner of Broad and Simmons Streets next to the Public Square. In 1843 he was the Illinois Anti-slavery Society delegate to the World Anti-Slavery Convention in London, England.

Gale, Kellogg, and Jonathan Blanchard, who became president when Kellogg resigned, were all staunch abolitionists. Reportedly the church belfry was an Underground Railroad hiding place.

Church members had different opinions on slavery and how involved they should be in UGRR efforts. These differences resulted in a split of the Presbyterian churches. One group became a Congregational Church, the First Church of Christ.

Knox College was the institution around which the town grew. A lot of history was made there. President Blanchard debated Senator Stephen A. Douglas over the issue of the Kansas-Nebraska Bill. It was believed that this debate was a model for the 1858 Lincoln-Douglas debates, one of which also took place on the college grounds.

During that same period (1856-1857) Hiram Revels was a student at Knox. He became the first black U.S. Senator in American history when he filled the seat vacated by Jefferson Davis of Mississippi.

There was much activity, especially Underground Railroad activity, elsewhere in the town of Galesburg. Many of the "passengers" had escaped from Missouri and stopped in Iowa at such Quaker settlements as Kossuth, Salem, or Denmark in southeastern Iowa. Friends would bring them to Galesburg at night. Samuel Hitchcock, Susan Richardson, George Davis, and Nehemiah West were station operators or conductors. The next stop might be Stark County or Ontario in Knox County.

Once on the college commencement day, Mr. Dilly from Warren County brought a load of oat straw to Samuel Hitchcock's farm three miles northwest of Galesburg. After Dilly and Hitchcock had exchanged a few words, one man, three women and three children crawled from under the hay. Hitchcock took them to the next UGRR station.

THE OLD FIRST CHURCH, GALESBURG, IL

Kennedy was a free black man whose parents had been enslaved in Kentucky. He came to Morris, Illinois, with the white man who had enslaved his family. They operated a blacksmith shop on the I & M canal. They knew the schedule of barges and the locations of stables along the canal, so they could tell UGRR passengers of safe travel times and resting places.

~ By providing free papers. As mentioned elsewhere, free black people, like Rev. Richard DeBaptiste of Chicago, sometimes loaned their own certificates of freedom to UGRR passengers.

~ By working with other abolitionists. For example, they cooperated with one another when slave catchers were near. A case in point was when Susan Richardson of Galesburg, a woman who had been enslaved/indentured, housed an Underground Railroad passenger whom agents Neeley, West, and Blanchard conducted to the next station.

~ By using one's place of business as a hiding place. No doubt a certain farmer transported an Underground Railroad passenger as he took corn to the mill operated by abolitionist Frederick Graue of the Hinsdale/Oakbrook area. The miller would grind the farmer's corn and secretly provide the passenger with lodging in the cold, but safe, basement of the mill. The passenger could then follow the nearby Salt Creek then follow the Des Plaines River northward.

~ By permitting one's place of business to be used as a secret meeting place, as was done by Henry O. Wagoner. Wagoner's mill was the setting in which Allan Pinkerton and John Brown met to clandestinely discuss a plan for safe passage from Chicago to Canada for Brown and the large group of slaves he had rescued.

~ By acting as decoys (as in cases of Rev. Batcheller in Harding, Rev. John Cross of Knox County, and an associate of Owen Lovejoy's in Princeton).

~ By being advocates in church pulpits, in courtrooms, anti-slavery tracts, and newspapers. Carver Tomlinson of Marshall County was one of many advocates. Rev. Milton Smith, who operated an UGRR station in Bloomingdale, narrowly escaped being thrown from a boat on the Ohio River for speaking out against slavery.

~ By purchasing train tickets for individual slaves, or financing flamboyant operations the "Secret 6" as was done by a group of backers of John Brown's Harper's Ferry raid.

The secret to the success of the Underground Railroad was the ability of conductors, agents, and passengers to be flexible and resourceful. For example:

~ Conductor Harriet Tubman was known to put her passengers on a train going back south to throw slavers off her trail. She once saw slave catchers board a train she was riding. Realizing they knew that she couldn't read, she got a newspaper and pretended to read it. Later, she realized she'd had the paper upside down, but her pursuers hadn't noticed. (Evidently they couldn't read either.)

~ Knowing that slave catchers were in the area, Rev. John Cross and a neighbor planned in advance for the neighbor to pose as the owner of some escaping slaves who were known to be in Knox County, Illinois. The neighbor was to pretend that he wanted to reclaim "his" property. As Cross approached with the slaves in his carriage, the neighbor lost his nerve and he rushed to Cross. They put the slaves into the neighbor's wagon, then Cross raced on as if he were trying to avoid being stopped. Finally he was stopped when both of his horses were tripped up with a pole. The neighbor, meanwhile, had gotten the slaves safely across the Spoon River.

~ The operator of a station in Plainfield hid slaves in a room built in the center of a woodpile.

~ While visiting Union troops in the South, Mary Livermore of Chicago hid and transported an abused slave child in her suitcase.

~ Israel Blodgett of Downers Grove wrapped slaves in buffalo skins and carried them into his blacksmith shop.

SUSAN RICHARDSON

Susan Richardson was brought into the Illinois Territory before it was a state. She was kept in bondage by Andrew Borders of Randolph County.

Her children and the Borders' children got into an altercation; Mrs. Borders was insistent that Susan Richardson be severely whipped.

Susan Richardson was able to escape with her two small children and a teenage son. First they went to Cairo then to Canton in Fulton County. They were taken by Mr. Wilson to the house of John Cross in the eastern part of Knox County. Susan Richardson and her children were arrested and imprisoned in the county jail. Andrew Borders learned of the arrest; meanwhile, some Galesburg abolitionists had arranged for the family to be released. Susan Richardson found work as a laundress and arranged for her young children to stay at the hotel during the day. Her teenage son worked on a nearby farm. One day she was informed that Andrew Borders was in town looking for "his property." Susan Richardson attempted to rescue her children but Borders recaptured them and she never saw them again. She learned that her son was killed while doing a dangerous job Borders had sent him to do.

After her personal tragedy, Susan Richardson operated an Underground Railroad station in Galesburg. Bill Casey was one of the people she helped. He had fled from Missouri with five other people. They were tracked down and two or three were shot and the others re-enslaved. Casey escaped through the woods and made his way to Galesburg unaided. He reached Susan Richardson's home on a Saturday night. His body was bruised, his clothes ragged, his feet swollen and bleeding, and he was starving. Susan Richardson provided food and clothing. The next day she left him at home while she went to church and informed other Underground Railroad workers Neeley, West, and Blanchard, that Casey was hidden at her house.

They went to her home. They attempted to get shoes for Casey, but his feet were so swollen that they had to go to the store four times before they could fit him.

That evening Casey was transported to the next Underground Railroad station.

~ In Farmington, Deacon Birges served sleep-inducing coffee to slave hunters and whisked slaves away while the hunters dozed.

~ Since slaves were considered to be property, the loss of the free services of a slave meant the loss of income for the enslaver. In addition to helping slaves escape, station operators (and abolitionists who were not directly involved in UGRR activities) often refused to use such slave produced items as cotton, sugar, rice, and molasses. For fabric the families of these abolitionists wore garments made of wool from sheep they raised or linen spun from flax they grew. They used honey instead of sugar or molasses. They ate potatoes instead of rice.

~ In Lake Forest, Roxana Beecher, a niece of author Harriet Beecher Stowe operated that town's first public school. Some of her students were former slaves who had been denied schooling while they were held in bondage.

~ Professor Jonathan B. Turner of Illinois College in Jacksonville was not always an UGRR agent. He said, "I took no interest in running slaves off to Canada because they were not needed there but were needed here to help us face the music around us ... " One cold December night while feeding his horses, he was approached by an abolitionist friend. The friend asked Turner's help in an emergency situation – three women had run away from St. Louis because they were about to be sold. The women were in need of a place where they could rest and care for their frozen feet. They had been sheltered in a black community in Jacksonville until slavecatchers drove them out into a hut in a cornfield where they would probably freeze during the night. All Jacksonville residents who were likely to be suspected of being UGRR workers were being closely watched. Turner's friend asked him to rescue the women. Agreeing, Turner got a stout stick that he could use as a club if necessary, and set out. When he found the women, he asked them to follow him with the understanding they would run into the cornfield if the slavecatchers returned. He tired to think of the safest place to shelter them. Knowing his home might be searched, he took them to the home of a pro-slavery Presbyterian elder and appealed to the elder's belief in the Golden Rule. The elder and his wife hid the women in their barn with warm quilts and ample food. The women remained there for two weeks until their feet were recovered enough to continue their journey. One of Turner's abolitionist friends took his horses and sleigh and transported the women to Farmington, forty miles away.

14. Were some Illinois locations especially well known for Underground Railroad activities?

Yes, however, Underground Railroad operators felt they had to be more secretive in some locations than others. The openness of operations ranged from to operators whose immediate family members did not know of their involvement, to the following accounts:

> Rev. Samuel Guild Wright wrote in his diary: "June 11, 1848. Tues. I brought a colored man from H. Rhodes to town, and he went on by day with a company from Osceloa, and the next day in the stage to Princeton. All which shows that the railroad has risen nearly to the surface here."

> And Ezra Cook, one of the Wheaton College students to volunteer in the Civil War later said, "The Underground Railroad was an above ground railroad at the college."

Perhaps the first UGRR stations in Illinois were established in Bond County around 1819 by a small colony of abolitionists who moved to the state from Brown County, Ohio.

Galesburg, Chicago and Quincy were probably the best known UGRR cities in Illinois. Along the Mississippi other cities such as Alton, Chester, and Rock Island were popular entry points to the state. Cairo was the entry point for freedom seekers from Kentucky and Tennessee.

Many routes converged in Bureau, Putnam, and LaSalle counties. Individuals and organizations there were very active. In 1831 there was a meeting at Shoal Creek Presbyterian Church in Boone County. Participants fasted and held prayer for the slaves. Two years later, in February of 1833, anti-slavery meetings were held in Putnam County. These meetings took place before the American Anti-Slavery Society was organized in Philadelphia in December 1833.

In 1836 and 1837, thirty-seven anti-slavery societies were formed in Illinois. These included societies in Putnam, Adams, Will, Madison, and Jersey counties.

The statewide Illinois Anti-slavery Society was formed at the stone house in Upper Alton shortly before Elijah Lovejoy's death in 1837. Lovejoy's murder motivated many people across the nation who had not previously taken action against slavery, to do so.

Residents of Brooklyn, the oldest black town in Illinois, had a strong association with the Underground Railroad. Many became members of the African Methodist Church. The town was platted the year of Lovejoy's death. The town's post office was named for him.

Anti-slavery societies were formed in Knox, LaSalle, and Warren counties in 1839. That same year Rev. Chauncey Cook, who later became Minister of Bristol (Yorkville) Congregational Church , organized three district societies.

Early black settlers worked with settlers of European ancestry in antislavery efforts. One example took place in Will County which was a center for abolitionist activity in the 1840's and 1850's. The small black community in Joliet worked cooperatively with white abolitionists in helping UGRR passengers to freedom.

The Kane County Anti-Slavery Society was most active in this same time period. Dr. Anson Root, better known for his role in the dramatic escape of Caroline Quarels, was chairman of this society in 1843.

The *Belvidere Standard* contained notices of anti-slavery meetings in Boone County which possibly were also attended by McHenry County residents.

There was antislavery activity at different locations in Lake County. The Lake County Anti-Slavery Society was named the Liberty Association. It convened in Libertyville in 1846. The Fox Lake Emancipation Society passed a resolution to denounce the Fugitive Slave Act of 1850.

The abolitionist movement in Chicago began following Lovejoy's death. The city became a hub of anti-slavery activity in the early 1840's. The Anti-Slavery Society was organized in 1840, and newspaper editor Zebina Eastman moved to Chicago in 1842 at the invitation of Dr. C.V. Dyer. Rev. Flavel Bascome, pastor of First Presbyterian Church, held monthly anti-slavery meetings to the displeasure of some of his members.

According to the "grapevine telegraph" in the years before the passage of the 1850 Fugitive Slave Act, if an Underground Railroad passenger could reach certain locations such as Chicago, or the North Woods, he or she was safe.

In his many years of study Underground Railroad researcher, Professor Wilbur Siebert of Ohio, also learned of other UGRR activity in these Illinois counties: Alexander, Bond, Cook, DuPage, Fulton, Grundy, Hancock, Henderson, Henry, Kane, Kendall, Lake, Lee, Livingston, McDonough, McHenry, McLean, Marshall, Mercer, Montgomery, Morgan, Ogle, Peoria, Randolph, Rock Island, Sangamon, Stark, Tazewell, Vermilllion, Washington, Wayne, Whiteside, and Woodford.

Philo Carpenter's House, corner of Randolph and Morgan streets, was an Underground Railroad station in Chicago.

MARY ANN SHADD CARY

One cold winter night in the mid-1850's Mary Ann Shadd stood on the train platform in Geneva, Illinois. She had traveled from Ontario, Canada, in an effort to get more subscribers to the *Provincial Freedman* newspaper that she edited.

Mary Ann was born October 9, 1823, into a free black family. She and her family had a history of dedication to the abolition of slavery. Her parents, Harriet and Abraham Shadd, operated an Underground Railroad station in Wilmington, Delaware.

Little is known about Harriet Parnell Shadd except that she was born in North Carolina in 1806.

Abraham Dorcas Shadd was born in Delaware in 1801. He was a shoemaker with a thriving business and a founding member of the American Antislavery Society and the Delaware delegate at the Improvement of Free People in rhe United States. He was an agent for William Lloyd Garrison's *Liberator* newspaper and he, like Garrison, believed in immediate emancipation. However, he believed that emancipation was only the first step. He insisted that education, thrift, and hardwork were the remaining steps. In fact, education was so important to Harriet and Abraham Shadd that when Mary Ann was 10, they left their family, friends, and property so that their children could attend school in Pennsylvania, because Delaware did not provide schools for black children. They enrolled Mary Ann in a Quaker school in West Chester.

After completing her studies, Mary Ann taught in Wilmington, and other cities on the East Coast. Soon after the Fugitive Slave Act passed in 1850, she went to Canada to attend a meeting of black people who wanted to find ways to meet the needs of the many UGRR passengers who would be seeking refuge in Canada. She found there was an urgent need for teachers, so she remained in Canada.

For a while she taught at a school operated by Rev. Henry Bibb, but Mary Ann Shadd felt that Rev. Bibb encouraged former slaves to become dependent refugees. She encouraged them to become self-reliant citizens as soon as possible. She taught the children the lessons she had learned from her father—to work hard and be thrifty.

Knowing that adults would need information as they began their lives as free men and women, Mary Ann Shadd wrote a 44-page guidebook on what to expect in

Canada, popularly known as *"Notes of Canada West."* She included information on climate, election laws, geography, business and educational opportunity. She also listed crops that would grow well there.

Rev. Bibb objected to her choice of a printer for that publication, and to the way she conducted her classroom. In addition to operating a school, he published a newspaper in which he was very critical of her.

Since childhood Mary Ann Shadd had known how important newspapers could be in shaping public opinion. She recalled what a teacher had once told her, "the printed and spoken word is never lost." She remembered how influencial the *Liberator* had been.

She knew that Jane Grey Swisshelm of Pittsburgh, Pennsylvania, published a newspaper devoted to abolition and other reforms, and decided to become the second woman in North America to publish a newspaper. She wanted to inspire her readers by featuring black progress in Canada. She also wanted a forum in which to voice her opinion of black or white abolitionists, who, like Bibb, she found to be hypocritical.

Realizing that her readers would object to having a female editor, Mary Ann Shadd worked out an agreement with noted writer and orator,Samuel Ringgold Ward, to list his name as editor. In reality she was the editor of the *Provincial Freedman*.

She began publication in March 1853. She not only wanted to promote abolitionism and racial uplift. She shared Jane Swisshelm's interests in reforms, especially women's rights. She often printed articles by Swisshelm and poems by Frances E. Watkins.

Soon after beginning publication Mary Ann Shadd began a tour in the United States. During the tour she sought subscribers to the newspaper, and she encouraged black people to emigrate to Canada. She was so successful in getting black people to move to Canada that her parents settled in about twelve miles from Chatham, Ontario, in the thriving black farming community of Buxton. The Buxton communit;y had been established by a Scotsman, Rev. William King. Rev. King had married the daughter of a plantation owner. When his wife died Rev. King freed fifteen slaves and took them to Canada where they could form the nucleus of this self-supporting community.

The school at Buxton was recognized throughout the

MARY ANN SHADD CARY (CONT.)

area for the high quality of education it provided. White neighbors enrolled their children. Many of the black graduates returned to the United States.

Mary Ann Shadd's younger sister, Amelia, and brother, Issac, emigrated to Canada with their parents. They joined her in operating the paper. At one point Mary Ann turned the day to day operations over to her sister. In the meanwhile, she married Thomas Cary, a Toronto barber who had been an active supporter of the newspaper.

Canada experienced a depression in the 1850's. This meant financial hard times for the paper. Mary Ann Shadd Cary had to resume traveling in an effort to get more subscribers. She was admitted as a delegate to the Colored National Convention in Philadelphia where she gave a speech that, according to a newspaper report, caused the crowd to be,"breathless in its attention to her masterly exposition."

She also visited a number of Illinois cities and towns. It was on one of these trips that she came to Geneva. She spoke at Wheaton College and to a small group in Rockford.

She spoke in Chicago on December of 1855, probably at Quinn Chapel. She returned a few months later after a shift in the ownership of the *Provincial Freedman*.

Issac Shadd was one of the new owners. The other two were Louis Paterson, about whom little is known, and H. Ford Douglass, a self-educated former slave.

Mary Ann Shadd Cary was joined by Douglass for a speaking tour in the Midwest. One or both of them spoke in Waukegan, and Kenosha and Racine, Wisconsin. They experienced the hardships of travel. Mary Ann Shadd Cary recalled a time when she reached a destination north of Chicago after "having made a bittter cold journey, by sleigh, of many miles, and having 'roosted' for one night on a very narrow platform at the Geneva station in the company of several belated snow-delayed mortals of both sexes."

The next years were filled with hope and disappointment for Mary Ann Shadd Cary and for the United States and Canada. She and her husband had a daughter and a son. John Brown went to Chatham to discuss his plans for Harpers Ferry and to draw up a Provisional Constitution for the free country he hoped to create. Issac Shadd and Thomas Cary not only

attended these meetings. John Brown may have stayed in the home of Issac Shadd while he was in Canada.

Osborn Anderson, a subscription agent and printer for the *Provincial Freedman*, was one of the few survivors of John Brown's raid on Harpers Ferry. Many of the details of the raid appeared in his memoirs which Mary Ann Shadd Cary edited.

When Thomas Cary died in 1860, the widowed Mary Ann Shadd Cary had two small children to raise and educate.

During the Civil War Mary Ann Shadd Cary crossed the border to join the Union efforts by becoming a recruiting agent. She canvassed states across the Midwest for black recruits who then reported to Martin Delaney in Chicago. The task of recruiting in the Midwest was complicated by the fact that Illinois, Indiana, and Iowa had Black Laws forbidding blacks from settling in those states. (Delaney, a former neighbor of the Shadd family's in Canada, later became the highest ranking black officer in the Union Army.)

In 1864 she became the travling agent for the Chicago based Colored Ladies Freedmen's Aid Society. She also helped recruit troops for the U.S. Colored Infantry based in Indianapolis.

When the war ended Mary Ann Shadd Cary recognized the great desire the newly freed slaves had for education. She taught in Detroit before going to Washington, DC where she was a school principal for seventeen years. She continued writing and studied law during the evening at Howard Universy. She was sixty one years old when she earned her law degree.

She utilized her new means of working for racial equaliy and women's rights. She started the Colored Women's Progressive Franchise Association. Her goals included working for equal rights, supporting black businesses, and opening up professions to women.

Despite serious health problems, Mary Ann Shadd continued to write and lecture as long as she could. She once said, "It is better to wear out than to rust out." She died on June 5, 1893.

CROSSING THE ROCK RIVER
Courtesy of Lucia Gates

"MOTHER" BICKERDYKE

Many women fought or were otherwise supportive of the Union and Confederate troops in the Civil War. A number followed their husbands or fiances. They sometimes worked as nurses and laundresses. Others like Jennie Hodges a.k.a. Albert Cashier of Belvidere assumed male names and enlisted in military units.

Mary Ann Bickerdyke of Galesburg was a 43 year old widow with three children when she served as a Civil War nurse. She cared for the sick and wounded in hospitals in Cairo and Memphis. She also raised funds and fought for improved sanitary conditions. She was highly respected by General Grant and General Sherman. She so endeared herself to the enlisted men that they called her "Mother Bickerdyke." There is an impressive bronze memorial to her located on the lawn of the Knox County Courthouse. The "Mother" Bickerdyke Historical Collection is a project in her honor. It gathers and publishes historical materials about the Knox County area. Its publications include Voices of the Prairie Land edited by Martin Litvin.

15.   Were records kept?

Most UGRR workers were law abiding, but they believed that the Fugitive Slave laws were very unjust. Although they were committed to a Higher Law, "Do unto others as you would have them to do unto you," they kept relatively few personal records since there were serious consequences for being involved in UGRR operations. There were, however, quite a number of legal documents in which court cases were recorded.

Some individual UGRR workers such as Dr. E. C. Guild of Wayne Center, Illinois, William Still of Philadelphia, and William Lambert of Detroit kept records in spite of the risks. The late Judge William Guild of Wheaton recalled seeing his grandparents' records showing the names of the people sheltered and the length of their stays. In his UGRR research, Dr. Charles L. Blockson learned that William Still hid his notes in a graveyard after interviewing slaves who passed through Philadelphia. In Detroit, William Lambert, secretary of the "Order of Men of Oppression," kept books that showed where journeys started and names, dates and origins of people he helped.

On February 6, 1843, Rev. Samuel Guild Wright, who was quoted in Question 14, wrote the following words in his journal, "Friday another Fugitive from slavery came along which makes 21 that have been through this settlement on their way to Canada." Although it is not known whether Wright was speaking of a period of fifteen or of thirty months this rare statistical record indicates there was a steady stream of UGRR passengers traveling through the corner of the Stark County near Peoria and the Knox County lines.

Zebina Eastman, editor of the *Western Citizen* newspaper, kept a scrapbook containing many accounts of the Underground Railroad and other anti-slavery efforts. He passed that scrapbook down to his son.

Old letters such as those found recently by three Illinois researchers, Ron Nelson, Jon Musgrave and Gary DeNeal, at the Illinois State Historical Library revealed how exploitative John Crenshaw, builder of the notorious Old Slave House (described later in this book), had been. In addition to making money from his salt works, Crenshaw, kidnapped free black people, indentured servants, and illegally held slaves, in order to sell them back into slavery. Crenshaw kidnapped and enslaved a black man named Frank Granger and a number of other people. These recent findings indicate that Crenshaw sold these kidnapped victims at $400 per adult and $200 per child and used his profits to buy the land on which he built the Old Slave House.

When Charles Gray was Poor Master for DuPage County, he usually kept detailed records of the people whom he assisted. These details included the full names and precise descriptions of the person's physical appearance, however, in one case he simply listed he first names of a man named "Doyle" and a woman named "Pauline." This led researcher Ann Hardy to believe that the man and woman were UGRR passengers.

WILLIAM WELLS BROWN

The Narrative of William Wells Brown: a Fugitive Slave was the autobiography of a man who had many different life experiences. The book was published in Boston in 1848. Unlike many formerly enslaved persons, Wells had a chance to learn to read and write. This made it possible for him to write, rather than dictate his life story. He also wrote an early novel entitled Clotel: The President's Daughter. He also wrote an account of black participation in the Civil War.

His accomplishments were not limited to writing. He was an Underground Railroad conductor and speaker.

Although he did not settle in Illinois, crucial events in his life took place in Illinois. In addition, he was influenced by two newspaper editors who did settle in this state.

William Wells Brown assumed this name as an adult. He was born in Lexington, Kentucky, the son of a white slaveholder and an enslaved African woman. When Brown was quite young he was one of forty slaves his enslaver took him to Missouri. Brown was hired out. He worked at various occupations. At one time he worked for newspaper editor Elijah Lovejoy. Another of Brown's employers was a slave trader named Walker.

Brown traveled to New Orleans with Walker. He, his mother, and his brothers and sisters were sold when Walker returned to St. Louis in need of money.

Brown and his mother decided to run away. They found and rowed a skiff across the Mississippi River and landed south of Alton, Illinois. They walked through the woods following the North Star. On the tenth day, they were 150 miles from St. Louis and out of provisions. They risked stopping at a farm to ask for food. Presumably feeling they would be safe travelling by day, they were overtaken by three men on horseback. The men showed Brown and his mother a handbill offering $200 for their apprehension.

Brown and his mother were returned to St. Louis and sold. Brown was put to work on board a steamboat. He saw his mother for the last time when she was on board another boat with fifty or sixty other slaves bound for New Orleans. His mother urged him to try to get his freedom.

Brown was sold to steamboat owner Enoch Price. He sailed to New Orleans on a steamer called the Chester. There the boat took on freight bound for Cincinnati, Ohio. According to Brown the girl named Eliza (in the book Uncle Tom's Cabin) was also on board.

The boat landed at a place which Brown determined to be a good point to make his getaway. The deck hands were unloading luggage. Brown carried a trunk onto the wharf and escaped into the nearby woods.

He said by then he'd made up his mind not to trust anyone. Finally, however, on the fifth or sixth day, he saw an elderly white man who was a Quaker. Brown asked him for help.

The Quaker warned Brown that he was in a pro-slavery neighborhood. He offered to transport Brown to his home in a covered wagon. The man's name was Wells Brown and gave his name to William Wells Brown.

William Wells Brown continued his journey. He reached Cleveland and found employment, first as a dining room waiter and later aboard a Lake Erie steamboat. He found that these jobs provided opportunities to make contacts with people who were escaping from slavery and to carry on Underground Railroad work.

In the meantime he read all he could about the anti-slavery movement. He subscribed to Benjamin Lundy's *Genius of Universal Emancipation* and William Lloyd Garrison's *Liberator*.

George Woodruff, a pharmacist with a passion for history, recorded much of Will County's history in three books. One of these books contains the story of Henry Belt, a popular barber and member of a viable black community in Joliet. Although Belt's background was not generally known, he claimed to be a freedman from Ohio. When some Missouri slave catchers passed through town and saw Belt, they wanted to sell him into slavery. They returned to Missouri and got falsified legal documents, and presented these papers to a Joliet judge who had a reputation for being easy to corrupt. The courtroom was filled with Belt's supporters one of whom was the sheriff. During the proceedings the sheriff eased Belt out of the courtroom as the crowd parted just long enough for them to escape. The slave catchers were furious when they realized what had happened and went from house to house searching for Belt, but his friends successfully hid him until the slave catchers gave up their search.

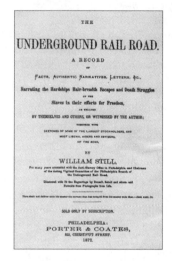

WILLIAM STILL

Pre-Civil War court records reveal many legal battles over issues related to the UGRR. The Anderson Fugitive Slave case involved international law. An enslaved African named John Anderson had been sold to a plantation many miles away from his wife and child. He escaped in an attempt to rejoin with his family. He encountered a slaveholder who had no claim on him, but who, with the help of four slaves, pursued him nevertheless. Anderson was cornered by his pursuers and killed the slaveholder while defending himself. He escaped from St. Louis to Alton, and reached Canada by way of the Underground Railroad. The governor of Missouri got the United States government to attempt to have Anderson returned under the extradition treaty between England and the United States. The outcome was that the Canadian government refused to surrender Anderson. However, his wife and child remained in bondage in Missouri.

JOHN HOSSOCK HOUSE
Courtesy of T.F. Godfrey

The efforts of James E. Burr, George Thompson, and Alanson Work, three Illinois men, to liberate some Missouri slaves, was a much written about interstate controversy which was recorded in history books. Another less well known interstate case had its beginnings in 1858. It centered around the escape of a young woman named Eliza from Nebraska when pro-slavery forces were attempting to introduce slavery into that state. Eliza successfully reached Chicago, but was followed by her enslaver, Stephen F. Nuckolls. Nuckolls was arrested during his attempt to recapture Eliza. He was brought before Chicago abolitionist Judge Calvin DeWolf, on a charge of riotous conduct. Nuckolls was locked up a few hours. In the meantime Underground Railroad workers helped the young woman set out for Canada. Following his release, Nuckolls filed suit in the United States court. He got an indictment against Judge DeWolf, George Anderson, H.D. and C.L. Jenks whom he believed had helped the young woman. Judge DeWolf and the other defendants held that, according to the Constitution , slavery was not permitted in Nebraska; therefore, Eliza had not been lawfully enslaved. This motion never came to trial, but in 1861, the case was dismissed by authority of Honorable E.C. Larned, U.S. district attorney.

Within the state of Illinois attempts were made to prosecute Underground Railroad workers. LaSalle, Will, Bureau, Cook, and Livingston were among the Illinois counties in which fugitive slave cases took place. Among the UGRR workers who were involved in court cases were John Hassock of Ottawa, Peter Stewart of Wilmington, Deacon Samuel Cushing of Crete, Owen Lovejoy of Princeton, Dr. Samuel Willard and his father Julius A.Willard of Jacksonville, Joseph T. Morse of Woodford County, Samuel Guild Wright of Stark County, Susan Borders (Richardson) and John Cross of Knox County.

The case of Dr. Richard Eells of Quincy was one of the most extensively documented cases. It, the Julius Willard case, and two cases involving the slaves of Andrew Borders were appealed and heard in the Illinois Supreme Court in the December 1843 term.

The case began one night when an enslaved man named Charlie escaped from the farm owned by Colonel Chauncey Durkee in Monticello, Missouri, and swam across the Mississippi River to reach Quincy. Arriving wet and cold, Charlie was befriended by Berryman Barnett, a free black UGRR agent, who "communicated his arrival" (that is, took him) to Dr. Richard Eells.

Slave catchers pursued Dr. Eells as he attempted to take Charlie to the next UGRR station. Charlie hopped out of Dr. Eells' buckboard wagon (and there's a marker at this spot in Quincy). Dr. Eells hurriedly returned his horses to his stable, but the horses showed signs of exertion when the slave catchers followed him home.

The William Hayes home, located outside Eden in the Flat Prairie, is the only documented Underground Railroad site in Randolph County. Mr. Hayes was sued by Andrew Borders, a wealthy, Randolph County slaveholder, for helping his slaves escape to Knox County in 1842. Mr. Hayes was subsequently found guilty of the charge. The home has been extensively remodeled and enlarged since the 1840's. The house is still occupied by the descendants of William Hayes and is not open for tours. *Courtesy of James and Phyllis Hayes.*

Dr. Eells was charged with illegally transporting a slave. Dr. Eell's abolitionist friends feared that the governor of Illinois would turn him over to the state of Missouri to be prosecuted for grand larceny. Dr. Eells escaped on the Underground Railroad route to evade prosecution. Rev. Samuel Guild Wright assisted him. When it became apparent that the governor would not turn him over he returned to Quincy to stand trial. Dr. Eells was brought before Circuit Court Judge, Stephen A. Douglas. Douglas fined him $400 and the costs of prosecution under the existing fugitive slave law. The case dragged on ten years. Dr. Eells died while the case was going through the various stages of litigation. The Illinois Supreme Court declared that only the Federal government had jurisdiction in fugitive slave cases. Dr. Eells' family's appeal eventually reached the U.S. Supreme Court.

Judge Douglas later became a United States Senator. He supported the extension of slavery in the Kansas-Nebraska Act in his debate with Abraham Lincoln, and in the Fugitive Slave Act of 1850. More than 100 years after Stephen A. Douglas served in the Senate, two U. S. Senators from Illinois took the leadership in assuring that the Underground Railroad received national recognition. In 1990 Senator Paul Simon authored legislation that directed the National Park Service to study and preserve the history of the Underground Railroad. Senator Carol Moseley Braun, the first African American woman to serve in the U.S. Senate, was the chief sponsor of the 1998 Underground Railroad Network to Freedom Act.

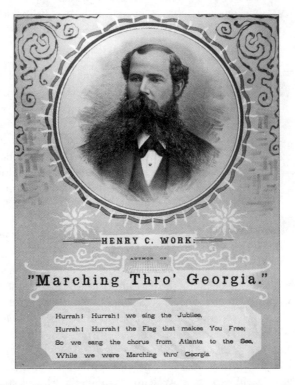

HENRY C. WORK

AUTHOR OF

"Marching Thro' Georgia."

Hurrah! Hurrah! we sing the Jubilee,
Hurrah! Hurrah! the Flag that makes You Free;
So we sang the chorus from Atlanta to the Sea,
While we were Marching thro' Georgia.

Most fugitives who came through Illinois had set out in Missouri, found their way to the Mississippi River, and crossed it, unaided. An exception to this took place in 1841, when George Thompson, Alanson Work, and James Burr attempted to rescue Palmyra slaves. Their plan was discovered and they spent several years in jail. Work's son, Henry Clay Work became the noted composer of "Marching Thro' Georgia" and "Kingdom Coming." *Courtesy of the Library of Congress*

16. What were the risks?

The UGRR was a dangerous activity for everyone involved in its operations. In the Foreword of his book, <u>Make Free: The Story of the Underground Railroad</u>, William Breyfogle states,

> The heroism of the Negroes themselves can scarcely be exaggerated. In spite of all the help that could be provided they were the ones who took the gravest risks and endured the worst hardships. A special handicap was the basic information that owners in the South withheld from them. All but a few of them, when they tried to escape were striking out into something completely unknown.

President George Washington signed the first Fugitive Slave Law in 1793. Then, in 1850, a second more stringent law was included in the Compromise of 1850.

Here are some of the provisions of this law.

~ The law provided that the runaway (or presumed runaway) be identified merely on the affidavit of the slave catcher, and no effort was made to prove true identification.

~ The runaway could not offer a defense, nor testify for himself. He was not allowed a trial by jury.

~ The fee of the commissioner who decided the case was ten dollars if he returned the slave, but five dollars if he freed him.

~ If a federal agent in any way interfered with the capture of the fugitive, he was fined one thousand dollars.

~ If the fugitive succeeded in his escape, with or without the federal agent's help, the agent was held responsible for the entire value of the slave.

~ Bystanders were often forced to lend a hand if a fugitive tried to escape.

~ Friends in the Underground Railroad work or casual humanitarians, were liable to a fine of one thousand dollars or imprisonment for six months if convicted of passing on a slave.

Instead of stopping escape attempts the Fugitive Slave Law inspired new, daring escapes. Abolitionists often lost their livelihoods and sometimes, their lives as a result of its enforcement. Many were socially ostracized.

Free black abolitionists faced the same consequences as their white counter parts, plus the possibility of their freedom papers being confiscated or destroyed by would-be slave catchers. This made them as defenseless as fugitive slaves. Slavery was the probable fate of any black person who could not immediately prove, by other witness or bond, that he or she was born free or had purchased their freedom. Anyone snared under these circumstances faced the most brutal punishment and possible mutilation or death as a "lesson" to other slaves.

Even so free and self-emancipated black people took dangerous risks. Ben Henderson of Jacksonville and the lodge members who helped Henry Stevenson (see textbox) are examples of such activities in Illinois. Rev. Richard De Baptiste of Chicago reportedly loaned his own freedom papers to help thirty-three enslaved people.

A number of white abolitionists faced grave consequences for their anti-slavery activities. Some like Elijah Lovejoy, of Alton, Illinois, sacrificed their lives. John Fairfield was jailed twice. He suffered 16 years of foul conditions in a Kentucky prison and eventually died in the struggle. Charles Turner Torrey, editor of the *Tocsin of Liberty*, was arrested, convicted, and sentenced to life imprisonment for "running off slaves." By some accounts he had possibly assisted 400 slaves before he was arrested in Maryland. He died of tuberculosis in a Baltimore prison a year later. Professor L.C. Matlack of Illinois Institute (which later became Wheaton College) spoke at Torrey's funeral.

DR. EELLS HOUSE
Courtesy of the Friends of Dr. Richard Eells House.

Some UGRR researchers have asked the following questions. Since city and church founders were often the anti-slavery leaders in a community, could they have been less likely to be prosecuted than someone less well known? Perhaps this was the case on occasion, yet, Rev. John Cross, James E. Burr, George Thompson, and Alanson Work all served time in prison, as did Benjamin Lundy. In Will County, Peter Stewart of Wilmington and Deacon Cushing of Crete were indicted, but acquitted.

Benjamin Lundy worked tirelessly — lecturing, forming anti-slavery societies, and publishing abolitionist newspapers. Walking or traveling on the poorest accomodations, he journeyed to Canada, Haiti, Mexico, and Texas in hopes of finding a sanctuary where emancipated slaves might live in a non-hostile environment. This grave marker was dedicated on the centennial of his death.

Dr. David Nelson was forced to make a hasty exit from the college he'd established near Palmyra, Missouri. He attempted crossing at a low point in the river and was met by Quincy residents who did not want problems with the Missouri slaveholders. Nevertheless, he established a Christian missionary college in Quincy. One of the college buildings later housed families of men who joined the Negro regiment organized at Quincy during the Civil War. The chapel was burned by a mob of Missouri slaveowners who crossed the frozen Mississippi River in March 1843.

Dr. Richard Eells, whose court case has already been described, fled Missouri with Dr. Nelson. His home in Quincy is still maintained by Friends of the Dr. Richard Eells House.

In 1844 John Hassock dodged hostile attacks from I. & M. Canal workers as he transported slaves to Dr. C.V. Dyer's "station" in Chicago. In 1860 he and ten to fifteen others, including Dr. Joseph and James Stout, were indicted. He was convicted and sentenced to 10 days, a $100 fine, plus court expenses of $591. John Wentworth, mayor of Chicago and proprietor of the *Chicago Democrat* newspaper; encouraged all patriots to visit the prisoners and pay their fines. He said they did "what every man with a heart true to humanity must have done".

Although Benjamin Lundy was not "caught" helping slaves, he devoted his life to trying to free slaves. He was an advisor to John Quincy Adams, inspired William Lloyd Garrison, John Greenleaf Whittier, and Zebina Eastman. By 1830, he had traveled 5,000 miles on foot and more than 20,000 miles by other means.

Of one trip to Texas he wrote, "I have traveled on foot, and alone often from ten to twenty miles without seeing a house...under rays of the burning sun...through drenching rains...with a knapsack...20 to 25 pounds and the cholera attacks frequently compelled me to stop for a day or two...Many a time while in this condition, I have been necessitated to sleep on the wet ground."

About 1858, Judge Babcock had recently purchased the Grove Farm in the Pontiac area.

47

One Sunday morning he heard "a terrible racket down the road" where upon investigation he came upon a covered wagon in which there were two Underground Railroad passengers. Beside the wagon were two pro-slavery men on horseback, demanding, according to the history of Livingston County, "in the most boisterous tones an unconditional surrender."

Between the men on horseback and the men in the wagon, there walked a man with a pistol in each hand. He alternately warned the pursuers not to come any closer, and the slaves not to get out of the wagon as their pursuers were demanding. The "man in the middle" was a black barber from Bloomington; the pursuers, two Pontiac citizens. Upon seeing the judge, the pursuers demanded his help. He refused. Thus, the judge was forced by circumstances to help the fugitives reach Colonel Stewart in Wilmington, although he had opposed the abolitionists until that time. He was forced to pay over $300 in fines and had to sell some of his farmland to do so.

PETER STEWART HOME

The Peter Stewart house overlooked the Kankakee River. Slaves walking or stowing away on barges were welcomed here. Stewart and Samuel Cushing of Crete were indicted for UGRR activities but were not convicted. The Daniel McIntosh home, constructed of native stone located (before demolition) on Route 53, was another UGRR "stop" in the Wilmington area. *Courtesy of Dorothy Kennard*

COLONEL PETER STEWART

Colonel Peter Stewart, of Wilmington spoke of himself as "President of the Underground Railroad." According to the 1878 History of Will County, this is how he got that title:

Once when in Washington, during the Presidency of James Buchanan, he happened to be riding from Washington to Baltimore in the same car with the President, and to be seated near him. A lady in the car asked Col. Stewart to exchange seats with her, saying that she wished to sit near the President. Mr. Stewart, with the bluff and hearty manner for which he was noted, says: "Madam, I am the President!" "Indeed!" said the lady, "Of what are you president?" "Of the Underground Railroad, Madam," he replies, as, with great politeness and good humor, he complied with her request.

Peter Stewart was the masonry superintendent for the Illinois Michigan Canal. He was born in Scotland and went to England as a child. He was an apprentice to a man who was both an expert horticulturist and student of engineering. The man taught Stewart everything he knew.

When Stewart was 19 he came to the United States. He settled first in the state of New York where he supervised the building of the Brooklyn Navy Yard and other building projects in the East.

In the early 1830's he, like Israel Blodgett who later moved to Downer's Grove, settled in the DuPage Settlement near Wheatland. In 1836 he built a large farm home in Wilmington.

The Stewart home sat on a hilltop between Stewart and North Streets. It overlooked the junction of Forked Creek and the Kankakee River. It was considered one of the finest in the country. It had a fine library. In addition to being a home for the Stewart family it was the location of a school taught by Miss Agnes Fonda from 1838 to 1840. The home was best remembered, however, as a station on the Underground Railroad.

This is how the History of Will County describes one day of Peter Stewart's antislavery activities:

He was an Abolitionist of the most ultra kind, and yet, always reasonable in his views and demands, commanded the respect of even those of contrary opinions. At one time, a company of men from the South visited Wilmington, in pursuit of a fugitive slave. When their business became known, they were at once surrounded by a mob of citizens, at whose hands they could not but expect violence. Having heard that Peter Stewart was a man of influence in the town, they sent for him to intercede for them. When Stewart arrived on the ground, the would-be slavecatchers implored him to use his influence with the people for their release, and were astounded to find that he was the leader of the Antislavery movement in this neighborhood. But, after learning that they would be only too glad to return to St. Louis, Stewart counseled the citizens to set them at liberty, with an injunction not to delay their return to their homes, which advice was duly heeded.

In 1854 the Stewart Hotel was built on the corner of Van Buren and Water Streets. A passage was dug from the house and beneath the limestone bed of Forked Creek to connect with an opening in the basement of the hotel. According to a writer who saw the supporting beams shortly before the old hotel was demolished this tunnel was little more than a crawl space. The last relic of the hotel was sold at auction in 1974. It was a copper bathtub in which Underground Railroad passengers could enjoy a hot bath after crawling from the Stewart house to the hotel.

Peter Stewart, a staunch Presbyterian, and Deacon Samuel Cushing of the Congregational Church were indicted for their UGRR activities. They were acquitted and resumed their work of harboring and assisting former slaves.

17. How did the passenger find out about the Underground Railroad?

Mostly by word of mouth.

~ From black sailors who knew how to navigate by the stars. This was such a significant source of information that Charleston, South Carolina, had ordinances requiring black sailors to be "lodged" in the jail whenever they were in port. This was done to prevent them from sharing knowledge with black people who lived in the city.

~ From slaves working on the Mississippi or Missouri riverfronts or steamboats who happened to meet abolitionist passengers.

~ From geometric designs in the quilts made by enslaved seamstresses. These designs, such as the "North Star" and "Flying Geese," were based on very complicated, traditional African methods of visual encoding. The book Hidden in Plain View contains pictures and tells the meaning behind many UGRR quilt designs. In an interview the book's co-author Raymond Dobard explained how the quilts were used to communicate information. First of all, an enslaved person, who was planning an escape, was taught the meaning of the instructive geometric shapes. After memorizing the quilt designs, he or she knew how to "read," or interpret, each quilt message. The quilts were hung on a clothesline one at a time to inform the person how and when to prepare and how to proceed even if he or she traveled away from familiar landmarks. Dr. Clarice Boswell of Plainfield, is the Illinoisan who is most knowledgeable about the secrets held within the UGRR quilts. She explains them in her presentations.

A Slave Auction

18.   What did it mean to be a slave?

It meant working ten to sixteen hours a day or more clearing fields, mining, harvesting crops or loading cargo, but not being paid for their labor. The owners kept all profits.

Slaves found it difficult to keep their families together. At any time their mother, father, brother or sister could be sold to a slave owner who lived far away. The parents of Lewis Howard Latimer, the inventor who made the drawings for Alexander Graham Bell's telephone patent, made a daring escape so that their children could be born free. Their escape is described in the book, <u>Lewis Howard Latimer</u> *(Turner)*.

They could not vote or own property—not even clothing.

Enslaved Africans had to have a pass to go anywhere off the premises. Without a pass they were subject to be caught and whipped by patrollers or "paddie rollers" as they were frequently called. In many cases they could not meet for church services (unless a white person was present).

If a member of the master's family tried to teach an enslaved person how to read or write, they'd both be reprimanded and/or severely punished. Reportedly, the great grandfather of Dr. Percy Julian who developed a medicine that has saved the lives of people across the world, had a finger cut off as punishment for trying to learn to write.

Even worse punishment awaited a slave who tried to organize fellow slaves. There is an account of another enslaved man being decapitated and his head placed on a stake at the crossroads to frighten other would-be organizers.

KING COTTON

Expectant mothers often worked in the fields and paused under a shade tree to give birth to their babies.

A slave could be beaten if he or she became tired or slowed down while working. It was reported that many men and women who were helped by abolitionists in DeKalb County arrived in Illinois covered with whip-inflicted stripes from head to foot.

Some slaves lived and worked in cities and could escape much easier than plantation slaves, especially if they lived in towns located near rivers.

*   *   *

You may think hard of us for running away from slavery ... To be compelled to stand by and see you whip and slash my wife without mercy. When I could afford her no protection, not even by offering myself to suffer the lash in her place ... This kind of treatment was what drove me from home and family, to seek a better home for them.

Letter from Charles Bibb, Windsor, Ontario, to his former owner, 1844.

A FUGITIVE SLAVE SUSPENDED
BY THE ARMS WITH BLOCK & TACKLE

19. What would happen if slaves were caught trying to escape?

Any of a number of things could happen to them.

They were forced to wear heavy neck irons with spikes sticking out in all directions, leg irons or ankle chains to prevent them from running away again.

They were frequently returned to their masters who might whip them or sell them "down the river," a term meaning the worst kind of enslavement.

They might be put on trial.

They might be beaten, buried up to the neck and covered in honey to attract ants, have toes cut off, or be killed.

FIGHTING TO BE FREE

20. What were some of the methods slaves used to keep from being caught?

~ Traveling by night on a cloudy or moonless night

~ Remaining very still all day

~ Moving as noiselessly as possible or imitating the sounds of birds or wild animals

~ Wading in streams to lose their scent, however specially trained dogs could pick up their scent—even in water

~ Rubbing the bottom of feet with onion or turpentine to lose scent

~ Hiding in caves or in forests

~ Riding out of the barnyard on a cow or horse

~ Staying close enough to a riverbank to use the river to get a sense of direction, but remaining out of view in the protection of trees and tall grass

~ Working on ship crews, sometimes substituting for another black person

~ Stowing away inside cargo holds

~ Imitating the characteristics of some animals (for example, taking a zigzagged route of escape like a wild rabbit would if chased by a fox)

~ Stringing a grapevine across road to slow down pursuers

~ Going south (then eventually making a U-turn), rather than north as a pursuer might expect

~ Disguising themselves (a man with a perfect set of teeth might knock out a tooth, or a light skinned mulatto would darken his skin so that he would no longer fit physical description in advertisements for his return.)

~ Defending themselves against would-be captors.

FUGITIVE LIVING IN A CAVE

WILLIAM M. CARNAHAN

In 1896 the son of Illinois abolitionist William M. Carnahan described an Iowa to Illinois route which crossed the Mississippi River between Burlington and Keithsburg, Iowa in great detail. The first station in Illinois was at Sunbeam, about 10 miles east of Keithsburg. William M. Carnahan operated the next station. It was located 12 miles northeast of Sunbeam and Midway between Aledo and Voila in Mercer County. The next station was 14 miles further ease at Elder James Oxford's in Henry County. The next station was kept by a Mr. Buck near Andover in Henry County. From there the route led into Whiteside County, but William Carnahan's son P.M. Carnahan, did not know who operated that station.

William M. Carnahan was born in Lawrence County, Pennsylvania and moved to Mercer County, Illinois in 1839. Soon after that he joined the Presbyterian Church but strongly disagreed with the position the General Assembly took at Louisville, Kentucky on the issue of slavery. He withdrew and became a charter member of the Free Presbyterian church. He served in the volunteer service during the Civil War. He and his children took pride in the role he had played in helping to end slavery.

Some other Underground Railroad workers in the Sunbeam area were John Sample, James Will, William Pinkerton, John and David Carnahan, Dr. Higgins, J.C. Graham, S.A. Markham, John Cowden and Henry Hoagland.

This Iowa-Illinois Underground Railroad route was most active in the decade before President Abraham Lincoln signed the *Emancipation Proclamation*. The most interesting and exciting incident took place in 1853 or 1854.

Iowa abolitionists tried to notify Illinois abolitionists about 10 days before the arrival of two men named George and Sam who had reached Iowa after escaping from slavery in Missouri. The Iowa abolitionists knew of the existence of abolitionists in or near Keithsburg, Illinois but did not know exactly where they were located. The Iowans went to Keithsburg and announced that they were trying to get subscribers for an anti-slavery newspaper. They figured this would put them in touch with abolitionists. They were directed to St. Clair Ross, the only black abolitionist in town. They told him their real reason for coming to town. They made a plan with him on the night of July 3rd. They were to take the refugees to Samuel McClure's house northeast of Sunbeam. Ambrose and Willis McCreight and some other abolitionists from Sunbeam waited at the place where they were to meet the Iowans.

The Iowans lost their bearings and crossed the Mississippi south of the planned meeting place. They spent almost all night searching for the place. It was almost a day before they found it.

The Iowans and Illinoisans then raced 14 miles to try to reach Samuel McClure's. It was daytime by the time they got to Sunbeam. They still had 2 miles to go, but they were able to stop at Samuel Dikel's.

P.M. Carnahan reported, "July 4th John Carnahan, Sr., and Dr. Higgins celebrated their country's independence by breaking it (Fugitive Slave) laws." They went on to the McClure's. No one was at home but by the morning of July 6th Sam and George had gotten that far safely.

21. How did Underground Railroad passengers know which way was north?

Many enslaved parents or adults taught children some method of knowing the four basic directions.

~ The sun rises in the east and sets in the west

~ You're walking north when the sun rises over your right shoulder and sets on your left, or if your shadow is on your left side in the morning and your right in the afternoon

~ When you're facing north, south is behind you, east is on your right, and west is on your left

~ The North Star is at the tail end of the Little Dipper

~ Moss grows on the north side of trees

~ Rivers usually flow south.

Nancy Hart Stieber

22. What kind of landscape did UGRR passengers find in Illinois?

Grassy areas or prairies covered much of Illinois between the Wabash and Mississippi River. For that reason, Illinois became known as the "Prairie State." The Indians called prairies, Mas-Ko-Tia. Prairies were also known as meadows, "openings," or savannas. While most prairies did not shield UGRR passengers as much as forests, they had their advantages. They were easier to walk across than wooded or rugged terrain. And they were easier to survey. A passenger who was hiding in the woods at the edge of a prairie could see anyone who approached. However, in the northern portion of the state, grasses sometimes grew to stand taller than a rider on horseback.

There were dense forests (timberlands) in the southern third of the state and areas near river forests provided natural shelter for UGRR passengers.

Typically, Native Americans settled near rivers to fish and have access to water supply and also near forests where they could hunt game for food. When Europeans came they sought these same areas. The prairie, with its grasses and wild flowers, was settled after the timberlands.

BELOW: THE PRAIRIE
Courtesy of The Morton Arboretum

Henry Stevenson

Henry Stevenson was born into slavery on the Stevenson farm in Old Franklin, Missouri. He was about 104 years old and living in Windsor, Ontario, Canada when he granted this interview to a researcher on the "The Negro in Illinois," Illinois Writers Project . Vivian G. Harsh Research Collection, Carter G. Woodson Regional Library, Chicago Public Library System.

Henry Stevenson explained, "My first master was Stevenson, he died and my mistress married three times." When Henry Stevenson came of age he was given to one of the slaveholder's sons, Mark. Mark traded him for a woman and a child. Later he was given to a second son, Gerrit, in Fayette, Missouri.

Henry Stevenson had married a woman by the name of Mandy. He reported that Gerrit treated him "pretty rough sometimes and pretty good sometimes." One morning, Henry Stevenson and an enslaved African named George were moving slowly. Gerrit asked why. Stevenson said it was because they were too weak. Gerrit told the cook to prepare some meat for them.

Stevenson continued his story, "After the Mexican War, they had gold fever and master Gerrit went out to California," Gerrit asked Stevenson and George if they wanted to go with him. George agreed to go. When Henry didn't, Gerrit told George, "Well I'll take you and leave Henry and if he doesn't make a good crop while I'm gone, I'll whip him when I come back in the fall".

Soon after that Henry went to round up the cattle. While he was away from the farm, a man named Andy and a woman named Margaret had tried to runaway from bondage. When Henry returned with the cattle a man named Butts or Botts asked where he had been and what he knew of the man and woman who had escaped. He said where he had been and that he didn't know anything about the escaped couple.

Botts was unsuccessful in his attempt to hunt for the couple. He wanted Henry to go after them, but he refused. He said, "The colored folk woulda killed me." However when he discussed it in the slave quarters, he

was told to go and watch all the roads and come back to report what he'd seen. A plan was made for Henry and as he stated it, "a gang of us (would) run away." Henry let Botts know he'd changed his mind and would go after the couple after all.

Botts hesitated, but the slaveholder who had enslaved the woman accepted his offer. That slaveholder provided him with a broad cloth suit and a knife and arranged for him to get $10.00 from Uriah (who was the stand-in for Gerrit and leader of the hunt.)

The search party started out from Adrian County, Missouri and headed for Palmyra, Missouri, less than six miles from Quincy, Illinois. They stopped overnight at Widow Sharpe's public house. Henry went to the kitchen, "as (he) was raised".

A black cook gave him his supper and said that she was a fortune teller. She said that he was hunting two slaves and asked what he planned to do if he found them.

Henry said, "to go with 'em if I find 'em." The next morning he and the search party continued their journey. He explained that they did not cross on the Quincy ferry because "it was an abolitionist ferry." They crossed the Mississippi River on a flat boat rowed with oars. He added, "On our side every teamster was a colored man, on the other side, every driver was a white man."

In Quincy, Henry was not allowed to go with the rest of the search party. Instead, he was sent to the black community to look for the man and woman who had escaped. He talked with Mrs. Seidner whose husband had been freed by his last slaveholder. Mrs. Seidner told Henry if he waited until 6 o'clock her husband would arrange for Henry to make an escape. At that time "a company" would transport him 75 miles and another "company" would take him 75 more and so on to Canada.

Henry Stevenson said that was the first time he ever heard of Canada. After dinner he stepped outside of the Seidner's house to smoke his pipe. He saw an

HENRY STEVENSON (CONT.)

elderly black man who motioned to him.

The man asked if he was making an escape. He told Henry, he was "in that business" and directed Henry to a Quincy abolitionist by the name of Miller.

Henry went to the Miller's. Mrs. Miller looked at his slave pass and she told him to go to the steam mill and ask for the head sawyer. Henry was still uncertain about what he should do. He had a dilemma. His wife was still in Missouri, should he try to escape in the hope she could join him? Meanwhile he knew that if he made his escape with the aid of the Seidner's and other Quincy abolitionists, he would be tracked by the search party that he'd accompanied to Quincy.

Henry was welcomed when he rejoined the search party. (He had been away so many hours that the leader feared that he had escaped.) He reported that the escaped couple had headed for Chicago, so he and the rest of the search party rushed in that direction. Their leader was unaware that the Maplesville farmer who provided overnight lodging operated an UGRR station. The farmer's name was Garner. The search party took a boat to Peoria. They took a tow boat.

(Horses were attached to the boats by ropes, they walked along a path beside the Canal). A man who worked on the boat told Henry, "You are free now, don't go back". Henry was still undecided. When the boat arrived in Chicago, Henry was met by a man with a dray who told him, "Jump on," Henry asked what the man knew about him and the man said, "We know all things here". The man took him several blocks to a very large hall where they were met by several men. A man in the hall gave Henry a letter to deliver to his father-in-law in Michigan. The men advised him to go on to Canada. One elderly man took him to his house. Later that evening another abolitionist gave him $4.50 and some clothing. He boarded a boat bound for New Buffalo, Michigan—about 40 miles from Chicago. At New Buffalo he was put on a train by a black man who told him the train would stop in front of a barber shop.

Henry found the barber whose name was Gordon in the process of shaving a customer. The barber took Henry Stevenson to a boat at the foot of Woodward Avenue in Detroit. Soon afterwards he arrived in Windsor. He remained in or around Windsor for the next 51 or 52 years. That's where he was interviewed at age 104.

Slave tags were worn by slaves in urban areas of the South when they were hired out as temporary labor. The tag distinguished "jobbing" slaves and runaway slaves and free blacks. Cities such as Charleston, South Carolina had slave badge laws. Note the name of the city, the number assigned to the slave and the kind of work he did (i.e. mechanic, porter or servant.) *Courtesy of The Chicago Public Library Special Collections and Preservation Division.*

23. What if passengers got sick?

Many enslaved Africans brought knowledge of medicinal plants and procedures from Africa and passed this knowledge on to their children. Others learned from Native Americans. Such knowledge was often life saving.

If a person traveling alone got sick or injured he or she might use these remedies. Knowledge and use of these African-Indian remedies often made the difference between life and death.

Women who were expecting babies often had difficulty keeping up with other group members. The climbing and other physical exertion experienced while escaping often caused them to go into early labor. This situation created a real dilemma for the woman, the baby, and other family members.

24. How or what did they eat?

The first day or so an escaping slave might have hard biscuits or other food he or she saved from daily rations. It was then necessary for escaping slaves to forage for berries and other edible fruits and nuts. It was important to identify plants correctly because misidentification could cause illness or death. Many slaves knew how to trap animals or catch fish, however there was danger that making a fire might attract attention of enemies and also the danger of starting dangerous prairie fires.

25. Were the plants and animals the same as those we see today?

Some were. Some were not.

The prairie has nearly disappeared since European settlement. Use of the steel plow, prevention of prairie fires, and introduction of weedy plants led to the destruction of the ecological system of the prairies. Today many organizations are working to restore prairie lands. Resources such as the Morton Arboretum and Chicago Botanical Gardens provide information on plants suitable for back yards and environmental education.

In Illinois there were three types of prairie:

1) Tall grass prairie, where grasses grew to 7 feet or taller. There were about 200 species of grasses and forbs, including the big tooth sunflower, compass plant, purple and white cloves, and prairie dock. These plants were helpful to the Underground Railroad passengers in various ways providing shelter, food and

medicine. The compass plant was helpful in yet another way. The vertical edges of its lower leaves turn in a north-south direction and so it could truly serve as a compass.

2) Sand prairie contained species adapted to dry conditions.

3) Hill prairie grasses grew to 2 or 3 feet tall.

Underground Railroad passengers saw many of the same types of animals scurrying across their paths as live in rural and suburban areas today. They saw raccoons, woodchucks, deer, brown bats, weasels, opossums, skunks, minks, foxes, bobcats, squirrels, rabbits, and beavers. When they reached a place where it was safe to make a fire, they hunted and cooked small edible animals.

At one time beavers were almost extinct in Illinois. The same is true of the bison (or buffalo), which provided the Indians with food, clothing and shelter. Successful efforts are now being made to protect these animals. A small herd of buffalo now roams the grounds of Fermilab in Batavia. However, the Wapiti (elks), the beautiful Virginia deer, cougars, timber wolves and black bears are all gone from the Illinois region.

FACING EVER PRESENT DANGER

Benjamin Lundy

After years of struggling to publish his anti-slavery newspaper under adverse conditions, Benjamin Lundy joined his relatives in the Quaker community of Clear Creek near McNabb, Illinois. He came there after spending almost half of his lifetime in anti-slavery activities.

He traveled over twenty thousand miles five thousand of which were on foot for the cause. He suffered at the hands of people who did not share his views. Once he was beaten by a slave trader in Baltimore just before moving to Illinois. His printing press and personal possessions had been destroyed by a mob in Philadelphia. He arrived in Putnam County almost a year after Elijah Lovejoy had been killed in Alton.

Soon after Lundy's arrival, The Illinois Anti-Slavery Society met in Farmington. Recognizing the need for an official newspaper, society members urged Lundy to resume publication of *the Genius For Universal Emancipation* newspaper. Lundy printed the paper in LaSalle County on a press owned by Hooper Warren in Lowell. Lundy died on August 22, 1839. The LaSalle County Anti-Slavery Society tried to continue publishing the *Genius* under the editorship of Lundy's former assistant, Zebina Eastman. Within the next two years the *Genius* ceased publication. Eastman moved to Chicago and with the assistance of Hooper Warren began publishing the *Western Citizen*. It became the Illinois Anti-Slavery newspaper.

Lundy began publishing the *Genius* in the Quaker community of Mt. Pleasant, Ohio. He had moved there to assist Charles Osborn in the publication of another anti-slavery paper, *The Philanthropist*.

Both Lundy and Osborn had organized abolition societies, which believed in destroying race prejudice, removing legal restrictions on black people, and the abolition of slavery. They differed in that Lundy believed in colonization and gradual emancipation. Osborn forcibly rejected colonization and called for immediate emancipation.

Lundy published the first seven issues of the *Genius* at Mt. Pleasant. He went from there to Jonesville, Ohio

where he published the eighth. He continued on to Greenville, Tennessee the center of anti-slavery, Quaker settlements in the South. Three years later he moved his publication to Baltimore, Maryland.

Two turning points occurred while Benjamin Lundy was based in Baltimore. One was a family tragedy. The other was an encounter that would have far reaching impact on the anti-slavery movement.

Esther Lundy died in Baltimore while her husband was in Haiti trying to establish a colony for freed slaves. The five Lundy children were raised by Mrs. Lundy's relatives who had moved from Ohio to Tozeville, then Putnam County. A number of Mrs. Lundy's relatives were involved and also active in the anti-slavery movement. Her uncle and aunt, John and Rachel Mills Lewis, operated Underground Railroad stations. So did her brother and sister-in-law William and Lydia Stanton Lewis.

Benjamin Lundy

While publishing the *Genius* in Baltimore, Benjamin Lundy listed a young man named William Lloyd Garrison as "Co-editor". Lundy was the person who got Garrison interested in the fight against slavery. The two men soon had differences of opinion. Lundy moved the *Genius* to Washington, D.C.

Garrison returned to Boston where he began publishing the *Liberator* and became a leader in the anti-slavery movement. Garrison's influence lasted long after Lundy's death.

26. Were there many stations in Illinois?

Yes. The UGRR was often more spontaneous, rather than highly organized.

Natural settings like forests, rock formations, and caves provided lifesaving shelter for many UGRR passengers. Such settings were utilized far more than buildings. Sometimes cornfields, haystacks, barns, or storage sheds on farms provided shelter with or without the farmer being aware of it. The first passenger to stop at David West's station in DeKalb County was a man who had tried to run away before but had been captured and flogged. He was so terrified by this experience that every little sound frightened him. He hid in the cornfield by day and slept in the barn or under the haystack at night. West loaded grain into his wagon, covered it and the frightened man, and set out toward Chicago, probably going as far east as Sylvanus Holcomb's UGRR station in St. Charles.

There are accounts of people hiding in such dangerous places as narrow ledges inside water wells.

There were, of course, more traditional structures that were stopping places. However the involvement of some of these structures, and their owners, was not always planned ahead of time. Such was the case with Professor Jonathan B. Turner at Illinois College in Jacksonville who became involved in the Underground Railroad, when a nearby station operator believed that slavecatchers were watching his house.

Other locations were regular stopping places. These included:

~ Mission Institute in Quincy, (one of the main points where slaves entered Illinois) called "Station #1".

BENJAMIN LUNDY (CONT.)

Reading the *Liberator* inspired eleven Putnam County men to establish the first anit-slavery society in Illinois in February 1833. Their goal was to accomplish equality of rights and privileges among all persons. The women of Putnam County founded the first Illinois women's anti-slavery society in 1842. Members of Esther Lewis Lundy's family played prominent roles in these organizations. These groups later disagreed with Garrison. He discouraged political involvement and they helped establish the Liberty Party in Illinois.

In the years after parting company with Garrison, Benjamin Lundy continued to publish the *Genius*. In the early days he had been one of few anti-slavery edi-

tors. His newspaper and later Garrison's were enthusiastically supported by black people. Philadelphia was Lundy's last location before moving to Illinois. The black community held a farewell for him at the Philadelphia Reading room. Speakers praised him as the father of the cause and otherwise expressed their gratitude. When he died 13 months later black groups in Boston and Philadelphia held memorial services in his honor.

He was buried in the Friends' Cemetery at Clear Creek in August 1839.

THE MILTON HOUSE

The Milton House in Wisconsin was on the Underground Railroad route on the territorial road from the Chicago lake port, and from Winnebago, Boone and McHenry counties in Illinois. It served as a stagecoach and Underground Railroad station.

On October 10, 1998 it was officially recognized as a National Historic Site by the National Park Service. This designation signifies its the site is of historic importance to the entire nation as well as to the state or region.

Joseph Goodrich , the founder of Milton, Wisconsin, built two structures on the site. He first built a log cabin in 1837 in which to house his family. In 1844, he built a six-sided grout (or concrete) building in front of the cabin. The new building served as a home and stagecoach inn. It is the oldest grout structure in the United States.

Both buildings figured in the UGRR operations. The log cabin was linked to the newer building by a hand-dug tunnel. Underground Railroad passengers first entered the log cabin, then stepped through a trapdoor in the floor of the cabin, climbed down a ladder, and crawled through the tunnel into the basement of the inn.

Like other stagecoach inns, the Milton House provided lodging for people who were traveling for various reasons. There was no way for innkeeper Joseph Goodrich to know how his "above ground" guests felt about slavery. Realizing the possibility that some of these guests might be slave catchers, he devised an escape plan. If he sensed danger he gave a signal to warn his "underground" guests.

The Underground Railroad passengers could exit from the basement of the inn by going back through the tunnel and cabin. They could then leave the cabin without being seen and escape by following nearby waterways to Fort Atkinson.

Andrew Pratt was an Underground Railroad passenger who decided to settle in the town of Milton. He participated in the life of the community and became a member of the Templar's Lodge.

Some members of the lodge made an attempt to trick Pratt into withdrawing his membership.

Joseph Goodrich's son, Ezra, wrote a lengthy statement in which he indicated many reasons why Pratt deserved to keep his membership in the lodge. Ezra Goodrich's writings describe Andrew Pratt as an intelligent, industrious man. They reveal that Pratt had escaped from bondage in Missouri and reached Wisconsin after having been imprisoned in Illinois because of the state's Black Codes.

It was very unusual for an Underground Railroad passenger to leave a handwritten record behind. There are two reasons for this. One, slaveholders forbade enslaved Africans from learning to read or write, and severely punished those who learned in spite of this restriction. Two, since reading and writing were forbidden, an Underground Railroad passenger who possessed this knowledge was unlikely to provide a clue for would-be captors.

There is speculation about whether Andrew Pratt wrote and left a rare note, the remaining scrap of which is pictured in this book. It was found among Goodrich family memorabilia and may have been written by a family member .

Courtesy of the Milton House Museum

~ A. A. Burlingame's house, one of several stops operated in the area of Sparta, Eden, Randolph County. (Fugitives came up the Mississippi River to Chester, then followed an old Indian trail there.)

~ Quinn Chapel African Methodist Episcopal Church in Chicago, where four women, "The Big Four," sheltered slaves.

~ Owen Lovejoy's home in Princeton and John Hossack's in Ottawa which provided refuge at key points near the Illinois River.

~ Probably Deacon Issac Kelley's log cabin in Alton. Issac Kelley organized the Brothers of Friendship, a black fraternal order which, like the Knights of Tabor, was serious about UGRR activities. His route was called the North Star Line. Its symbol was the daisy. Kelley was one of the few people who knew the location of Elijah Lovejoy's original burial site, and served on the Lovejoy Monument committee.

~The Blazer or Allison homes in McDonough County were on a line between Quincy and Fulton County. The route led through Hancock County with stops at the Pettyjohns or Burtons on Round Prairie then to McDonough and Fulton counties.

~ The homes of Philo Carpenter, founder of the first Sunday School in Chicago, and John Jones, a black businessman whose picture is seen at Chicago Historical Society. Dr. C.V. Dyer, sometimes called "President of the UGRR," operated Underground Railroad stations in Chicago. Peter Stewart, an engineer for Illinois and Michigan Canal, operated a station on the Kankakee River in Wilmington.

~ The First Baptist Congressional Church, which Philo Carpenter used as an UGRR station.

According to local legend, the A.A. Burlingame house, located in Eden, Illinois in Randolph County, was an integral part of the Underground Railroad in the years before the Civil War. A.A. Burlingame, a wagon and farm pump manufacturer, hid slaves in the basement of his house, rolled them in carpet to discourage any scent which could be picked up by dogs, then hid them beneath the pumps he carried north to Carlyle. The home is privately owned and is not open for tours. *Courtesy of Carol Pirtle.*

ILLINOIS-WISCONSIN CONNCETION

A number of Wisconsin people and events have Illinois connections. The stories of Caroline Quarrels and Andrew Pratt are told elsewhere in this book.

Jeremiah and Eliza Porter shared the fervent religious belief that slavery was a sin. For a time they lived and worked in Chicago, which was still a frontier village. He was pastor of First Presbyterian Church and she was the first public school teacher. In 1836 they went to Peoria and then to Farmington in 1837. That same year Jeremiah Porter had participated in the formation of the Illinois Anti-Slavery Society in Alton. The following year he persuaded the Society to meet in Farmington. He and Eliza provided lodging for Benjamin Lundy and Edward Beecher, who was the president of Illinois College in Jacksonville and brother of author Harriet Beecher Stowe.

After leaving Illinois the Porters went to Wisconsin. Green Bay was a small settlement at that time. The Strongbridge Indians lived nearby on the eastern shore of Lake Winnebago. They were a proud people who had been forced from their lands in New York and Massachusetts. Although it was at great risk, they broke civil laws to shelter a bereaved father and two children who had escaped from slavery. They did not know whether the children's mother had died or been sold.

When the Strongbridge spotted slave catchers prowling around their land they knew their guests were in danger. They sent a letter to Jeremiah and Eliza Porter asking the Porters to receive them and send them on the next steamboat.

The Porters were sure the captain of the Michigan steamship would take the family to Canada. They did not have any room in their home and hid them in the bell towers of their church. From the bell towers the father could look down on Green Bay and the surrounding area. He had escaped from slavery with three children; one had died on the way. He could only hope the ship would arrive soon and that he could reach Canada with his two surviving children. Having sacrificed much in the effort to be free, he felt desperate when the steamboat did not arrive on schedule and the slave catchers were nearby.

Days later the ship arrived. An abolitionist deacon let the captain know the father and children would be boarding. The Porters led the family down to the harbor and another abolitionist rowed them out to the steamboat.

The father and children safely reached Canada with the cooperative efforts of the Strongbridge Indians, the Porters, other abolitionists in Green Bay and the ship captain.

Hiram Foote had attended the Illinois Anti-Slavery Society meeting in Farmington, Illinois. He studied at Lane Seminary in Ohio. Beginning in 1839 he pastored and established churches in Joliet, Illinois and five cities in Wisconsin. At the same time he established Underground Railroad stations.

Hiram and Eliza Foote also operated a "station" in their home in Janesville. One night they were awakened by a knock on the door.

A black man named George was standing outside. He was leaning on a crutch and in pain. He had been shot as he fled from slave catchers near the Illinois -Wisconsin border yet made his way to the Foote's Underground Railroad station. He rested there two days, but the slave catchers who shot him were still looking for him.

Hiram and Eliza Foote supplied him with clothing and luggage so he looked like a well-dressed freedman as be boarded a steamboat bound for Canada. Hiram and Eliza were eager to find out whether or not George arrived safely. Knowing that enslaved Africans were denied a chance to learn to read or write they couldn't expect him to write them a letter. They solved the dilemma, however. They gave him an envelope that was addressed to themselves and asked him to mail it when he reached Canada.

George arrived safely and he mailed the envelope back to the Footes. Eliza Foote later wrote about this. She said it "meant as much to us as though containing an account of the journey. We knew George was safe."

Other stories of the Underground Railroad in Wisconsin can be found in Freedom Train North by Julia Pferdehirt.

27. What was the role of the African-American church in community life?

Black people settled in various locations early in Illinois. Churches served as anchors in the formation of African American communities. In addition to being places of worship, they were centers of social, civic, and political activity. Many churches provided reading and writing instruction to adults and children.

Because many members of early black churches had been enslaved or had family members in bondage, their leaders and members were particularly dedicated to helping fellow black people escape to freedom and better life. They provided food, clothing, lodging, and helpful information.

BISHOP PAUL QUINN
Courtesy of The DuSable Museum of African American History

Reportedly, African Methodist Episcopal churches were located relatively near each other in order to form a chain of Underground Railroad stations. Legend has it that the black Baptist ministers stood on the banks of the Mississippi River and preached to slaves on the Missouri side. They knew how to hold an iron skillet in such a way that it would amplify the sound of their voices.

Black congregations worked alone or with members of white churches. Even if they felt free to worship they thought of their brothers and sisters who were not.

The Wood River Baptist District Association grew out of the cooperative efforts of black and white religious leaders in the Alton area, including George James Leman, John Mason Peck, John Livingston and Alfred Richardson. The Colored Baptist Association, which later became known as the Wood River Association, was originally a branch of

MOSES DICKSON

Reprinted from The Story of a Rising Race *by Rev. J.J. Pipkin.*

Rev. Moses Dickson was born in the city of Cincinnati, Ohio, April 5, 1824. He was the son of Robert and Hannah Dickson, natives of Virginia. His father died in 1832, and his mother in 1838. He learned the barber's trade while he as a young man and at the same time attended school and mastered all the branches of study that were taught at that early day. At the age of sixteen, he secured employment on a steamboat and for three years traveled in various boats upon the different Southern rivers and bayous. In these travels through the South, he saw slavery in all its aspects, and what he saw in these three years of travel made a lasting impression on him and determined him to devote his best efforts to secure freedom for his race. He had made the acquaintance of a few true and trusty young men, who were ready to join with him in any plan that seemed feasible and likely to assure freedom to the slaves. Eleven of these young men met with him and agreed to form an organization for that purpose. Knowing that the work was one of great magnitude and would require time, courage and patience, they took two years to study over it and planned to meet again in St. Louis on the 12th of August, 1846.

Mr. Dickson embarked on the steamer *Oronoco* at New Orleans in May, 1844, and made a trip to St. Louis, where he remained during the summer. He then traveled for two years through Iowa, Illinois, Wisconsin and other Northen States, and in August, 1846, was in St. Louis prepared to meet his friends with an outline of the plan to be submittted to them. The twelve met on the second Tuesday in August and Mr. Dickson unfolded to them his plan which was adopted. This meeting resulted in the formation of the "Knights of Liberty." The twelve organizers went actively to work and formed local organizations in every slave State except Missouri and Texas. Mr. Dickson remained the head of the Order with headquarters in St. Louis. The Knights of Liberty were not to commence active operation for ten years from the time of organization, the intervening time to be used in making preparations. When the ten years were ended, in 1856, the trend of events was such that it was not thought advisable to carry out the plans of the organization, inasmuch as it seemed probable at that time that freedom would come in the natural course of events.

During the ten years of preparation and up to the breaking out of the war, the Knights of Liberty, in connection with their other work, were actively interested in the "Undergroung Railroad," and in ten years transported more than 70,000 slaves from bondage to freedom. The organization was so compact and its affairs so secretly conducted that for years nobody knew the names of the original twelve organizers, or that such an organization existed. The methods by which the Knights of Liberty expected to accomplish their object will probably never be known, but the extent of the movements and the secrecy maintained proves Mr. Dickson to have been a past master in the art of organization.

Mr. Dickson was actively engaged in the field during the war, and was in thirteen hard-fought battles, returning home in 1864 without a scratch from the enemy's bullets.

After the war, he turned his energies and efforts to the education of the freed men and their children. He led a powerful lobby to Jefferson City, Missouri, and worked hard for the establishment of schools for colored children. His efforts were successful, and, under the administration of Governor McClurg, the present school laws of Missouri were adopted. This being achieved the next movement was to procure colored teachers for colored schools. After a hard fight, he was successful in that also.

He took an active part in the founding of Lincoln Institute, at Jefferson City, Missouri, and was trustee and vice-president of the board for several years until the success of the institution was assured. He has given his time largely since the war to educational movements for the benefit of the colored race.

In 1878, he became president of the Refugee Relief Board in St. Louis, and the board under his management cared for about sixteen thousand people. These refugees were comfortably clothed, given provisions to last them several months, and forwarded to Kansas, Nebraska, Colorado and other Northern States, where

the Friends of Humanity, a white Baptist organization. Rev. John Livingston who organized Union Baptist Church in Alton led the Association. Rev. Alfred Richardson was the first minister of that congregation. Elijah Lovejoy was a close friend of the organizers of Wood River Association and shortly before he was martyred he was chosen to be secretary of the Association.

Rev. Livingston organized black churches in other Illinois cities beginning in the late 1830's. Two of these churches were in St. Clair County—Mount Zion Baptist in Ridge Prairie and Salem Baptist in Ogle Creek. Rev. Livingston also organized Emory Baptist Church in Jacksonville, and Zion Missionary Baptist Church in Springfield.

In 1837 seven formerly enslaved people founded the Mount Emory Baptist Church. The church was built in the part of Jacksonville once called Africa. Zion Missionary Baptist Church in Springfield was called the Colored Baptist Church when Rev. Livingston organized it in 1838. Its seven founding members were all former slaves.

MOSES DICKSON (CONT.)

they settled and became good citizens. More than ten thousand of these refugees settled in Kansas.

Mr. Dickson was prominent in politics in his State. He was a delegate to every Republican State Convention of Missouri from 1864 and 1878, and during several campaigns stumped the State in the interest of his party. He was elector at large on the Grant ticket in 1872.

He was converted and joined the A.M.E. Church in 1866, and in 1867 was licensed to preach. He has held a number of large and small charges, and was well known as a successful manager of churches, and particularly as a church builder, a debt payer and a revivalist. During his several pastorates about fourteen hundred persons have been converted by him.

After the war, when the work of the "Knights of Liberty" was ended, he decided to institute a beneficial order in memory of the twelve original organizers for that society. After three years of preparation he organized, in 1871, the first Temple and Tabernacle of the "Order of Twelve of the Knights and Daughters of Tabor," which has for its object the encouragement of Christianity education, morality and temperance among the colored people. Its object is to teach the art of governing, self-reliance and true manhood and womanhood. Part of its work is to encourage home-building and the acquiring of wealth. The Order in

twenty-seven years, has taken its place with the greatest organizations of the world. It now has more than sixty thousand members, and wields a powerful influence for good among the colored people.

M. Dickson was married on the 5th of October, 1848, to Mrs. Mary Elizabeth Peters. She died in 1891. The couple had one child, Mrs. Mamie Augusta Robinson, and one grandchild, who was adopted by the Knights of Tabor, and bears the title of "Princess of the Knights and Daughters of Tabor."

After a long life spent in the service of his race, Mr. Dickson died in the early part of 1902.

Rocky Fork was a community in the Alton area where freedom seekers could rest and recuperate after escaping from bondage by crossing the Mississippi River into Illinois. Some stayed long enough to rest then set out again to put more distance between themselves and slavery. Others remained, and together with free black people, organized the Rocky Fork Church, since renamed New Bethel A.M.E Church.

Founding members, Eurastus Green and George Hindman, both served in the Civil War and resumed leadership roles when they returned. A.W. Hasley, a white cattle farmer in the area, gave them an opportunity to work and then allowed them to purchase land in 40-acre parcels. Eurastus Green, George Hindman, and other members of the Rocky Fork congregation are buried in the church cemetery. Reverend Wilkinson was one of the early pastors of the Rocky Fork church. He organized churches at Sorrento (south of Litchfield) and also Collinsville.

Some of the UGRR passengers who continued their journeys after taking a rest in the Rocky Fork area became founding membrers of Baptist churches under the umbrella of Friends of Humanity mentioned above. Wherever the people went, a church was established. Reverend George James Leman, an abolitionist, brought this concept from Kentucky. Reverend John Livingston was the agent who organized the churches in Piasa, Shipman, Bunker Hill, and Jerseyville, Jackonville, and Springfield.

Antioch (Missionary) Baptist Church of Decatur was organized in 1857, the year of the Dred Scott Decision.

Pre-Civil War efforts to form a Baptist church in Champaign resulted in the founding of Second Baptist, renamed Salem Baptist Church.

People of African descent have played a central role in the history of Batavia ever since the town's early days. The 1850 Census includes the names of black residents. The A.M.E. church began in 1860.

Ward Chapel A.M.E. Church, which was organized in 1846, is Peoria's oldest African American church. This church was the location that city's first school for black children. An African Methodist Episcopal Church was also organized in Jacksonville. A circuit preacher served congregations in Galesburg.

Campbell A.M.E. Church in Alton was the first A.M.E. church in Illinois to be organized by Bishop Paul Quinn who was noted for the large number of churches he organized in Illinois and Indiana. Like many ministers of that time, he was a circuit rider, serving a number of churches and riding from one church to another on horseback. Pricilla Baltimore had been a member of the church in St. Louis that Quinn organized. She rowed him across the Mississippi River in a rowboat to take him to a gathering at her home in Alton where Campbell A.M.E. was organized. Eurastus Green who was also a circuit rider organized Bethel A.M.E. Church in Champaign in the midst of the Civil War.

Local residents under the leadership of Reverend Paul Quinn established the Wayman Avenue A.M.E. Church in Bloomington in 1843. The original church was built in 1859 and is now the home of the Faith Baptist Church. It which once housed the A.M.E. Publishing Company.

In Illinois many other churches including those in Lovejoy and Eagle Park Acres are named for Bishop Quinn. In Chicago Rev. Abraham Hall and six other founding members of Quinn Chapel started meeting in homes in 1844. In 1847 Bishop Quinn held a meeting and organized the church in downtown Chicago. The church was at a number of locations before building on its present site.

The Liberty Association was the first organization established within the church. It was a vigilance committee composed of the men of Quinn and other black men in the community. They served as watchmen walking the streets of community each night so that they could alert sleeping residents if slave catchers were in town.

The Fugitive Slave Law of 1850 interrupted these efforts. After it became law the entire congregation of Quinn Chapel AME Church migrated to Canada overnight.

28. Were UGRR passengers the first Black people in Illinois?

No. The French enslaved black people in Illinois. As far back as 1712, a French Jesuit priest made a large dictionary of the Illinois Indian language. In his dictionary there was a word for which the literal translation is "black men".

Within the next decade a Frenchman named Philippe Francois Renault purchased workers from the French in Santa Domingo and brought them to the area near Fort de Chartres and to Galena. He had hoped to develop mining operations. He was unsuccessful in his venture and sold the Santa Dominicans to other French slaveholders. Some of the French valued and treated slaves humanely. The "Code Noir" or Black Code regulated slave owners as well as slaves. It was severe but provided some minimal protection for slaves against cruel masters.

In 1763, after the French and Indian War, the British ruled the Illinois Country . They were noted for being even less considerate than the French.

Meanwhile, a free black Haitian (sometimes called a Santo Dominican), Jean Baptiste Pointe DuSable had developed a thriving business with the Ottawa, the Illinois, and the Miami tribes in the St. Louis area. He earned their respect by dealing more honestly than some other French traders. DuSable left St. Louis after the death of Ottawa Chief Pontiac and also after France ceded Louisiana. He settled in the Chicago area, having seen it while on a peace making mission that Pontiac had requested from his deathbed.

DuSable was the first permanent settler in Chicago. Historian Milo Milton Quaife and others found a corroded plaque on a dilapidated old soap factory building in downtown Chicago. The words on the plaque were: "On this site, in 1772, Jean Baptiste Pointe DuSable, a Negro from Santo Domingo, built the first cabin at Chicago." Quaife described DuSable as "a true pioneer of civilization, leader of the unending procession of Chicago's swarming millions."

DuSable had established a trading post on the north bank of the Chicago River near Lake Michigan. He chose this most strategic site because it linked the Great Lakes with the fur-rich lands of the Illinois, the Mississippi, and Missouri rivers with the Gulf of Mexico.

DuSable's trading post consisted of log homestead that included a bakehouse, smoke-house, dairy, workshop, gristmill, barn, and stables. Tradition claims that DuSable's home was the site of the first wedding, the first recorded birth, first election, and first court session in the area. In 1778, an early British commandant, Colonel Arentschuyler de Peyster, described DuSable as a French speaking "handsome Negro well educated and situated at Chickagou."

Most accounts of the American Revolutionary War focus on events that took place in states bordering the Atlantic Ocean. However, in her research, DuSable scholar Virginia Julien learned that in the (Middle) West, Chicago was the sought after prize of the Revolutionary War. France, Spain, and England all wanted to control this strategic location.

The British at Mackinaw in Upper Michigan viewed American General George Rogers Clark and DuSable, whom they felt influenced his Indian allies to support the American side, as obstacles to their gaining control. In 1779 they arrested DuSable with supplies intended for Clark. Knowing that DuSable was a skillful trader, they took him to Mackinaw and had him operate their trading post. The Ottawa Indians interceded on DuSable's behalf and he was released.

DuSable and the Native Americans were a major force in holding access to Lake Michigan after Clark left the (Middle) West in 1780. They had high expectations when in 1787 the American Continental Congress enacted the Northwest Ordinance banning slavery in the Northwest Territory (the Great Lakes region). Article IV of the document stated,

---

ARTICLE VI
"There shall be neither slavery nor involuntary servitude in the said territory, otherwise than in the punishment of crimes, where of the party shall have been duly convicted"

When these terms were not enforced, on May 17, 1800, DuSable sold his property to an employee, Jean LeLime, for 600 livres (in French money). The itemized bill of sale is on file at the Wayne County Document Building in Detroit, Michigan. John Kinzie who purchased the DuSable homestead from LeLime three years later witnessed this sale.

DuSable retired to Peoria and later moved to St. Charles, Missouri. He died on August 29, 1818 and was buried in the Catholic cemetery in St. Charles.

* * *

When Hugo Leaming taught at the University of Illinois at Chicago he conducted research on another cooperative interracial effort. He found out that around 1790, indentured whites, Native Americans and enslaved Africans who had escaped bondage in Maryland, North and South Carolina, Virginia, and Tennessee met in Kentucky. There they formed a community where they felt safe from capture, and became known as "The Tribe of Ishmal." (A Biblical name which means "Wanderer"). They made their living by hunting, fishing and growing vegetables.

Unfriendly pro-slavery settlers moved nearby and the Tribe crossed the Ohio River hoping to settle on the north side of the river. However, the Fugitive Slave Law of 1793 made it unsafe for them to remain there. They continued westward, arriving in Illinois in the 1820's. Native Americans welcomed the fugitives and gave them permission to establish settlements in Illinois and Indiana.

One Ishmael settlement was at the town of Mohamet, Illinois. Settlement members with African ancestry recalled words from their native languages. At one time there were quite a few Arabic surnames in the Mohamet city directory.

Three other settlements were near Bloomington, Peoria, and Decatur. When early European immigrants arrived, they were amazed to find tri-racial farm communities, complete with cabins and meeting halls.

By the 1840's, most of the black people who lived in these communities had been born there—not in slavery—so if slave catchers appeared, all the people could claim to be free.

One of their favorite customs was an annual summer journey. It was three hundred fifty miles long—from settlements in Indiana, up to what is now the, Chicago area then down through Illinois. The children and elderly people rode in little carts drawn by donkeys or horses, and the men and women walked along side.

These communities continued until after the Civil War. Finally, by about 1910, the people moved into the cities, joining the rest of the population.

ELGIN

Elgin has a "two track" railroad story. One is about events traditionally related to the Underground Railroad. The other relates to the contraband trains which brought women and children displaced by the Civil War to Elgin.

Dr. Anson Root and the Gifford family are people who link Elgin with the Underground Railroad. Dr. Root is listed in Wilbur Siebert's Underground Railroad book as an operator in Kane County. He was chairman of the Kane County Anti-Slavery Society meeting in 1843. He is associated with the Caroline Quarels case (described elsewhere in the book). He is believed to be the Dr. Root visited by Waukesha abolitionists and Caroline Quarels on the escape to Canada.

Harriet Gifford, Elgins's first teacher and Louisa Gifford were the sisters of Elgin founder, James T. Gifford. Lousia's husband was Dr. C.V. Dyer, and their home was a "central depot" in Chicago.

Other Elginites including storekeeper William G. Hubbard, and Congregational minister Reverend N.C. Clark, took a stand against slavery. Before becoming pastor of the Baptist Church in Elgin, James T. Gifford was on the state central committee of the Liberty Party. Rev. Adoniram Judson Joslyn had been secretary of the DuPage County Anti-Slavery Society and helped edit the *Western Christian* anti-slavery newspaper published in Elgin.

In 1847 Owen Lovejoy spoke at an anti-slavery convention in Elgin. Some of the other prominent anti-slavery speakers who came to Elgin were Wendell Phillips, Icabod Codding, Cassius M. Clay of Kentucky, and John P. Hale, presidential candidate for the Free Soil Party.

After the battle of Shiloh, large numbers of newly freed slaves escaped to or were captured by the Union forces. These war refugees were called contraband. The men joined the Union army or provided it with much needed labor. The women and children were not as easily absorbed into war effort. In 1862, the Secretary of War authorized their transfer to northern states. During the time the order was in effect, John Wilcox, Commander of the 52nd Infantry, wrote his wife, Lois. He told her of the miserable, unhealthy conditions the contrabands were living in although he revealed his own prejudices in his letter. Plans were made to bring some of the contrabands to Elgin. The order was rescinded two weeks later. (Opponents argued that it was in conflict with the Illinois Black Codes and notified the sheriff.) In the meantime, Benjamin Thomas the chaplain of the 52nd Illinois was en route to Elgin with two carloads of contrabands amidst much controversy. Chaplain Thomas told the sheriff that these people were traveling under military orders and that those orders superseded the Black Codes.

Many of the contrabands had been enslaved on plantations near Cherokee, Alabama. They received a mixed reception in Elgin. William Bent built an addition to his farmhouse to provide a home for one family. On the other hand, Lois Wilcox whose husband had written her did not welcome the new arrivals. The contrabands had been exposed to such communicable diseases such as scarlet fever, small pox and diphtheria. As a result, an epidemic erupted through Elgin and the contrabands were blamed and further isolated.

After President Lincoln signed the *Emancipation Proclamation* the black freed men who had stayed in the South with the Union army were able to join their families in Elgin. They too faced treatment as second class citizens. However a local lumber merchant, Lansing Morgan, provided building materials. Under the leadership of Arthur Newsome and others, black Elginites built homes, maintained churches and assumed responsibilities in the city. A park near downtown Elgin is named Newsome Park as a tribute to Arthur Newsome.

In an interview Newsome's nephew, Edward said that he was fifteen years old when he had his first opportunity for education. He, like other former slaves, craved education, so he entered first grade at that time. Although he must have felt self-conscious to be a teenager starting school with six year olds, he remained until he finished eighth grade. He later became a homeowner and respected citizen, his son, LeVerne, became a highly accomplished musician and educator.

In recent years Elgin has become a model city where white, black, and Hispanic people live in harmony. Its schools have received national praise and in 1996 *Money* magazine called Elgin a "mirror of America."

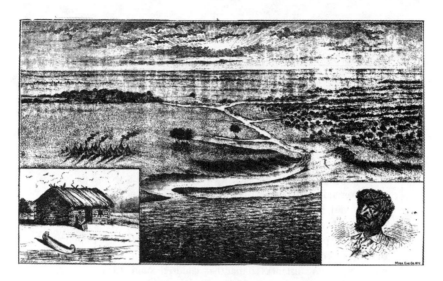

JEAN BAPTISTE POINT DUSABLE'S TRADING POST
AT LAKE MICHIGAN AND THE CHICAGO RIVER

Carrier Mills, Brownville, and Miller Grove are early black communities in Illinois. The settlers of Carrier Mills migrated from North Carolina to Southern Illinois in oxen drawn covered wagons soon after the War of 1812. In the mid-nineteenth century they purchased government land. One of the first settlers, Zachariah (Byrd) Taborn donated land for the church and cemetery. The main blacktop road is named for him. Each year families who trace their roots to Carrier Mills come from all directions for a community reunion.

Fort Allison, near the Indiana border, served as a refuge during the War of 1812. One of the African-American families that came with that group has maintained a farm in Lawrenceville known as the Morris Centennial Farm.

"Free Frank" McWorter (see the "Introduction" to this book which was written by his great granddaughter, Dr. Juliet E.K.Walker) arrived in the then-huge but sparsely settled Pike County in 1830.

In 1834 Amos Bennett was the first African American resident of Lake County.

The U.S. Forest Service is conducting an archaeological dig in the Shawnee Forest at what was once the site of the all black settlement of Miller Grove. The settlement was established in the 1840's by a group of free black people from Tennessee. When they entered Illinois they were required to post a bond to indicate they would not become a burden to the state. Two white men, Henry Fides and a man named Dabbs, accompanied the group consisting mainly of the Miller and Ellison families, posted their

Terre Haute

Two churches were in the forefront of anti-slavery activities in Terra Haute, Indiana. They were the Allen Chapel A.M.E. (African Methodist Episcopal) Church and the First Congregational Church.

Allen Chapel A.M.E. was founded in 1837. It was an UGRR station and is listed on the National Register of Historic Places. Its second pastor was Reverend Hiram Revels who attended Knox College in Galesburg, Illinois and later became United States Senator from Mississippi. Reverend Revels started the Allen Chapel School a decade before Indiana had public schools. The Church's school provided a rare opportunity for formerly enslaved people to get an education. Black families moved from long distances so that their children could attend. One of the families was that of P.B.S. Pinchback who became Lieutenant Governor and for a short time, Governor of Louisiana. In 1825, John Roye moved his family to Terra Haute from Ohio. He and a white farmer named James Farrington, operated a ferry boat across the Wabash River. (Might this ferry have provided transportation for people escaping bondage soon after Missouri became a state?) James Roye bought many acres of land in Illinois in addtion to his land in Indiana. When he died in Vandalia, Illinois, in 1829, he left his property to his son Edward. Edward attended Allen Chapel School and Ohio University then taught in Chillicothe, Ohio. He and his bride moved back to Terra Haute so they would be able to send their children to the Allen Chapel School. Edward later sold the Illinois and Indiana properties he had inherited and moved to Liberia in West Africa. He became Chief Justice of the Liberian Supreme Court and the 5th President of Liberia.

There is a framed copy of a sermon hanging on the walls of First Congregational Church of Terra Haute. It is a sermon made by Reverend Lyman Abbott. His sermon is significant because of the courage it took to make it. In the 1860's, he was one of the few ministers to speak out against slavery. He continued in the strong abolitionist tradition. After serving in Terra Haute, he became pastor of the New York Church that Elijah Loveoy's friend Edward Beecher has pastored.

No written documentation has been found indicating that the First Congregational Church served as an UGRR station. Certainly some of its members were strong UGRR supporters.

bonds and declared them free. These records are on file in Pope County Court House in Golconda.

The town of Brooklyn, in Saint Clair County was platted in 1837, although not incorporated until 1874. Its post office was named Lovejoy in honor of abolitionist editor, Elijah P. Lovejoy.

James Henry Johnson was a resident of Alton in 1837. In 1850 he purchased a farm from the U.S. Land Bank. The farm has remained in his family and is one of the oldest working African-American farms in Illinois.

George Washington Foster was born in Hennepin County, Ohio, in 1822. He and his parents migrated to Indiana where he became a barber's apprentice. He went to work on riverboats serving as barber, cook, steward, engineer, and waiter. He settled in Morris in 1857 and opened a barbershop. Abraham Lincoln stopped in Morris on his way to his first of his famous debates with Stephen A. Douglas and he went to "Wash" Foster's shop to get a shave. Foster lived to be 95 years old and fascinated generations of children with stories of his days on the riverboats and his conversation with Lincoln.

OVERTON MARKER AND THE GRAVE OF FRANCIS OVERTON

Escaping slaves were sometimes escorted from Overton's to the Stone Castle by way of a ravine that extended part of the distance between the two "stations."

29. Were young people involved in UGRR operations?

Yes. During his formative years American hero Wild Bill Hickock helped with his father's Underground Railroad activities. Bill became aware of the mysterious activities at the Green Mountain House in Troy Grove, Illinois. Once he learned that their business was a cover for UGRR operation, his father allowed him to help transport slaves. Driving the wagon helped Bill become an expert in handling horses.

Handling horses was how another young person, Harriet Overton, rescued her father, who was an UGRR operator near Bernadotte, Illinois. One day when Harriet and her father went to town pro-slavery men attacked her father. She mounted a horse and armed herself with a lead bar, then she rode into the group and obtained her father's release.

Charley Love's quick thinking saved another adult. Charley was a young black man. Written records do not indicate whether he was born free or in bondage. One day two strangers came to Galesburg hunting for Bill Casey, a man who was the only survivor out of a group of people who escaped from slavery in Missouri. Charley didn't provide any information to his questioners; instead he gave the alarm, so Casey had time to safely escape.

Once when his father was not at home to do so, fourteen year old Elias West, hitched up the wagon and transported seven UGRR passengers from Sycamore to St. Charles. It was an overnight trip. En route, one of the men in the group told Elias that he had rubbed onions on his feet and waded in water for miles to escape the bloodhound dogs. On another occasion Elias West and Hiram Kellogg, who was also in his teens, transported six more UGRR passengers in a covered wagon that Elias's father had made.

Soon after Annistine Waterbury returned to Buffalo Grove from school in the East her uncle, John Waterbury, came to her parents' house and told her father, "Samuel, we've got company at our house. A woman and ten children came last night ..." Her uncle and her father helped that family escape. The next year Annistine accompanied her father as he transported two young UGRR passengers to Byron, possibly to the home of Jared Sanford.

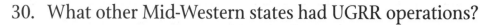

30. What other Mid-Western states had UGRR operations?

Iowa, Missouri, Michigan, Wisconsin, and Indiana. The section of the country now called the Middle West was called "The West" at that time.

~ Iowa

There were Missouri patrols along the Des Moines River. The Quaker settlements of Salem and Denmark were havens for slaves who escaped across that northeastern border of Missouri. The Lewelling Quaker House in Salem is open to the public.

Enslaved Africans from Missouri frequently passed through Harrison County (which borders the Iowa line) and after entering Iowa, received assistance from local families. Several short Underground Railroad "roads" started at Corydon, Bloomfield, Lancaster, and Cincinnati.

In 1864, Laura Haviland (1808 -1898) discovered these "iron arguments" used by slave owners to keep slaves under control. In Haviland's hands are handcuffs and a knee stiffener. The rough iron collar under her foot was worn by a slave as a torture device. Haviland, a devout abolitionist, dedicated her entire adult life to helping others. *Courtesy, Lenawee County Historical Museum.*

One Iowa route passed through Lewis, Des Moines, Grinnell, Iowa City, West Liberty, Tipton, DeWitt, and Low Moor. This route was essentially that of present day Intestate 80. Slaves crossed the Mississippi River at Clinton to connect with Illinois routes in the Quad City area. Guided tours are conducted at the Hitchcock House in Lewis.

In southwest Iowa Underground Railroad passengers came to Todd House in Tabor after stopping at the Allen B. Mayhaw Cabin and John Brown Caves across the Missouri River in Nebraska City, Nebraska.

BEN HENDERSON

This excerpt of an interview with Benjamin Henderson, a black UGRR conductor in Jacksonville, Illinois, is reprinted from "The Negro In Illinois," Illinois Writers Project. Vivian Harsh Collection, Carter G. Woodson Regional Library, Chicago Public Library System.

Question(Q). "How long was the Underground Railroad kept up in this place?"

Response(R). "Until about 1855 or 1857, though with intermissions, as the slave catchers would sometimes watch my father's house so closely that some other place had to be chosen for a depot for a while.

One afternoon I saw a colored man whom I believed to be a runaway slave. I asked him in and in the evening started off with him on horseback. It was raining hard and was very dark with occasional vivid flashes of lightning. We soon heard steps behind us and I told my companion to lie down on his horse and conceal himself which he did so completely that when the next flash of lightning came I thought he had dropped off entirely. Our pursuer turned out to be a cow and we were much relieved.

I remember after the southerners had been busy looking elsewhere for a time a large party of fugitives was brought to my father's barn about the year 1853. I shall never forget the sight; strong men and women hungering for freedom, boys and girls hardly realizing the situation, and one infant in its mother's arms, looked around the bewilderment at its strange surroundings. They were in due time successfully removed and sent on their way to the North Star."

Q. "Mr. Henderson, in what year did you begin your labors in the cause of freedom?"

R. "I came here to live in the year 1841 and was soon at work on the Underground Railroad and kept it up more or less until 1857 or '58. My house was a regular stopping place for fugitives, though at intervals it had to be abandoned, as it would be watched too closely by the slave catchers. I did a great deal of teaming in those days and so was called on to transport the fugitives frequently. Sometimes I made two trips a week carrying all the way from one to sixteen."

Q. "Where was your next depot?"

R. "We generally went to Springfield, Farmington and other places."

Q. "Who were your best friends here?"

R. "Elihu Wolcott and Ebenezer Carter were always the main pillars of the enterprise, sparing neither trouble nor expense, always acting as though they knew nothing of fear. Next to them came T.W. Melendy, Dr. Reed and several others who have been mentioned previously. When we wanted supplies for the fugitives we always found friends in Joseph and Horace Bancroft, J.W. Lathrop T.D. Eames, Asa Talcott, Mr. Hoyt, Mr. Burdette and others. Henry Irving was always ready to go on the road or entertain parties, and Rev. Mr. Kirby often proved himself a friend in deed."

"Considerable driving was also done by Washington Price of this place."

Q. "Please tell me some of your adventures."

R. "My first experience was in a small way. A fugitive came in one Saturday evening and we carefully secreted him a short time and then put him on the road to the next station. Next, a man came to my house from Mississippi, and as I was not well acquainted with the road to Springfield I tried for two days to get someone else to go but couldn't, so I got a buggy one night and started. Indications of day appeared before we reached the city, and my man began to get uneasy. I lost the way and hardly knew where to go, but finally made a successful turnaround found the town. Daniel Callahan and William Butler were our station keepers, and without very much trouble I found the letter and left my charge with them.

Walden Steward, E.B. Shedeker and a Mr. Pitman used to operate below here and for a time the fugitives they sent north to the house of a colored man whom they trusted were never heard from.

~ Missouri

Within the slave state of Missouri, Moses Dickson and eleven other free blacks organized the "Knights of Liberty". (It later became the "Knights and Daughters of Tabor Society".)

They operated in St. Louis, the city where the Missouri River meets the Mississippi. There was brisk slave trading here (e.g. at the courthouse where the Dred Scott case was filed.) In order to help fellow blacks they risked having their own freedom papers destroyed, or being enslaved, and "sold down the Mississippi River" and sent so far South that escape would be nearly impossible.

Rev. Benjamin Meacham conducted another daring endeavor. Knowing that slaves were forbidden to learn to read and write while on the plantation, he had a boat built. He conducted a floating school on the Mississippi River near St. Louis. More details about this school and other examples of activities on the Illinois-Missouri border can be found at Black World History Wax Museum in St. Louis.

Meramec, the five-story cavern in the Ozarks, was an UGRR hiding place. It was also a hideout for outlaw Jesse James.

~ Michigan

In Marshall, Michigan, a boulder in Triangle Park marks the site of the cabin of Mr. and Mrs. Adam Crosswhite and their children. The Crosswhite family had escaped from slavery in Kentucky in 1846. Knowing that their former slaveholder might come after them, Crosswhite arranged for his neighbors to signal him if someone

---

BEN HENDERSON (CONT.)

"One night they sent two men on to this man who received them all right and started on with them the next night. They were soon met by white men who halted them, handcuffed all three and started toward St. Louis. The man who received the fugitives was sent off by himself and the other two taken on to St. Louis and thrown into the slave pen. One was sold to a party who took him to New Orleans, but he managed to escape and return to St. Louis on the very boat which had taken him away. Meanwhile, his comrade escaped from the slave pen, and the two made another start for the north. On their way up they met their old friends and told them of the treachery of the man who had been trusted and he was severely let alone. The city of St. Louis offered a reward of $100 for each fugitive returned and the owner generally gave an equal amount and for this paltry sum, or a part of it, these and others had been betrayed.

Henry Irving was one of the bravest men connected with the Underground Railroad and did good service on it from 1843 until the war. Though his principal work was that of conducting he always did what he could in the way of entertaining fugitives. Once he kept a man in the garret of his house for a week, the roads being watched so closely that it was unsafe for anyone to start away with his guest, and so cleverly did he manage the affair that he finally got away with him in spite of the vigilance of the slave catchers.

THE JESSE WHEATON HOUSE

In 1837, Jesse Wheaton traveled to Warrenville to join his brother, Warren and the Erastus Gary family, who had been neighbors in their hometown of Pomfret, Connecticut. Jesse married Orinda Gary between the time that the Indians of this region were forced to cede their lands and when the federal government surveyed the newly available lands. He took a preemption claim for a total of 300 acres. He later paid the government for them at $1.25 per acre.

Many historic events took place in the home of Jesse Wheaton. In fact, it was the meeting there with John Ogden, President of Galena and Chicago Union Railroad, that resulted in the naming of the town. Ogden intended to have the railroad follow the old Galena stagecoach road (now Lake Street) across northern DuPage County. Tracks were already laid as far as present day Maywood. Jesse and Warren Wheaton offered Ogden free right-of-way if he would reroute his railroad through their property. Ogden accepted and built a station near the boundary of the Wheaton farms.

The city of Wheaton was organized in Jesse Wheaton's living room. So was the College, which was also eventually named Wheaton. The first Milton Township meeting was held there as well.

The house was also an Underground Railroad stop. Jesse was a carpenter and had a secret attic in addition to the main attic. This was the Underground Railroad hiding place. There was a section of wall between the two attics. The attic has since been remodeled.

When the college was first established it was called Illinois Institute. It operated under the auspices of the Illinois Wesleyan Methodists whose members had broken away from the Methodist General Conference over the issue of slavery.

The school's first instructor was John Cross, who had come to Illinois as an agent of the American Anti-Slavery Society. As is stated elsewhere in this book, Cross was involved in many aspects of anti-slavery activities in Illinois and other states. He was also a signer of the city of Wheaton's Papers of Incorporation.

An early president, Lucius Matlack, was active in UGRR operations at the college. It is believed that he "forwarded" passengers to Thomas Filer in Glen Ellyn.

When Jonathan Blanchard became president, he re-named the college in honor of its founder. Wheaton College was a hot-bed of anti-slavery activity. In fact, Ezra Cook, one of the sixty seven students who left to join the Union forces, said that there was an "above ground" rather than (underground) railroad at the school.

Reportedly, UGRR stations were operated in Blanchard's home, other homes in the area, and the school's first building (now the totally remolded Blanchard Hall).

came looking for him. The slaveholder did come. The Crosswhite's neighbors gave them a warning signal and they were able to escape to Canada. The neighbors were arrested and received heavy fines.

According to Underground Railroad authority, Dr. Charles L. Blockson, this incident was a factor in the 1850 Fugitive Slave Act and in the Dred Scott Decision of the U.S. Supreme Court.

Towns on or near Lake Michigan and the Huron River were on the route. Recently when an old building in Ann Arbor was being remodeled, workers discovered a tunnel leading to the Huron River. It is believed to be a remnant of the UGRR.

Main routes from Indiana converged at Battle Creek, where residents Erastus Hussey and Sojourner Truth were noted for their anti-slavery work: Erastus Hussey as the main station operator and Sojourner Truth for her extensive lecturing for human rights, including women's suffrage. Both are buried in Battle Creek where they are each honored with a monument.

SOJOURNER TRUTH & ABRAHAM LINCOLN
Courtesy of DuSable Museum of African AmericanHistory.

In Detroit, freedmen William Lambert and George DeBaptist founded the Fraternal Order of African American Mysteries. They had two main objectives. The first was to make it possible for escaped slaves to reach a free territory. In her research, Mary Edmond, the person who is most knowledgeable about the UGRR in Michigan found that members of the Order established a series of farms, which functioned as UGRR stations along the route between Chicago and Detroit. Laura Haviland and Sojourner

Truth were integrally involved in these UGRR operations, because they lectured to help raise money for these stations. The second objective of the order was to prepare ex-slaves for a new life. It provided a special ceremony that symbolized the ending of a slave's dependence on a master, and the beginning of independence as a free person.

UGRR passengers who had traveled by way of Wayne and Ann Arbor met at different stations in Detroit. One station was at the home of J.G. Reynolds. Levi Coffin sent Reynolds there. Reynolds was a black man who worked for a company that was constructing the Michigan Central Railway. Another UGRR station was in the barn of white agent Alderman Seymour Finney. Finney, who owned a hotel one block from the barn, was connected with the UGRR for more than 30 years. Today a plaque on the Detroit Bank and Trust Company marks the location of the hotel.

Perhaps the largest UGRR station in Detroit was at the Second Baptist Church. This extremely active station has been preserved and can be visited by appointment. The last part of the journey was by boat. George de Baptiste owned boats, which were concealed under the docks. By morning they had taken all the fugitives over to the Canadian shore. He and William Lambert had put carpeting on the hooves of horses to muffle the sound as they transported groups of former slaves through the city streets to the banks of the Detroit River. William Webb, John Richards, Dr. Joseph Ferguson, and Rev. William Monroe were other conductors in Detroit. Many attended a meeting at the home of black grocer William Webb, where John Brown first discussed plans for his 1859 raid on Harper's Ferry.

~ Wisconsin

If persons who followed the Rock River through Illinois continued northward, they would reach Janesville, Wisconsin. The town of Milton and Milton House located a bit northeast of Janesville, was an UGRR station which was designated as a National Historic Landmark. Slaves were hidden in the basement of this hexagon-shaped inn. A tunnel, which could be entered from behind stacks of grain, connected the main building with a log cabin.

CAROLINE QUARLES
Courtesy of Julia Pferdehirt.

There were no steps from the tunnel to the small trapdoor in the floor of the cabin; slaves climbed a rope to get out of the tunnel. The Milton House is open to the public. Check times and dates before going.

JOHN JONES

The name John Jones appears in many accounts of the Illinois Black Codes, Chicago history and the Negro convention movement.

In 1996, a high school student named David Joseph Carnegie II did an in depth study of Jones which showed how these various activities were related to the Chicago tailor's best known efforts to have the Black Codes repealed. Although Jones was an extremely successful businessman, a freeman, and tax paying property owner these laws denied him the right to vote. Like the early American patriots, Jones objected to taxation without representation. John and Mary Richardson Jones knew the unfairness of such taxation applied to women of all races as well as to men. They entertained suffragettes Susan B. Anthony, Carrie Chatman Catt and Emma Chandler at their home on 119 Dearborn.

Jones objected to other provisions in the law. These included the fact that any slaveholder who freed an enslaved black person in Illinois had to post a $1,000.00 bond. Free black people had to get a certificate testifying that they were free.

John Jones had personally been subjected to this provision. He was born free in Green County, North Carolina in 1816. Although born free, he was tricked into becoming a bondsman in Memphis, Tennessee.

He was able to win his freedom in a Tennessee circuit court. Later he and Mary Richardson married and lived for a while in Alton, Illinois. While there, John Jones obtained the required certificate of freedom from the clerk of Madison County.

In 1845, the Joneses moved to Chicago. The trip took almost a week. En route they were nearly arrested on suspicion of being fugitive slaves.

John Jones opened his tailor shop with only $3.50. The business thrived although Jones had been denied an education. Before learning to read and write, Jones dictated correspondence to attorney L.C. Paine Freer. These two men were also associated through their Underground Railroad activities.

John Brown and unknown numbers of escaping slaves found shelter at the Jones' Underground Railroad station.

Jones was deeply involved in the Negro convention movement through which blacks worked for full citizenship. The main issues were voting rights, fair legal treatment and education.

Jones was elected to be a delegate at the Colored National Convention in Cleveland. Prior to that he spoke at the state Convention of Colored Persons in Alton. Jones subsequently attended and took a leadership role in other national and state conventions.

He persisted in his efforts to have the Black Codes repealed. He spoke, he lobbied, he petitioned and in 1864, he published a pamphlet detailing why these laws should be repealed. Finally in 1865 they were. The repeal was celebrated with Jones participating in a sixty-two gun salute. (One for each legislator who had voted for repeal.)

Jones took an active part in the civic and political life of Chicago. He became the first black person to be elected to public office in Cook County, when in 1871 he became a county commissioner. He died on May 21, 1879 and is buried at Graceland Cemetery, Chicago.

The town of Waukesha had a reputation of helping runaway slaves. Caroline Quarels was a former slave who was aided by a citizen of Waukesha. Gloria Urch of McHenry County is the most knowledgeable contemporary expert on the story of Caroline Quarels. By one account, Caroline's long hair had been cut off by her slaveholder in a fit of temper. Caroline, who looked white, crossed the Mississippi River on a steamboat. She entered Illinois at Alton, but was hunted by slave catchers when her mistress offered a $300 reward for her return. A free black man put her on a stagecoach bound for Milwaukee, Wisconsin. She arrived in Milwaukee, but her pursuers persuaded a black barber to betray her. A young black boy foiled the barber's plans and abolitionists soon spirited Caroline out of Milwaukee. UGRR conductors passed Caroline along until she reached Waukesha. There, Lyman Goodnow escorted her safely over a dangerous 600 mile journey to Detroit. Their journey led them into Illinois. Documents suggest that they stopped at the home of Dr. Anson Root in Elgin. Gloria Urch reports that Allan Pinkerton helped finance the escape. Lyman Goodnow's heroism is honored with a bronze plaque in Waukesha.

LEVI & CATHERINE COFFIN
Courtesy of the Levi Coffin House

~ Indiana

Crossing points on the Ohio River from Kentucky included Jeffersonville, Madison, West Franklin, Evansville, Little Pigeon Creek, Rockport and Indian Creek. Boats were hired by the Indiana Anti-Slavery Society to cross the river. Mysterious signal fires would alert boatmen.

One prominent Negro conductor was Reverend Chapman Harris. He was a blacksmith in Eagle Hollow near Madison. Reportedly, he signaled across the river by ringing on his anvil.

The area around Louisville, Jeffersonville and New Albany was also a busy crossing point, as was Cincinnati (Ohio). Many slaves who entered there took Indiana routes northward.

Communities of black free persons in Jenning and Tippecanoe counties hid would-be free persons. In Marion County, Hiram Bacon, a wealthy white dairy farmer, was chief conductor.

SAMUEL DENT

The Union Army functioned as a "moveable Underground Railroad." Enslaved people who could reach its encampments did so. They often joined and fought with the army. Others served as laborers. Sam Dent is an example.

Samuel Dent was born and enslaved in Tuscumbia, Alabama in 1841 on the plantation of John Horry Dent. In 1862, he escaped from bondage. He joined and fought in the Illinois Infantry of the Union Army. He served there with the rank of private until the end of the Civil War.

His whereabouts for the following five years remain a mystery. What is known is that he married Eliza Jane Weaver of Virginia during that time. He, his wife and two daughters are listed on the Chicago Census in 1870. His family moved within Chicago several times until 1872 when they moved to Lake Forest.

A teamster by trade, Sam Dent continued to work in Chicago for a period of time after his move. He eventually established his own livery business in Lake Forest.

Sam Dent transported commuters from the train station to their homes. He also had an express wagon used to haul luggage. He was so identified with the railroad station that, according to historian Edward Arpee, someone had claimed, "The Northwestern Railway people talk of putting Dent's picture in a panel on the station house, instead of the Lake Forest sign."

He was known to be an independent man. If he took passengers to a dinner party, he would go to pick them up when he was ready to turn in for the night. He would whistle loudly at the front door, and if no one answered, he drove his carriage back to town. Sometimes Sam Dent took sightseers through large Lake Forest estates. He described the homes in great detail. This made him the town's first tour guide.

Dent was very popular with children. He often gave them free rides. Once a youngster wrote a school composition stating, "There are two important men in Lake Forest—Dr. McClure (the Presbyterian minister) and Mr. Dent."

Having been enslaved and denied schooling, Sam Dent could neither read nor write. He was known for his keen wit and sense of humor. Once when he was driving a passenger home from the station, his sleigh was upset in a snow drift. He refused to charge the passenger stating that a tip over was payment enough.

Mr. and Mrs. Dent were active in the African Methodist Episcopal Church. They were the parents of seven children. The youngest, a daughter named Eliza Jane after her mother, became a seamstress in Evanston, After her death the Jane Dent House for elderly in Chicago was partly established from her life savings.

After Sam Dent died, fellow townspeople had a massive tombstone erected in his honor. It is at the Lake Forest Cemetery. The inscription on the monument:

> *"To the memory of Sam Dent, Born in Tuscumbia, Alabama.*
> *Escaping from slavery he entered the Union Army in 1862.*
> *Died at Lake Forest June 9, 1890*
> *This monument is erected by the citizens of Lake Forest in token of their esteem for*
> *A humble Christian, A respected citizen, A faithful friend"*

Reportedly Sam Dents' freedom papers were placed in the cornerstone of the Presbyterian Church; however, when the cornerstone was opened the documents it had contained had disintegrated beyond recognition.

Years later Brooks Smith and Gordon Neal selected "Samuel Dent Memorial Jazz Band" for their musical group. Sam Dent's name became known wherever the group appeared in Europe and the United States.

SAM DENT'S LIVERY SERVICE IN OPERATION
Courtesy of Lake Forest College

Levi and Catherine Coffin (Levi was often called the President of the UGRR) operated an UGRR station in Fountain City (then called Newport) on the eastern route. Some estimates indicate they may have helped 2,000 slaves escape. It is one of the Indiana UGRR sites on the National Register of Historic Places.

Two other Indiana sites are on the National Register. They are Bethel African Methodist Episcopal in downtown Indianapolis, and Eleutherian College in Lancaster, which is now closed, but available for tours by appointment.

The Indiana route closest to Illinois passed through Evansville, Vincennes, Terra Haute, Bloomingdale, Crawfordsville, Darlington, Lafayette, Rensselaer, and South Bend. It is possible there was some zigzagging across state lines. Paris, Illinois, is one of several black communities that were near the Indiana border.

Although less trafficked than routes to Chicago, at least two East-West routes ran through Illinois and into Indiana. One route connected St. Louis with the Indiana border town of Terra Haute. The other extended from the Rock Island area through or just south of Chicago and into northern Indiana.

You can learn more of UGRR activities by checking histories of specific counties and cities.

CROSSING THE BAY

James McGruder

When the Union Army took possession of Kentucky, James William Henry McGruder escaped from bondage and joined the 102nd U.S. Colored Troops. He had experience in the care and training of horses and was detailed to the the officer's horses at the military hospital in Vicksburg, Mississippi. In addition to caring for the horses he cooked for the sick and wounded soldiers.

He met Major Surgeon Harris Burnette Osborne of Elburn, (then called Blackberry Station) Illinois. They thought highly of each other. When Surgeon Osborne resigned from the Army and returned to Elburn after the Civil War in 1867, James McGruder accompanied him. Dr. Osborne went to New York to further his medical studies.

James McGruder remained in Elburn with Osborne's relatives. (These relatives, the Warne family, had operated an Underground Rail station in previous years.) McGruder continued working with horses. The Osborne family made him a gift of a spirited horse which he named "General Moultrie." McGruder and his horse raced and won prizes at the Kane County Fair.

McGruder became so well known for his veterinary skills that horse owners from elsewhere in Illinois and parts of Wisconsin brought their animals to him.

He was a well known for his kindness to children as for his skill in caring horses. Two stories have been passed on.

Ernie, one of the Warne children, injured his knee. When the town's medical doctor examined the boy's injury, he said that Ernie would never be able to run and play again.

James McGruder visited the boy when he heard what the doctor had said. He took a look at the knee and said he could repair it. He soon returned with sticky black ointment he had mixed at the local drug store and plastered on the injured knee; and it healed! This fete and his ability as a veterinarian earned him the name "Doc" McGruder.

The following story demonstrates what a friend he was to children. An extremely sick little girl wanted some strawberries more than anything in world. It was not strawberry season and there weren't any available in the Elburn area. Knowing that a greater variety of fresh produce was available in the big city of Chicago, James McGruder caught the train to Chicago located some strawberries, and brought them to the dying girl.

James McGruder never married nor was reunited with his family in Kentucky. When he died, the Elburn school children took up a collection to purchase a marker for his grave. That marker deteriorated over the years. In later years, school children in Mrs. Donna Blankenship's class raised money to replace the weatherworn marker.

James McGruder with General Moultrie.
Courtesy of Elburn Historical Society.

31. What are some other ways blacks and whites cooperated?

An example found in <u>Kane County History</u> tells of an episode in which a white couple by the name of Miller helped a black woman, whose name was unrecorded, to escape. Mr. Miller of Aurora borrowed a carriage. Mrs. Miller and the woman who was escaping dressed alike. Both women wore veils. The men in the party were in the back of the carriage.

When the party got to Naperville, they met two slaveholders heading for Chicago and looking for escaped slaves. Mrs. Miller moved her veil to one side. Seeing that she was white, the slaveholders assumed they had the wrong carriage and rode on.

The carriage proceeded to Deacon Philo Carpenter's house in Chicago. Evidently other slaves were in hiding at Deacon Carpenter's. The house was being watched by slaveholders, as were boats and trains out of Chicago.

Mrs. Miller called on Mr. Isbell, a black barber who had a shop in the Sherman House Hotel, and a Mr. Lucas, a black merchant tailor; Mr. Miller requested them to get the prominent black men together. He stated, "We met in a private house." The black men told him of a man in the lumber business who had land in Michigan and was loading vessels in Chicago. The lumberman was not known as an abolitionist, but as a friend to blacks. To get slaves to the lumber warehouse, forty black men went to Deacon Carpenter's house. The slaveholders fled, thinking the men were after them.

The slaves escaped safely and became successful farmers in Michigan.

MAYWOOD

Between the 1840's and 1927, there was a house at the intersection of Lake Street and First Avenue, Maywood. If the house known as the River House or the Noyesville Post Office could have talked, it would have "told" many stories.

It started as a roadhouse where farmers, taking produce to Chicago could find food, drink, lodging, and news of the day. Because roadhouses were usually built about ten miles apart—the distance a team of horses could pull a wagon between rests—the house was sometimes called "the Ten Mile House."

Located on the overland route from Rockford and other towns to the west, it became a stagecoach stop. Being situated at the point where the Desplaines River crossed this road, it was ideally situated as an Underground Railroad station. Like Jean Baptiste Pointe Du Sable, Native Americans, and other early travelers, Underground Railroad passengers could follow the river this far north and the road eastward toward Lake Michigan.

Out buildings and brush near the house provided good hiding places.

Underground Railroad passengers could rest before continuing their journey toward Chicago. Once there they might remain, or board a sailing ship bound for Canada.

Some old newspaper accounts shed light on the story of the house. The house was built by a Mr. Tater. There was a sawmill up the river. It may be that some of the men who were escaping bondage found work there.

The house had a series of owners and was eventually deserted for many years. It was shrouded in mystery. Rumors ranged from the belief that a smallpox victim had died there to reports that it was haunted. The house was removed in 1927. The land where it stood was included in the Maywood Company's original land purchase in 1869.

As in its early days the location is a busy location. A McDonald's restaurant now stands on this historic site.

The West Town Historical and Art Museum spear-headed the effort to get the site designated a National Historic Landmark.

Courtesy of the West Town Museum of Cultural History.

32. Were all blacks and whites helpful?

No. Some blacks and some whites were very tempted to "cash-in;" they could get $100 or more for selling a person into slavery. Free and fugitive blacks were subject to kidnapping at river entry points and at every stop along the way.

Even very young children were abducted and sold into slavery. There were some men who were full-time kidnappers. They would capture anyone who could not prove his or her identity. They knew that there were many slaves who were light complexioned children of slaveholders and enslaved women. No one will ever know how many blacks or whites were "sold down the river."

Northern whites that were pro-slavery opposed anti-slavery activities. During the Civil War they were known as Copperheads.

UGRR passengers could never be sure of whom they could trust. Henry Miller was the son of Rev. Ebenezer Miller whom slaveholders had driven out of North Carolina for preaching anti-slavery doctrine. The Miller family settled in Waverly where the father and son conducted UGRR activities. Once when a family of freedom seekers named Washington was being hotly pursued, a church elder betrayed the family. The elder had agreed to shelter the family. Instead of befriending the family, he and another church member turned them over to slave catchers for $40.

Then, as now, there were people who didn't pay much attention to things that were going on around them. There were people who felt slavery was against their religion and/or morally wrong but they did nothing.

Courtesy of the George Eastman Collection

HORRID OUTRAGE!

WAS KIDNAPPED, in the neighborhood of the Saline, a NEGRO GIRL, named MARIA, about eight years of age, dark complexion, nearly black, well grown of her age, has a dent or small hole in her face just below the cheek bone, she had strings in her ears, though the Thieves may use the precaution to take them out, her ears however have been pierced, and they cannot destroy that mark. The clothes she had on when taken off were very ragged, and it is presumed will soon be changed. She was taken from the spring on Saturday evening the 25th inst. by two ruffians who are unknown. This girl is one of the negroes emancipated by the last will and testament of John M'Alister, of Montgomery county Tennessee and moved here about a year ago, and some time last spring some scoundrel - probably one of these - stole two horse creatures from them, and thereby prevented them from making a crop, and now returned to steal the children. The uncle of the girl, a black man of the name of DRYAS, offers a reward of FIFTY DOLLARS for the girl, and a *Subscription* is now making up for the Girl and Thief or Thieves, and I am of opinion that TWO HUNDRED DOLLARS will be raised.

LEO D. WHITE

Equality, 27th July 1829.

33. Did all UGRR "stations" have specially built hiding places?

No. Actually many did not.

Take the Graue Mill in Oak Brook for example. This mill is situated on York Road about a block off of the old southwest stagecoach road (now called Ogden Avenue). UGRR passengers may have arrived at the mill on foot, or been transported there in the wagon of the village blacksmith John Coe. They were sheltered in a basement which had no tunnels or secret nooks or crannies while Frederick Graue conducted his milling business upstairs. A plaque beside the basement stairs tells of other stopping places along the route leading to the mill. An interpreter, displays, and a film provide further details about the Graue Mill and the Underground Railroad.

Not all UGRR stations were structures. Oakwood Cemetery in Waukegan was reportedly a station stop. Attics, barns, ditches, haystacks, cornfields, empty wagons, and any other available places were also used as hiding places. There were instances, however, where features were added to provide greater soundproofing, secrecy, or comfort. For example, a barn near Harding had a plastered room in the hayloft. One "station" in Plainfield was a room built inside a woodpile. Other ingenious hiding places are described in Question 34.

THE GRAUE MILL AND MUSEUM, OAK BROOK, ILLINOIS

34. What were some of the features in homes that had specially built structures?

In Glen Ellyn, the Thomas Filer House had a space several feet wide between walls that could accommodate quite a few people. Reportedly the home had a window bench that was built on a stair landing. It was said to have a seat that was actually a trap door to the basement from which a tunnel led to the barn.

A home that had been an Underground Railroad station near Quincy had a secret room behind the fireplace. The family who bought the home in the many years after the Civil War did not know of this. Then one day their child disappeared, but they could hear his voice. After much searching they found a hidden stairway and an entrance from the basement to this secret room.

STAIRCASE AND TRAP DOOR

In the days of the UGRRoperations, the underside of these stairs could only be entered from an adjacent room. It is the author's understanding that the little door at the side of the steps was cut by later owners. The full extent of secret hiding places will never be known. Most of these buildings, if still in use, have been modernized. Wood paneling or carpeting covers tunnel entrances or trap doors. Some of these openings made the homes hard to heat.

In Warrenville, the John Fairbank house has a stone basement. There is one very large stone which has no mortar around it like the other stones. When Horace "Ace" Hardy was a teenager growing up in that house, he removed that stone and crawled into the hole in the wall. He found that hole opened onto a tunnel just large enough to wiggle through on his stomach. The tunnel ended in a man-made cave. Knowing that the house had been built before the Civil War and that John Fairbank opposed slavery, when "Ace" Hardy read about the research for this book, he wondered if there could be a connection.

He gave permission to four teenage camp counselors to investigate. Some of them crawled in and found a number of items including stew bones and chicken or pheasant bones that had been cooked, a stone marble probably of Indian or African origin, a boot of the Civil War era, and an old bone button. An archeological field team from Northern Illinois University had, in cooperation with the DuPage Forest Preserve, conducted a "dig" at the log cabin where the Fairbank family had lived before they built the house with the stone basement. Dr. Milton Deemer, curator of the NIU Anthropology Museum identified and did preliminary dating of the items. He believes the "new" information indicates that the Hardy's house was probably an UGRR station. This was an unusual find.

James T. Wheeler operated an UGRR station in his home later known as the "Wild Rose Inn," on the west bank of the Fox River just north of St. Charles. The house had a little door in the kitchen from which a person could enter a tunnel. At the end of a tunnel there was a large removable stone that looked as if it was built right into a stone wall. After replacing the stone, an UGRR passenger had to walk only a short distance to Ferson's Creek and follow the creek to the Fox River. In the early 1900's the tunnel holes were sealed off to provide the home with a stronger foundation. The tunnel was "rediscovered" almost 100 years after the UGRR had operated by a man who was digging a well. The man dropped through a hole "into nothing."

JOHN HUBBARD BARN
Barn on the John Hubbard farm near Harding, Illinois contained a plastered room upstairs in the hayloft. The room had trap door and could be surrounded by hay to hide it and deaden sound.

In Fulton County, one house had a stair landing that was actually a trap door to the basement. From the basement a tunnel is believed to have led to a creek. A real railroad track and depot were also located nearby.

Near Roselle and Aurora, there are homes that had trap doors leading from the ground floor to little rooms in the basement that could not be reached in any other way. In the Enos Apartments in Alton there are underground tunnels 15 feet below ground level.

B.G. Root, the Illinois Central Railroad surveyor in Tamaroa, had a secret passage in the fireplace of his home which led to the attic. He also had a hidden chamber beneath the barn floor and used cisterns as hiding places.

In Pana, the Dr. Bullington house has a multi-level basement. There is a little door on the lower level.

The James Cory house in Waukegan and at least one other Illinois house had double brick walls along the foundation of the house. Seeing that these walls were constructed with secret compartments and knowing the anti-slavery views of its builder, convinced James W. Dorsey College of Lake County professor and author of <u>The Underground Railroad, Northeastern Illinois-Southeastern Wisconsin</u>, that the Cory house was an UGRR station.

A room was found beneath the front lawn of a house in Marengo. There is evidence to suggest there was also an underground room adjacent to the residence of Frederick Graue in Oak Brook. Its use is unknown. A 1929 article in the *Hinsdale Doings* indicates there was a tunnel between the Fuller Inn and Fullersburg Tavern near Ogden Avenue and York Road. Houses in the area are rumored to have had tunnels linking them to the Graue home.

The full extent of secret hiding places will never be known. Most pre-Civil War buildings, if still in use, have been modernized. Very few home owners have found a way to preserve trap doors and other Underground Railroad related features. The Tunnicliff home in Macomb is a rare exception.

Wood paneling or carpeting has been placed over entrances to old hiding places. Tunnels often caved in or weakened during the digging for sewer systems or new buildings. The installation of indoor plumbing and central heating have further altered former "stations".

While many of the UGRR "stations" and hiding places no longer exist, The Milton House in Milton, Wisconsin and the Owen Lovejoy House in Princeton, Illinois not only exist. Both are National Historic Landmarks that are open to the public. The Milton House is an example of how two structures were connected by a tunnel. An entrance in the Owen Lovejoy house connects the bedroom to a hall closet. The entrance is hidden behind a dresser that could be moved to one side when necessary. (NOTE: When the author wrote <u>Running for Our Lives</u>, she had her fictional characters use this "exit".)

GEORGE WASHINGTON

The name George Washington was, of course, that of the first President of the United States. It was also the name of a young black boy born into slavery in the mountains of Virginia.

Although the boy's mother was also enslaved, she had learned to read. She never met President George Washington but having read good things about him she named her son after him.

The slaveholder sold young George's mother when he was about six years old. George cried so much for his mother that no one could console him. One version of this story says that the slaveholder soon sold the little boy to a slave trader for a bargain price.

The trader tied one end of a rope to George's wrists and threw the other end over the saddle of his horse. The boy was still crying and was covered with dust as he ran behind the trader's horse. They eventually stopped to rest under a shade tree.

There they met another traveler. That traveler was a medical doctor, Silas Hamilton, who operated a Mississippi plantation on which he demonstrated his belief in fair and considerate treatment of slaves. Dr. Hamilton saw that George had a severe cold and chronic eye inflammation. He asked what the trader would charge for George and purchased him for $100.

(Another version of the story says that Dr. Hamilton heard the continuous crying of a child as he neared a plantation. Believing the child was sick and in need of a doctor, he asked the plantation owner about the boy. When Dr. Hamilton learned the boy's mother had just been sold, he offered to buy the boy. The price was $100.)

By the early 1830's Dr. Hamilton was widowed. In the meantime he had realized that his views of plantation management were not popular with other plantation owners. He sold his plantation and took twenty eight slaves up the Mississippi River and across the Ohio River to Cincinnati. He freed them and paid their freed men's bond. An elderly couple and George Washington, who was about eleven years old by this time, asked to remain with the doctor. They settled near the village of Gullom, an early name for Otterville, Illinois.

The town was about ten miles from the Illinois and Mississippi rivers. The doctor bought a large amount of land and practiced some medicine. George expressed his wish to have some schooling.

Dr. Hamilton died before he was able to see that George received an education. He, however, provided in his will for two things.

The first was the establishment of the first free and integrated school in Illinois and probably in the nation. The school was built of stone and was called the "Stone School House." Its charter stated that it admitted everyone regardless of age, race, or previous conditions of servitude. Not only did George Washington receive an excellent common school education, many immigrant families moved from the East so their children could attend this school. The Hamilton Memorial School is now listed on the National Register of Historic Places and is visited by hundreds of people at the annual fall festival.

The second provision of Dr. Hamilton's will was a bequest of $3000 for George Washington who worked as a farm hand until he was able to buy an 80 acre farm. According to accounts of his life he was an excellent businessman, and his advice was sought by less educated immigrants in the community. He was vice president of a local debating society and recognized for his ability and fairness when conducting a meeting.

He was assistant superintendent of the Baptist Sunday School and served as the local "grave digger". He was thoughtful of the sick and shut-in. Yet this model citizen was wrongly arrested in a nearby county that had a reputation for smuggling Missouri slaves across the Mississippi River and selling them to southern slaveholders.

George Washington never married. When he died he left a nuncupative will. Like Dr. Hamilton George Washington had two provisions in his will. The first was that $1,500 be appropriated to the construction of a monument for Dr. Silas Hamilton which was built in front of the school. It has a shaft above a base block. The inscription on the shaft is:

GEORGE WASHINGTON (CONT)

ERECTED BY GEORGE WASHINGTON-
BORN IN VIRGINIA A SLAVE DIED AT
OTTERVILLE, IL
APRIL 15, 1864
A CHRISTIAN FREEMAN

The wording at the base of the
block is:

TO THE MEMORY OF DR. SILAS
HAMILTON HIS FORMER MASTER
BORN IN TINMOTH, VT.,

MAY 19, 1775
DIED AT OTTERVILLE, ILL.
NOV. 19, 1834

HAVING GIVEN FREEDOM TO TWENTY-EIGHT SLAVES. AT HIS DEATH BEQUESTED FOUR THOUSAND DOLLARS FOR THE ERECTION AND ENDOWMENT OF THE HAMILTON PRIMARY SCHOOL.

The second provision of his will was that "whatever be left of said estate shall be appropriated to the education of colored persons, or Americans of African descent."

George Washington's will was especially significant. It was made by an ex-slave, who was separated from his mother in childhood, and had little opportunity to get acquainted with other black people. Yet George Washington wrote the will before the end of the Civil War with a knowledge that having an education had helped him acquire property, manage his business affairs, and contribute to this community in a meaningful way. He wanted to make it possible for future generations of African Americans to develop their potential. His generosity has given generations of students the opportunity to attend college.

With Dr. Hamilton's and George Washington's views on slavery it would seem likely that they might have taken part in Underground Railroad operations. This would be even more likely since there were Underground Railroad stations in Alton, Jerseyville, and Jacksonville.

Lila F. Melcher gives a detailed account of the lives of Dr. Hamilton and George Washington in her book, <u>Noble Master, Noble Slave</u>. Her book includes references to an earlier work called the <u>Reminiscenses of Mary Chandler Hamilton</u>. When describing Underground Railroad operations Mrs. Melcher

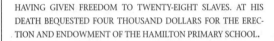

states,

"George Washington may have worked with or supported the Otterville stations of the underground railway according to Mary Ann Chandler Hamilton.

'This is the only railroad that ever ran through Otter Creek Prairie and in fact, no more important road was ever built. Well do I remember one of those bands of fugitives. They were carefully hidden away in a closet with a secret door under the stairway. On the following night father took his two horse wagon and carried them on to the next station."

In her chapter entitled "The George Washington Story," Mrs. Melcher explains, "This Otterville depot was on the 'Main Line' between St. Louis, Missouri and Jacksonville, Illinois. From Jacksonville, then one of the most important cities in Illinois, the route led to Canada via Chicago."

In the "Hamilton School" chapter, Mrs. Melcher again quotes Mary Ann Chandler Hamilton: "Our home in Otter Creek'was built at a time when slavery was agitating the entire country. Only a short time before Nov. 7, 1837 Owen [sic] [Elijah] Lovejoy the noted abolitionist was killed at Alton only twenty miles away. Several people among them were Hiram White, Adam Waggoner, Asher Chase, were entered into a compact to assist Lovejoy. And this foul murder made a profound impression on them. The anti-slavery sentiment was rapidly crystallizing into the formation of well organized societies. The fugitive slave law was becoming more and more obnoxious, for very frequently southern slave-holders accompanied by their officers of the law, came through the country and searched the premises of our citizens for fugitive slaves. These slaves were advertised in the public press and large rewards were offered for their capture. A picture of a negro with a knapsack on his back, fleeing for life and liberty, always accompanied these advertisements. This only intensified the opposition to the whole slavery business. No one can wonder that otherwise law abiding men engaged in a determined effort to defeat the fugitive slave law and assist in the escape of the fugitives. My father was one of the most active in this work and our house became one of the stations of the famous Underground Railway"

BASEMENT

Some UGRR agents had specially built features designed for their work, but others adapted common features to uncommon uses. The exceptionally large basement windows opened onto the underside of a large circular porch. Why? Do you imagine that these windows might have been used by arriving UGRR passengers?

35. Were any of the UGRR sites noted for anything else?

Yes. Here are some examples.

The Castle Inn, which stood at the intersection of Ogden and York Road in Fullerburg (now Hinsdale), was the birthplace of the internationally known dancer Loie Fuller. It is also one of the many stagecoach inns where Lincoln was said to have stopped.

Inns were sometimes called taverns, and spaced relatively close together along routes such as the Indian trail that later became the old Southwest Plank road, and is now Ogden Avenue. The travelers found food and (less than plush) lodging. Drivers got fresh horses. The inns also served as meeting houses for the surrounding communities. Some even had ballrooms, as did the Halfway House near Ottawa.

In Cairo, General U.S. Grant occupied Room 215 of the Halliday Hotel, the largest, most elegant hotel between Chicago and St. Louis or Memphis. General Grant's room overlooked the confluence of the Ohio and Mississippi River. In the cellar were dungeon-like chambers rumored to have concealed fugitive slaves. The hotel no longer stands. The chambers were excavated in 1998.

The Tremont House was a Chicago stop for fugitives passing through West Chicago, Wheaton, Glen Ellyn or Lombard. It was campaign headquarters for the Illinois Republicans in 1860 when Lincoln was nominated for President.

John and Mary Jones' home was in Chicago, the location of meetings where plans for repeal of the Illinois Black Codes were made. Mary Richardson Jones was a pioneer in the suffrage movement and entertained Susan B. Anthony, Carrie Chatman Catt, Emma Chandler and Mrs. John Brown.

In Byron, the Ercanbrack barn was the site of an ill-fated experiment with flying.

WILLIAM deFLEURVILLE A.K.A. "BILLY THE BARBER"

The barbershop of William deFleurville was the popular meeting place for Illinois politicians, business and professional men. Known as the Palace, it was the "clubhouse" where men would gather to announce and hear the latest news.

It was Abraham Lincoln's second home. He often went there to swap stories with the owner and other patrons, to make new business contacts, and to discuss current events.

Lincoln and deFleurville had known each other longer than either of them had known anyone else in Springfield. They met quite by chance. deFleurville had been born in Cap-Haitien, Haiti about 1806. For many years slave labor had made his island homeland one of France's richest overseas possessions. About five years before de Fleurville's birth a former slave and soldier, Toussaint L'Ouverture, led a revolt which resulted in abolishing slavery there, and resulted in conquering the island, putting a new constitution into effect. His country gained its independence in 1804 making it the second free republic in the Americas. Some scholars believe the loss of the important possession was the main reason that France was willing to sell the Louisiana Purchase to the United States.

Like many Haitians deFleurville was Catholic. He and his godmother went to Baltimore where he attended St. Mary's Convent. When his godmother died, the Orphan's Court bound him out as an apprentice in a barbershop. He had also worked as a handy man in the home of a doctor who later moved to Springfield.

After mastering barbering he left Baltimore for New Orleans and St. Louis thinking he would find the French atmosphere more like that of Haiti. He found instead that New Orleans and St. Louis were dangerous places for a man of color. He saw black people bought and sold at large slave markets. Although deFleurville had been born free in Haiti he knew that slave traders would seize any black person and place him on the auction block and that person could not appeal to the laws of Missouri or Louisiana.

In 1831 deFleurville was on a hunting trip during which he sailed up the Mississippi River, then into the Illinois and finally the Sangamon River. When he got to New Salem he met a tall stranger who turned out to be Abraham Lincoln. Lincoln was staying at a boarding house where he helped deFleurville get work. DeFleurville earned enough money to go on to Springfield two days later. The first person he met there was the doctor he had worked for in Baltimore.

DeFleurville found work in Springfield. He married Phoebe Roundtree who had been born in Glasgow, Kentucky. They became parents of five children, Samuel, Alseen, Sineet, Varneel, and William.

The following year deFleurville opened the first and only barbershop in Springfield. He was creative in the ways he advertised his business. In newspaper ad he sometimes spoke of himself as "the barber king of the village" and of his shop as the "Palace". He was best known for his poetry such as this verse which appeared in the *Sangamon Journal* in March 1837.

> They who would get the public favor must learn to utter some palaver; sound their own fame or at least show they'll hold the trump while others blow.

He charged fifteen cents for cutting men and boy's hair and twenty cents for cutting girls' hair. In addition to the barbering business deFleurville opened Springfield's first cleaners.

He was thrifty and became one of the wealthiest men in Springfield. At one time he owned almost the entire block between 8th and 9th Streets on Washington Street. DeFleurville was noted for sharing his wealth with the Catholic Church, other churches and individual people who needed assistance.

DeFleurville was also known for his musical talent. The flute and violin were two of the instruments he played at social gatherings in Springfield.

Abraham Lincoln was deFleurville's attorney and advisor in all legal matters. References to his real estate transactions on deFleurville's behalf can be

Abolitionist Jared Sanford unsuccessfully launched his homemade flying machine from the roof of the barn.

The house on the Guy Morse farm (also known as the John Cragg Cabin) in Grundy County was a stagecoach inn on the Bloomington-Chicago road. Reportedly it was also an UGRR station. Small upstairs rooms are believed to have been used by UGRR guests.

STAGECOACH INN
A former stagecoach inn on the old Lincoln Highway near New Lenox, IL, which is believed to have been an UGRR station. Reportedly, seven fireplaces were used to heat this inn (or tavern) back in the days when travellers sought food and shelter here.

WILLIAM deFLEURVILLE A.K.A. "BILLY THE BARBER" (CONT.)

found in some of Lincoln's correspondence.

Their association gave Lincoln a firsthand experience of knowing a hard working and civic-minded black man. It also prompted Lincoln to receive the black Minister from Haiti with all diplomatic honors.

DeFleurville never recovered from the shock of Lincoln's death. Although he could have joined the party of Lincoln's old political friends, he joined all the other black people as they stood in line to see the funeral procession.

Upon his own death he left all his personal property to his widow. After her death the real estate holdings were divided equally among their children. One granddaughter, Mrs. S. A. Ware eventually inherited the mirror that originally hung in front of the barber chair in which Lincoln sat when William deFleurville was giving him a shave or a haircut.

ABRAHAM LINCOLN AND BILLY THE BARBER.
Courtesy of The DuSable Museum of AfricanAmericanHistory

36. Are all the Pre-Civil War houses part of the UGRR?

No. There's a house just east of Equality, in Gallatin County, Illinois that was just the opposite. It is a 3-story mansion built by John Hart Crenshaw in the 1830s. It overlooked former salt beds along the Saline River.

At one time these saltworks were reported to be the only source of salt west of Marietta, Ohio. They brought such great revenues to the state of Illinois that although the Ordinance of 1787 prohibited slavery into the Northwest Territory, the Illinois Constitution of 1818 permitted slavery at the saltworks.

The salt was produced by boiling salt water from the river into crystals. At the end of the process workers scooped the salt onto barrels which they had made on the scene. They produced eighty to one hundred bushels of salt per day. The salt was loaded onto wagons pulled by oxen. It was taken first to Shawneetown, then loaded onto keelboats and sold in Indiana, Missouri, Kentucky, and Tennessee.

Many black workers were brought in to cut down trees and feed the fires under large iron kettles. Some of these workers were indentured servants. Slaveholders in Missouri and Kentucky rented others out. Still others were enslaved by Crenshaw under the Illinois law. In addition, Crenshaw hired men to pose as UGRR conductors and kidnap black people who had escaped from slavery in other states. He also took babies born to enslaved mothers and sold them into slavery.

To this day the house is known as the Old Slave House. In front it has huge wooden columns and a wide expanse of porches. At the back there is a doorway wide enough for a carriage to be driven through the house.

Enslaved people were secretly unloaded. They were forced up a narrow staircase to the third floor where unimaginable cruelties awaited them. They were kept in small rooms or cells for the housing and breeding of slaves. Some of these rooms contained two shelves that measured six feet by twenty inches. They were used as bunks. Two wooden racks are thought to have been used as whipping posts.

Profesor John W. Allen wrote in <u>Legends and lore of Southern Illinois</u> that the salt-making industry near Equality was important far beyond the income it produced. He stated it, more than any other one factor, served to shape the policy of the new state concerning slavery and encouraged the movement in 1824 to open Illinois to slavery."

OLD SLAVE HOUSE IN EQUALITY, ILLINOIS
Courtesy of James T. Ransom, Sr.

JAMES BOLVIAR NEEDHAM

Chicago never looked the same after the Great Fire of 1871. The picturesque waterfronts, the hustle and bustle of city streets, and historic old buildings of post Civil War Chicago were gone forever.

Fortunately, James Bolviar Needham had captured these images of early Chicago in his oil and watercolor paintings. His work preserved scenes of the ships – including schooners and three masters that sailed into Chicago; the sailors and dock workers; the gingerbread architecture reflected in the water; women with bustles and men in tall hats; horse drawn surreys and coal wagons.

Unfortunately, although James Needham and his many and varied views of the city had survived the Great Fire, he and many of his paintings did not survive the fire in his loft room sixty years later.

Needham was born in Chatham, Ontario, Canada in 1850. (Chatham and nearby North Buxton were havens for black people who had escaped from bondage in the United States. It is possible that was why his parents had settled in Chatham.)

As a youngster James Needham and his brother, Will, used to drive cattle and horses to the province of Manitoba, Canada. Will continued doing this for the rest of his working life. Jim was restless. At age 14 he went to work on old lumber schooners on Lake Huron and Lake Michigan. He sailed out of American cities of Detroit, Bay City, and Saginaw. When he heard of Chicago he set out for it, leaving his life as a sailor on the Great Lakes.

He fell in love with Chicago. He moved to town at age 17 and lived there until he died at 81. He took jobs as a painter and decorator. In fact, he fell off of a ladder and broke his leg while working as a decorator at the Chicago World's Fair in 1893. Later he worked as a part-time janitor.

He had no wish to make a lot of money, in fact although he was skillfully painting Chicago scenes from the time he arrived until he lost his sight in 1925, he never sold any of his work. (And presumably never wanted to.) He worked in order to be able to afford a place to live, food to eat, an occasional trip to the theater, and most of all, the chance to paint.

He had high standards for himself. He threw away pictures that he was dissatisfied with—possibly 60%. He kept the remaining ones stacked, propped up or hung on the walls of his loft room.

He was such a shy person that he lived in one loft for 25 years without ever meeting the real estate agent. He simply left his rent payment in an envelope.

One person Needham did meet was Chicago based sculptor Lorado Taft. Evidently Needham studied with Taft and at The Art Institute briefly.

Needham was so unassuming that he seldom signed his paintings. Instead he often placed a unique diamond design on the back of his paintings.

He cared deeply about his paintings. He was eighty one years old and no longer able to see well enough to paint when fire broke out in his small room on New Year's eve 1930. He inhaled so much smoke in his desperate effort to save his beloved paintings that he died of pulmonary tuberculosis.

James Needham's brother, Will, came from Canada to bury him. Will arranged for two commercial artists, Anders Haugseth and Theodore Firks, who had lived across the hall from James to sell the pictures he had been able to rescue.

37. Was there ever slavery in Illinois?

Yes. In 1848 slavery ended legally after at least 170 years of existence. When French explorers Father Jacques Marquette and Louis Joliet arrived in 1673 they found that the Illinois Indians enslaved other Indians captured in war. Many of these captured people were originally members of the Pawnee, a tribe west of the Mississippi River. The French Jesuits also enslaved Indians.

In 1719 a Frenchman named Philippe Francois Renault left France with two hundred miners. He was in search of precious stones and metals in the Louisiana Territory. He brought five hundred black workers from the Santa Domingo to what is now Monroe County Illinois and took others as far as Galena. As stated in Question 28 Renault had planned to develop mines in Illinois and Missouri. He had intended to have these enslaved people grow food for other slaves and laborers at these mines. The mines were not profitable and the enslaved people were sold to farmers in the Kashaskia-Cahokia region.

Black families who had remained in the area of Fort de Chartres followed French customs and spoke a mixture of French and English into the twentieth century. The area around Lake Peoria was also under French control. In his work, The Negro in Peoria, Dr. Romeo B. Garrett states, "There is evidence, too, that Negroes were stolen and brought South and sold into slavery," Dr. Garrett quotes a letter that was written to the mayor of Peoria by a black Texan named Charlie Borzele. Borzele had been born three miles from Peoria. His parents were farmers who spoke French.

He had been kidnapped at age 9 or 10 and had never spoken a word of English until that time. As an adult he wrote the Mayor to ask him to give the letter to "some colored minister of any church" who might aid him in finding his family.

The French King issued edicts legalizing slavery in the territory. The French also established regulations known as Code Noir or Black Codes to control enslaved people and the slave trade. While less harsh than later black laws, these codes still allowed brutal and severe punishments, even death for minor infractions.

In 1844, Peter White was ten years old. He and three other children were kidnapped in Equality, IL and taken to Arkansas where they were sold for $800. They were later rescued and returned to Equality.

ZEBINA EASTMAN

Zebina Eastman like William Lloyd Garrison was a most influential editor of an anti-slavery newspaper. Both men had been assistants to Benjamin Lundy on *The Genius of Universal Emancipation*. Both were born in Massachusetts and began journalism careers as young men.

Zebina Eastman was born in North Amherst, MA September of 1815. His parents died when he was young. He was still in his teens when he decided to become a journalist.

ZEBINA EASTMAN

He got some training in the printers' trade and friends gave him a chance to work on newspapers. Between the ages of nineteen and twenty-one, he published *The Vermont Free Press*. That paper failed and he headed West. He stopped for a while in Ann Arbor, Michigan, then continued on to Illinois. He passed through Chicago and settled in Peoria where he worked on the *Peoria Register*, which was owned by Samuel Davis.

Eastman joined Benjamin Lundy in Illinois after the death of Elijah Lovejoy. After Lundy died, Zebina Eastman and Hooper Warren attempted to continue publishing the paper under the auspices of the LaSalle County Anti-Slavery Society. They renamed it *The Genius of Liberty*.

During this period Eastman went to Vermont to marry Mary Jane Corning and the center of anti-slavery activity shifted from Putman Counties to LaSalle counties to the Chicago area. Dr. C.V. Dyer, Philo Carpenter, Calvin DeWolf and other prominent Chicagoans wanted an anti-slavery newspaper to be established in Chicago. They asked Zebina Eastman to be the editor.

By the spring of 1842 Eastman had moved to Chicago and published the first issue of the *Western Citizen*. The Illinois Anti-Slavery Society held its meeting in Chicago that same year. A large number of delegates represented northeastern counties for the first time. The *Western Citizen* became the leading anti-slavery newspaper in the (Middle) West through the efforts of such men as Eastman, Warren, and Henry O. Wagoner.

In 1850 Zebina Eastman was the Illinois delegate to the World Peace Congress in Frankfort, Germany. He made valuable contacts there.

Readers of the *Western Citizen* respected his editorial opinions. He was influential in getting fellow abolitionists to vote for Henry O. Wagoner's friend from Galena, Elihu B. Washburn.

In 1853 the newspaper's name was changed again, this time to the *Free West*. Increasingly the slavery issue was being widely discussed in general interest newspapers, and the *Free West* was absorbed by the *Chicago Tribune*. Eastman attempted to publish a magazine, which he called the *Chicago Magazine*. It never became popular.

After the Civil War, Eastman was appointed Consul to Bristol, England where he remained for eight years. When the returned to Illinois he lived in Elgin for 4 years, then moved to Maywood where he lived until his death in June of 1883.

MARY BROWN DAVIS

Mary Brown Davis agitated for abolitionism in one of the few public ways permitted to women: in the presss. She, more than her husband, Samuel Davis, Peoria newspaper publisher, was a staunch believer in the anti-slavery cause. She was an unlikely abolitionist. Her husband owned two slaves in Virginia and she was born on a plantation where her father owned forty-five slaves. She was raised by a black nursemaid who may have taught her that everyone wants to be free.

In any event, she began to agitate against slavery in the late 1830's. She published essays, letters, and news from Peoria and later Galesburg and Chicago. She signed her writing with the initials M.B.D. rather than spellng out her full name. She helped develop the anti-slavery movement in Galesburg while her family lived and cooperatively published the *Peoria Register.*

Mary Brown's first anti-slavery articles appeared in 1839 in Benjamin Lundy's newspaper the *Genius for Universal Emancipation* during the last months of his life. The titles ofher articles were "The Cause of the Oppressed" and "Cruelty of Slavery."

Although Mary Davis' husband was not an abolitionist his was one of only three newspapers to speak out against Lovejoy's murder. He did so to support the protection of property and freedom of speech rather than Lovejoy's view on slavery. While he included reports of state and local anti-slavery societies along with of her news in his Peoria paper, he did not change his own opinions.

For a short time Zebina Eastman worked on the Davis' newspaper. He went, at Mr. Davis' suggestion, to help Benjamin Lundy publish the *Genius of Universal Emancipation* in Lowell. Several years after Lundy's death Zebina Eastman became editor of the *Western Citizen.*

M.B.D.'s articles appeared in the *Western Citizen* on a regular basis. Fifty-nine of sixty of her articles dealt with slavery.

The Davis' were members of the Main Street Presbyterian Church pastored by Rev. Jeremiah

Porter, a strong anti-slavery leader. His wife, Eliza Chappell Porter was later an aggressive worker in reform activities, however she was engaged in child rearing when the couple first moved to Peoria. Fellow church member Lucy Pettingil was as devoted to abolitionism as Mary Brown Davis was. Her husband, Moses Pettingil, had joined Rev. Porter in going to Alton when Elijah Lovejoy and Edward Beecher organized the Illinois Anti-Slavery Society.

Jeremiah and Eliza Chappell Porter moved to Farmington and Rev. William T, Allan became the new pastor of Main Street Presbyterian Church. Rev. Allan was an agent for the Illinois Anti-Slavery Society and according to Knox College Prof. Hermann Muelder, considered to be "one of the most notorious abolitionists in the state."

There was an increased interest in abolitionism in Peoria. However, a mob attempted to prevent the formation of a local anti-slavery society. The disturbance and the mob's efforts to suppress free speech changed Samuel Davis' opinion. He became an abolitionist.

Three weeks after these events took place in Peoria, anti-slavery leaders from Galesburg called for an anti-slavery convention. Delegates from Peoria, Knox, and Fulton counties met in Farmington, which was midway between Peoria and Galesburg. Their main topics of discussion were the violation of free speech, free assembly, and the free press.

Samuel Davis, Moses Pettingil, and Rev. William Allan were among the men who attended from Peoria. Later in the spring of 1843 President Hiram Kellogg of Knox College traveled from Galesburg to board a steamboat in Peoria. He was starting his journey to the World Anti-Slavery Convention in London, England. He spoke the Main Street Presbyterian Church and got copies of a pamphlet on free speech to distribute during his trip.

Meanwhile Mary Brown Davis and Lucy Pettingil formed a Female Anti-Slavery Society in Peoria. Female societies were also formed in Putnam County,

A section of wooden pipe used in the Salt Works at Equality.

When the Illinois Country passed into British hands, slavery continued. Later when Illinois became part of Virginia during the American Revolution, slavery was not automatically abolished here.

The Northwest Ordinance of 1787 decreed "There shall be no slavery or involuntary servitude except as punishment for a crime where the person shall have been duly con-

---

MARY BROWN DAVIS (CONT.)

in Jerseyville, and in Galesburg. Mrs. Kellogg was president of the Galesburg society. They formed the Illinois Female Anti-Slavery Society in May of 1844.

The education of black children was the first undertaking of the new state organization. This project was of particular interest to Mrs. Irene B. Allan. In addition to sharing; the anti-slavery views of her husband, Rev. William Allan, she had attended Oberlin College in Ohio, the first college to become co-educational and admit students of all races. Eventually a lack of funds prevented the Illinois Women's Anti-Slavery Society from accomplishing all it had set out to do.

The organization was most active in the late 1840's. Mary Brown Davis and Mary A. Blanchard, whose husband, Jonathan Blanchard was the new president of Knox College, were officers of a meeting held in Farmington in 1847. They circulated a statewide petition agsinst the Illinois Black Codes. The got five to six hundred signatures. In his book Fighters for Freedom, Prof. Muelder states that "the unpopularity of something tainted with feminism" might have been one reason for it being less successful than they had hoped to be.

Mary Brown Davis continued to publish articles in the *Western Citizen*. Her topics included the rights of women,and the fact that her husband and other Peoria men had formed an anti-slavery society. She also reported that new members of the Main Street Presbyterian Church led an effort to keep the building from being used by abolitionists. The anti-slavery mass meeting was then held in a room above Moses Pettingil's store. Knox College president, Jonathan Blanchard gave a lecture on "American Slavery." Another speaker, noted abolitionist Ichabod Codding, was scheduled to speak after Blanchard, but a mob broke up the meeting.

Jonathan Blanchard published a strong protest in the *Western Citizen*.

Samuel Davis who had become politically active in the Liberty Party reported this violation of constitutional rights at the party's state convention. Later Davis was seriously beaten.

victed." The governor, Ninan Edwards of the Illinois territory decided the Ordinance did not apply to slavery already in existence.

In 1818 when Illinois became a state, the slavery question was hotly contested. Finally, a compromise was reached. Slavery was forbidden, indentured servitude, which in many cases was exactly the same as slavery, was permitted. The next year a series of laws were passed which denied Negroes full citizenship rights. These Black Codes were made even harsher in later years.

The records of some southern Illinois counties show that laws to regulate slavery were openly flouted before and after Illinois achieved statehood.

At the time of the Civil War, the most southern 100 miles of Illinois were considered to be in the South. When the war started, President Lincoln asked the Governor to send troops to Cairo to take control.

Both the pro-slavery and anti-slavery factions were dissatisfied with the constitutional compromise. In 1823, Governor Edward Coles, who had freed his slaves upon coming to Illinois, asked the legislature to:

1) Free slaves and indentured laborers

2) Abolish the Black Code

3) Protect Negroes from being kidnapped

The legislature wanted to call for a convention to try to revise the constitution and legalize slavery. Cole led the great struggle against the convention. His side prevailed. However, the census continued to show slaves until the 1840s, and indentures into the 1880s.

The Illinois Constitution of 1848 provided that the " ... General Assembly shall at its first session ... pass such laws as will prohibit free persons of color from immigrating to and settling in this state and to effectively prevent owners of slaves from bringing the into this state for the purpose of setting them free."

In 1853 the General Assembly enacted a law that implemented that provision. During the Civil War the Black Code article in the proposed Constitution of 1862 was put to a vote. It won at the polls.

Restrictive provisions in the Black Codes limited the ability of black persons to establish homes and support themselves in Illinois. For example they:

~ subjected persons of color who entered the state to arrest and fine. In case they could not pay the fine, they could be required to pay costs in labor.

~ denied persons of color the right to vote and the opportunity to hold office

LUCRETIA MOTT (1793-1880)

Reprinted courtesy of Margaret Hope Bacon

Lucretia Coffin Mott, traveling Quaker minister, abolitionist, and pioneer of women's rights was born in 1793 on the island of Nantucket. Educated in Boston and at Nine Partners School in New York. She became a gifted teacher. At the age of eighteen she married James Mott of Long Island, a fellow teacher and an abolitionist. Together the couple had six children of whom five survived to adulthood. After the death of her second child, Tommy, she turned more deeply to the Bible and Quaker writings, and became at age twenty-eight a recognized minister and thereafter traveled in the ministry all her life.

In 1833 Lucretia Mott helped to organize the Philadelphia Female Anti-Slavery Society, an interracial, interdenominational organization which played an important role in the anti-slavery struggle. She also became a member of the Pennsylvania Anti-Slavery Society and the American Anti-Slavery Society. In 1840 she was sent as a delegate to the World Anti-Slavery Society Convention in London, but not seated because of her gender. This led her and Elizabeth Cady Stanton, the wife of another delegate, to plan the Seneca Falls Convention of 1848 at which the world's first declaration of women's rights was made public.

Following the London Conference, Mott traveled and lectured widely against slavery, speaking to the U.S. Congress and to President John Tyler in 1845. At the same time, she organized workshops and day care for poor women in North Philadelphia. She supported the first women's medical college, organized in 1850, and defended African Americans accused of treason under the Fugitive Slave Law in 1851. She assisted Harriet Tubman and William Still in helping escaping slaves, preached to the African American troops being trained in Camp William Penn during the Civil War, and protested racial discrimination on the city's trolleys, refusing to ride inside until her black sisters were also permitted to do so.

Mott was also an advocate of nonviolence, or peaceful settlement of conflicts, and an end to capital punishment. She espoused the rights of the Native Americans, and was concerned with temperance and prison reform. Her courage was matched with a sweet spirit which made her a beloved figure both within and without the Society of Friends. She died in 1880 and was buried in Fair Hill Burial Ground in North Philadelphia, an interracial cemetery where lie many of the pioneers of abolition.

~ placed a heavy fine on any white person bringing free or enslaved persons of color into the state.

~ permitted slaveholders to claim and repossess fugitives upon payment of costs.

Free blacks, of which there were several groups in Illinois, were subjected to kidnapping.

John Jones, a skilled tailor, worked especially hard to get the Illinois Black Codes repealed. His home was an Underground Railroad "station." He owned real estate valued at $85,000. After the war he became a Cook County commissioner, and later, a member of the Chicago Board of Education. His portrait and that of his wife, Mary Richardson Jones, are displayed at the Chicago Historical Society.

Proponents of the Black Codes assumed that if blacks settled in the state, they would not know how or wish to earn a living. This assumption was later proven to be false as the examples in Question 38 indicate.

Although John Jones and other critics worked for the repeal of the Black Codes, it was 1865 before these laws were repealed. In the meantime, free blacks lived within these restrictions, and still made contributions to their communities.

EDWARD COLES FREES SLAVES
Courtesy of the DuSable Museum of African Amerivan History

JOHN JONES TEARS UP RESTRICTIVE BLACK CODES
Courtesy of The DuSable Museum of AfricanAmericanHistory

38. Did all Blacks go to Canada?

African Americans settled in various locations before and during the Civil War, and in the years that followed.

There were black residents of East St. Louis, Carlyle, Lebanon, Belleville, and Alton by 1839.

The 1850 census listed 5,000 black residents in the state of whom three hundred seventy eight settled in Chicago. A sizeable number of these African Americans were free. They and former slaves worked together and with white abolitionists. After the Fugitive Slave Act was passed, concerned black and white Chicagoans protested vigorously. Illinois Senator Stephen A. Douglas was requested to appear before the Chicago Common Council. He defended the unpopular bill. Local blacks formed a vigilance committee to assure safe passage of fugitive slaves who reached Chicago. They worked cooperatively with whites who objected to the Act. In spite of these efforts, the Fugitive Slave Act finally made life for black people so perilous that many migrated to Canada.

A number of free black people settled in Galesburg. In 1857, a festival was held there on the anniversary of emancipation in the West Indies. Black people from Quincy, Monmouth, Kewanee, Burlington, and Cole and Edgar counties attended.

Early black communities are described in Question 28.

THE GEORGE WASHINGTON JONES FAMILY
OF PRAIRIE CENTER
George Washington Jones, born in Raleigh, N.C. came North with the aid of a Union soldier. In the South, slaves had operated an Underground Railroad in reverse, feeding Union soldiers and guiding them through Confederate lines. Possibly, Jones and the soldier he accompanied met under such circumstances, and each extended a human kindness to the other.

Black people have long inhabited the Robbins area. A number of former slaves settled there and in surrounding communities.

George Washington Jones was born a slave in North Carolina. He and his wife operated an eating establishment in Prairie Center. Diners from as far away as California, New York and Washington signed the Jones' guest book. The Jones' home was a favorite place for people who lived within a day's carriage ride.

In Mendota, elders remembered a former slave whose twin had been sold and sent to Cuba. Fearing that he too would be sold, he escaped. His mother bid him farewell and told him, "Always be honest and do what is right." He traveled on the Underground Railroad until he reached Union Army lines. There he became an attendant. Later he went to St. Louis, Centralia, Amboy, Chicago, and finally settled in Mendota. He was janitor at Graves Public Library and the Presbyterian Church.

Israel Blackburn had also served in the Civil War, however his former master tried to collect the military pay that Blackburn had earned. Blackburn was a signer of the Downers Grove papers of incorporation. He made his living as a farmer specializing in growing celery.

Germanius Kent had purchased Lewis Lemon of Rockford for $450.00. The price for buying his freedom was $800.00. Lemon paid this amount, received his free papers, and became a truck farmer. A Rockford school is named for him. He is buried in Greenwood Cemetery. Kent returned to Virginia in debt.

Ruben Armstrong provided the first barbershop or "tonsorial parlor" to Rockford. Ike Williams operated a lunch counter and fruit stand there. His nephew, Daniel Hale Williams, joined the family in Rockford. Later, at Provident Hospital in Chicago, Daniel Hale Williams performed the world's first open heart surgery in 1893.

DR. DAN HALE WILLIAMS (L) AND FATHER TOLTON OF QUINCY (R)
Courtesy of The DuSable Museum of African AmericanHistory

Father Tolton was the first black priest in Quincy. He had been born in slavery, but when he was a boy his mother escaped to Quincy with the children in the family. His father served in the Union Army after which he was able to join his family. Father Tolton was buried in St. Peter Cemetery. There are plaques in his honor at St. Boniface Church in Quincy, and at Brush Creek, Missouri, where he was born.

John Lawson was born in Virginia and served in the Union Army as a sergeant in

ELIJAH LOVEJOY

The death of Elijah Lovejoy was a turning point in the Underground Railroad in Illinois and elsewhere around the nation. Lovejoy would have been 35 years old in two more days. He was corresponding secretary of the recently formed Illinois Anti-Slavery Society and editor of the *Alton Observer*.

He was born in Albion, Maine on November 9, 1802. He attended China Academy and Waterville College where he'd graduated with the highest honors. He headed west in May 1826 to teach in St. Louis. The following year he became editor of a political newspaper.

In 1832 he decided to enter the ministry. He went to New Jersey to train at Princeton, afterwards he returned to St. Louis as a Presbyterian minister and editor of a religious newspaper, the *St. Louis Observer*. He would often preach in the countryside near St. Louis. He considered slavery to be a sin. He stated this in his sermons and newspaper editorials.

He and Celia Ann French were married in St. Charles, Missouri on March 4, 1835. In October of that year he announced in the *Observer* that he would be going out of town for church meetings. During his absence the newspaper's publisher received complaints about Lovejoy's anti-slavery articles from patrons and owners of the building which housed the newspaper. The publisher promised to stop these articles in the future, however, it printed an article Lovejoy had written before leaving town. A mob threatened to destroy the newspaper office.

Lovejoy was threatened when he returned to St. Louis. He did not agree to stop expressing his anti-slavery views. In his memoirs he said that he could not as an American citizen, and Christian patriot in the name of the Liberty, and Law, and Religion. He solemnly protested against all these attempts to "frown down" on the liberty of the press, and forbid the free expression of opinion. He declared, "I am prepared to abide the consequences."

Elijah Lovejoy made a distinction between being an uncompromised enemy of slavery and an abolitionist.

He wrote to his brother saying, "I am not an abolitionist—at least not such a one as you are."

Even so Missouri newspapers threatened him. He resigned as editor of the *Observer*. The owners wanted to sell the paper at auction, instead the seller offered it to Lovejoy if he would move it to Alton.

Lovejoy decided to do this. Five or six persons who objected destroyed the printing press the night after it arrived in Alton. Lovejoy's friends pledged to replace it. Lovejoy went to Cincinnati, brought back a new press, and published his newspaper. Circulation more than doubled after the move to Alton.

In June 1837 the secretary of the American Anti-Slavery Society asked Lovejoy to send him names of two people from each county in Illinois who would circulate a petition to abolish slavery in the District of Columbia. Lovejoy wrote an article to ask interested readers to submit their names. He also asked if it was time to form an Illinois Anti-Slavery Society.

There was objection from some citizens. A meeting was held and Lovejoy was criticized. Lovejoy replied by defending liberty of the press and freedom of speech.

A St. Louis newspaper fostered a spirit of lawlessness among Lovejoy's pro-slavery critics. On August 21st, *Observer* materials were destroyed, but Lovejoy's supporters in Alton and Quincy encouraged Lovejoy to re-establish the paper.

ELIJAH LOVEJOY (CONT.)

Lovejoy appealed to "all friends of law and order to come to the rescue." They did and he was soon able to order a new press in Cincinnati. In the meanwhile, a minister from Mississippi published a pamphlet claiming that the Bible sanctioned slavery. Lovejoy responded by writing a letter to the Christians of Alton refuting those claims.

Lovejoy was out of town attending a Presbyterian Church meeting when his third press arrived in Alton. The mayor had the press taken to a warehouse that was guarded until a certain hour. When the guard left ten or twelve men who had covered their faces with handkerchiefs, broke into the warehouse, rolled the press to the riverbank, smashed it and threw it into the Mississippi River.

A drunken mob later went to Lovejoy's house. Two men struck Lovejoy and tried to drag him outside. Mrs. Lovejoy struck then in the face. She, her mother and sister forced them to leave.

Lovejoy sent a note out to the mob saying he would leave town the next day. After the mob left he slipped out of town but returned the next day. Friends of his armed themselves and guarded his house.

In mid October, Lovejoy ordered a fourth press. Meanwhile friends in Quincy urged him to come there. On October 26th the state Anti-Slavery Convention met in the Presbyterian Church in Upper Alton. There was some disturbance. The group adjourned until the next morning when it organized. Against the wishes of the majority the report of the anti-abolition faction was adopted. Members who objected, gathered at a private house the following day. They formed the Illinois Anti-Slavery Society. They decided the *Observer* was to remain in Alton and chose Lovejoy as the corresponding secretary.

A series of meetings and discussions followed. Lovejoy declared his right under the Constitution to print his opinions. Other speakers violently disagreed.

Lovejoy's fourth printing press reached Alton on the morning of November 6, 1837. The mob was alerted. The press was stored in a warehouse, a group of armed citizens stood guard inside.

About 10:00pm a mob came and demanded the press. They threw stones, they shot into the building, the defenders of the press returned fire. The mob left but soon returned with ladders and set fire to the roof of the warehouse. The defenders refused to leave. Lovejoy and others went to the door. A sniper shot and killed him. The mob sent up a yell of exhilaration.

Lovejoy was buried on November 9th. A black man by the name of Scotty Johnston is credited with having protected Lovejoy's body from his enemies.

Lovejoy's murder was deplored and his courage praised in resolutions by anti-slavery societies and black and white abolitionists in many states. His death changed the minds of many people who believed that slavery was wrong, but too large of an institution to challenge.

Courtesy of the Greater Alton Area Visitors and Tourism Bureau.

Company G 16th U.S. Colored Infantry. While in the military he changed his last name to Killibrew. Later he changed it back to Lawson. He worked in Belvidere, and in 1870 returned to Virginia to marry his childhood sweetheart, Luella Spurlark. Other family members settled in Belvidere, and nearby in Garden Prairie and Rockford. For years, he was janitor of the Belvidere public school. Relatives tell how he'd start up the heat at 4 A.M. so the school would be comfortable when the children arrived. He was the town's official parade marshal. His bummer cap and GAR hat are part of the Civil War display at the Boone County Historical Museum.

Martha Johnson, who also came to Belvidere from Virginia, worked as a domestic after settling in Illinois. During the Civil War she belonged to the W.R.C. (the Woman's Relief Corps).

Rachel McCullom Harris was born in Holly Springs, Mississippi. She was working as a cotton field hand when Vicksburg came under siege and captured by Union troops. She was detailed as an army nurse and attached to the 127th Illinois Infantry led by Colonel Frank Curtiss of Marengo. According to one account she saved the life of Colonel Curtiss or that of his brother, Ira. A 1902 edition of a Marengo newspaper reported that in addition to being a nurse Rachel Harris was a spy for the Union cause—traveling through Confederate lines with important dispatches hidden in her hair. At the time of her capture she was the wife of John Tyler and the mother of two daughters. Her husband was killed in a battle at Milliken's Bend. In 1863 she came to Marengo to care for the Curtiss brothers' ailing mother. She was reunited with her daughters and in 1865 married Josephus Harris. When they moved to Deitz and Forest streets another black couple, Jack and Nancy Ford, were their neighbors.

Mrs. Emily Gain, Mrs. Gilbert Vernon, and B. Carr were founding members of Antioch (Missionary) Baptist Church. The church provided schooling for adults and children. It is probable that two men who enlisted in the Civil War from Decatur were members of Anitoch. The agricultural research of another black man, George Washington Carver at Tuskegee Institute, Alabama helped make Decatur the "Soybean Capital of the World."

In Peoria, Thomas Lindsey was well known to fight for freedom. He came to Peoria from Kentucky in 1826 and became the first market manager. Mrs. Dorothy Davison and attorney Don Jackson are descendants who followed his example.

In 1892, Charles H. Smith had the reputation of the "wealthiest black plasterer west of Chicago." A photo of this early homeowner and businessman is on display at the Elmhurst Historical Society.

Louis Spurlock crisscrossed America before settling in Peoria. He was born in West Virginia where his father maintained machinery used in the coal mines. Louis' older brother taught at Tuskeegee Institute in Alabama and encouraged Louis to attend college there. After finishing his studies Louis got a job repairing steam engines for a lumber company near Seattle, Washington.

MARY JONES

Reprinted from Discovery and Conquest of the Northwest, by Rufus Blanchard, 1900.

In interviewing Mary Jones, widow of the late John Jones (colored), her words are herewith reported verbatim, to better express her recollections of the eventful period of the anti-slavery issue:

About the time we came to Chicago in 1845, there were three girls who escaped from slavery in Missouri who came here in a wagon covered in straw. As late as the fall, they remained here until navigation opened, and then they were sent on to Canada.

At one time, Dr. Dyer told a slave in front of the old Tremont house, "You don't belong to anybody. Go about your own business." His master heard what the doctor said, and he rushed up and struck him, which caused a fit. In the disturbance, the doctor broke his cane over the slave owner's head. After that friends of the doctor made him a present of a fine gold headed cane, which is now in the Historial Society.

The fugitive slave law was passed on a Saturday night. On Sunday, after the law had been passed, the Friends of Freedom chartered cars enough to send every fugitive slave from here and around the country, out of this country into Canada. They went out and loaded up the cars at what I believe was then called the Sherman Street station. I remember at that time, a man came along who looked as if he might do a great deal of fighting. He told the slave owners and friends that if they would bring one man at a time he would not leave one of them. The men who got these cars together, what few I now remember, were Charles V. Dyer, Zebina Eastman, John Jones, L.C.P. Freer, Calvin DeWolf, Henry Bradford, Mr. Bridges, Louis Isabell, H.O. Wagner and others.

The first time I ever met John Brown, he came to our house one afternoon with Fred Douglass. They sat up until late and John Brown stayed all night. Mr. Douglass said that he was a nice man, and Mr. Jones wanted to know if I could make some provision for

him to stay all night, that he did not want to send him away. He remained all night. I told Mr. Jones that I thought he was a little "off" on the slavery question — - that I did not think he was right — that I did not believe he could ever do what he wanted to do. Somebody would have to give up his life before it was done.

The next morning I asked him if he had any family. He said, "Yes, madam. I have quite a large family, besides over a million other people I am looking out for. Some of these days I am going to free them, if I live long enough." I thought to myself, "How are you going to free them?" After that time, until he went to Kansas, he dropped into our house most any time, generally in the morning, and stayed until long in the afternoon.

He would talk about the slavery question, about war, and say what might be done in the hills and mountains of Pennsylvania. Mr. Jones would say, "Why, Mr. Brown, that is all wind, and there is nothing to it; and besides, you would lose your life if you undertook to carry out your plans." And I remember how Mr. Brown looked when he snapped his finger and said, "What do I care for my life?" He spoke low and distinctly, and said with a snap of his finger, "What do I care for my life, if I can do what I want to do ... if I can free these negroes?" But Mr. Jones told him that he did not believe his ideas would ever be carried out. During the several times that he was coming to our house, and in these talks, I remember that he also said to Mr. Jones, "I tell you what you do Mr. Jones. You lay in a supply of sugar, corn, coffee and cotton, because I am going to raise the price of it" — meaning, of course, that he expected to stop slavery, and that more would have to be paid for raising these articles.

After being in Kansas awhile, he came in here with thirteen slaves. One morning someone rang the bell, and Mr. Jones went down and answered the bell. About daylight, I heard several men talking. I had been reading about how many men he had around him, and I said to my husband, "I do not want John Brown's fighters. I am willing to take care of him, but

MARY JONES (CONT.)

not his fighters. He will lay himself liable." But he said, "They are here, and I am going to let them in."

I don't know how many, but four or five of them were the roughest looking men I ever saw. They had boots up to their knees, and their pants down in their boots, and they looked like they were ready to fight. They behaved very nicely, and I came downstairs right away.

Mr. Brown said, "Now, Mr. Jones, if you will give my men a little bite, as they have had nothing to eat, we will go away from you, and won't be heard of anymore today. Just give them a little bite of something." So, we did, and Mr. Jones came downstairs, and we all had breakfast.

So then, Mr. Brown went away, or started, and I asked him if he would not have some more coffee. He said, "Yes, I will take a little more coffee, because I ate very little dinner yesterday, and will have some more coffee." That shows he had a system in all things. Sure enough, these men went away and my husband left, and nobody was left at the house but John Brown and me.

By and by, a boy came to the door. I think he was a train boy who peddled books, and asked for Mr. Jones. I told him he was not in. He said the conductor told him to come to Mr. Jones and see where he was, because he said all the people who came in this morning were suspicious looking people and had negroes with them.

The conductor thought they were going to take the negroes down to Missouri and sell them, and he did not want it that way. I did not say to him that John Brown was in the house. I kept that a secret, and I did not tell him that I knew about these men, because I did not. I told him where to go to find the anti-slavery people, Mr. Freer and Dr. Dyer. What he wanted was someone to look after these slaves and see that they were not sent to Missouri. He said there was a very suspicious white man who had these negroes, and it

was supposed they intended to take them to Missouri, while the negroes believed they were going to be taken to Canada.

The boy left, and by and by, I answered the door again. There was Mr. Pinkerton, whom I had met before, and I began a conversation with him. Just at that time the fugitive slave law was in force and altogether, it made me feel a little nervous, as I did not know whether he was on the right side or not. He spoke, "This is Mrs. Jones, I believe. Is John Brown stopping with you?" I thought the truth was the best, anyhow, and asked him to come in. I did not know what the result might be. But as soon as he saw John Brown, I knew they were friends, and Mr. Pinkerton was on the right side.

They were very friendly together and were very glad to see each other. Mr. Pinkerton said that he had been to see the slaves Mr. Brown had brought in, and he said they were going to be looked after. " I am going to get enough money to send these negroes out of the city." He said, "Mrs. Jones will take good care of you today." Of course I said, "Yes." Then their anti-slavery friends came up to see John Brown and Dr. Dyer suggested giving him a suit of clothes and said that would be a good disguise for him. Dr. Dyer, Mr. Freer, and I do not know how many, were there. One man whose name I cannot remember, was about the same size as John Brown, and he went down in town and fitted the clothes on himself, because they did not want to send John Brown . He brought them to John Brown, and I guess John Brown was hung in these same clothes.

One of the girls which I told you about that came here from Missouri covered with straw, is now living in Chicago. They were all sent away from Chicago. One got married and died, and I do not know what became of the other. One drifted back to Chicago. Her husband had been in the war, and she came here to see if Mr. Jones could identify her to get a pension. She had four girls. One of the girls lived with us for five years, went to school and was accepted as a teacher.

Louis' work was seasonal and he decided to work his way back East hoping to find year round employment. He stopped at a farm in Kansas and took a job maintaining the huge threshing machine during harvest. While there, he met the owner of a straw board factory in Peoria who had come to Kansas to buy straw. The owner offered him the job of maintaining machinery at his factory. Louis Spurlock accepted and remained at the factory the rest of his working years.

Four brothers, Nathaniel Williams, Reuben Reed, Jerry M. Burkhalter, and John T. Williams, who were all craftsmen during slavery established prosperous homes, farms, and families in Elkville, north of Carbondale, although penniless when freed. Family members provided lumber for the Mount Zion Missionary Baptist Church, and land for a cemetery, and a school.

Mr. David Janes' parents had been enslaved in Kentucky. After the Civil War the family moved to Illinois when his older brother, Ward, came to the state as a pastor. The family lived and worked mostly in Onarga and Pontiac, however, David Janes worked at the Illinois State Library at one time before he returned to Pontiac. Always a book lover and avid reader, he collected an outstanding personal library. He wrote and published a number of short stories.

Census records indicate that black people were early residents of Fairbury along the Chicago and Alton Railroad line near Lexington and Pontiac. Their grave markers in Graceland Cemetery there indicate that they were substantial citizens of this farming community.

In Broadlands, in the Champaign-Urbana area, George W. Smith, an ex-slave who served in the Union Army, purchased 80 acres of land. He and his son farmed it. The old farm was later relocated and has remained in family ownership ever since.

Dr. Romeo B. Garrett (right) who spent many years ferreting out documents in order to write <u>Early History of the Negro inPeoria</u>. Dr. Garrett's grandfather (left) was born in Mississippi. *Courtesy of the Garrett Collection, African AmericanHistory Museum, Peoria, Illinois.*

SENATOR LYMAN TRUMBULL

The name Lyman Trumbull is not as well known as the names of many Illinois politicians, yet Senator Trumbull was the author of at least two crucial documents which shaped the U.S. law from the end of the Civil War to the present day.

The first of these documents was the 13th Amendment to the *Constitution of the United States*. Adopted in December of 1865, these relatively few words freed the slaves in all states not included in President Lincoln's *Emancipation Proclamation*.

Senator Trumbull also wrote what many historians consider one of the most significant pieces of legislation of the nineteenth century; the *Civil Rights Act of 1866*. In it Senator Trumbull defined the fundamental rights of every man as a freeman. It held that all persons born in the United States were natural citizens with the right to make contracts, bring lawsuits and otherwise enjoy equally, without regard to race, the "full and equal benefits of all laws and proceedings for the security of person and property." This law and the *Fourteenth Amendment* which was ratified in 1868 transformed the legal status of black people in the United States.

Although the 14th Amendment was intended to protect the rights of citizenship, for more than fifty years it had little effect on Supreme Court decisions. The most famous example of this is the 1896 *Plessy v. Ferguson* decision. In this case, the Supreme Court decided state laws allowing for separate railroad accommodations for black and white people did not violate the 14th Amendment if facilities were separate but substantially equal. The result was that black passengers had separate accommodations which were not equal in comfort or size to those of white passengers. It was the basis for separate "Jim Crow" accommodations in dining, lodging and other aspects of everyday life. This 1896 decision was struck down by the Supreme Court in the *Brown v. Board of Education of Topeka* (1954) although compliance to this ruling has not been unanimous.

Anyone who had followed Illinois Senator Lyman Trumbull's career knew that the documents he wrote were consistent with his earlier actions. For example, when Elijah Lovejoy was killed in Alton, Trumbull who was then a young lawyer in nearby Belleville, wrote a letter to tell his father of "this awful catastrophe."

As a lawyer he fought against indenture system in Illinois which in practice was slavery. He was the lawyer for Susan Richardson who had escaped from Andrew Borders in Randolph County, but lost that case in the Illinois Supreme Court. Soon after that he appeared before the same court in the case of *Jarrot v. Jarrot*, (Joseph Jarrot was a black man who sued his mistress Julia Jarrot for wages. He alleged that he had been held in servitude contrary to the *Northwest Ordinance* and the *Constitution of the State of Illinois* . His grandmother had been enslaved by a Frenchman before the Illinois Country passed under the jurisdiction of the United States. Joseph Jarrot and his mother were passed by descent to Julia Jarrot.) Fifty-seven years after the Ordinance of 1787, Lyman Trumbull argued and won Joseph Jarrot's case. This victory practically put an end to slavery in Illinois.

When author Ruby Berkley Goodwin of DuQuoin asked about her family history she learned that her parents' ancestors had very different experiences. Soon after the Civil War her father's family had come from Island Number 10, an island in the Mississippi River where the Union kept escaped slaves in protective custody so that slavecatchers could not recapture them. During the war, her father eluded slave hunters and the Confederate Army to reach Union lines. He kept up with them until he reached the island. Her father's mother was of black and Indian ancestry. She was the first black woman in town to purchase an organ. Mrs. Goodwin's maternal grandfather was set free at age nine, injured his leg in a fall and had to have an amputation. He became a shoemaker's apprentice and learned to read. He gained the respect of the slaves, became a minister and married a young woman from a nearby plantation who was given her freedom when she married. The couple settled in DuQuoin.

JARROT MANSION STATE HISTORIC SITE
Courtesy of the Illinois Historic Preservation Agency

Thomas Jefferson Houston escaped to Cairo from slavery in southern Missouri. He got a job on the Illinois Central Railroad, but returned to Missouri for his mother and brother. The brother also got a job on the I.C. Charles was a minister; he carried a gun in his Bible. He moved to Springfield where he pastored the church then called the Colored Baptist Church, now Zion Missionary Baptist Church. Some members had come to Springfield on the Underground Railroad. The early members met in a house on Vinegar Street, then built a church on Ninth and Carpenter with bricks that were hand moulded and baked by members of the church who were part owners of a brickyard. The church has since relocated. There is a marker at the site of the corner where the original building was located. Thomas Jefferson Houston's great great grandson Charles Hamilton Houston worked with the NAACP and helped shape the legal strategy for the famous *Brown v. Board of Education* case. He was teacher and mentor to Thurgood Marshall who argued that case before the U.S. Supreme Court and later became Associate Justice on the Supreme Court.

In Bloomington the McLean County Historical Society has conducted extensive oral history interviews and prepared an exhibit which includes significant African American artifacts and archival material.

121

JOHN LAWSON
WEARING A G.A.R. HAT
*Courtesy: Boone County
Historical Museum*

BELVIDERE SCHOOL
John Lawson is second from right in
the third row. *Courtesy: Boone County
Historical Museum*

FREDERICK DOUGLASS VISITS AURORA

Frederick Douglass and Sojourner Truth appeared in many towns in Illinois. Accounts of one particulary eventful visit by Frederick Douglass are recorded in the history of the Aurora Congregational Church, in two issues of the *Aurora Beacon News* (April 17, 1927 and January 3, 1937), and in the Kendall County Bicentennial book. The accounts differ in some details, but this appears to be essentially what happened. Frederick Douglass, who was usually associated with East Coast abolitionist activities, learned that Senator Stephen A. Douglas was speaking to audiences the Middle West trying to explain why he had sponsored the controversial Kansas-Nebraska bill of 1854. Frederick Douglass strongly opposed the bill which allowed the extension of slavery into Nebraska. He arranged to debate Stephen Douglas at a meeting to be held at the Congregational Church in Aurora. When the two men arrived in town, both were very ill. Neither felt well enough to speak, but the debate had attracted large numbers of people, some had come from out of state. Frederick Douglass was persuaded to attend the meeting but was carried to the platform and laid on the pulpit sofa until time to speak. Some members of the audience wanted to hear Senator Douglas' views. Other members of the audience began "booing" when a Mr.

Chapman, stood in for Douglas but failed to address the Nebraska bill. They demanded to hear from Beman, the diminuitive hunchbacked orator who had accompanied Frederick Douglass. Judge Benjamin Parks, who was a supporter of Senator Douglas, sprang to his feet and insisted that the audience let Chapman continue. According to the news article which written closest to the time of the event, Parks who as six feet tall and sturdily built, pointed to Beman who was little more than four feet tall, and called him "an insignificant pigmy." The newspaper account continued, Beman "planted his fist in Parks' face." Most of the audience shared Beman's views, and after a good deal of noise and confusion, the second news article reported, "Parks was forcibly ejected. He went out . . . through a window. Eager hands then lifted the hunchback to the top of the communion table in front of the altar, from which commanding position, he burst forth in a flood of eloquence denouncing the slave power." He explained that he had received and resented insults since his birth in Georgia and apologized for temporarily forgetting he was in a church. His speech was well-received. He, Frederick Douglass, and Stephen Douglas left Aurora the following day.

39. Did the Illinois indenture laws subject both white and black children to servitude?

Yes. Any child could be "bound out" with parental consent, as could orphans and other dependent children.

White children were bound out to be indentured servants, apprentices, or clerks. They were entitled to "meat, drink, lodging, washing, clothing suitable for working and for holy days...reading, writing and the ground rules of arithmetic, and a new Bible...".

This same form of indenture could be used to bind black children, but other procedures allowed black children to be held for longer terms of service. Most would-be masters preferred the latter procedures. In cases when children of African descent were bound by the provisions used for white indentured children, masters were permitted to omit "reading, writing and ground rules for arithmetic"... a provision legally required for whites.

Bound children were subject to discipline and "suitable punishment" from their masters. They had recourse in law if they received cruel or inhumane treatment, but, there were so many requirements that the apprentices were practically helpless unless some adult male citizen served as "next of friend". There were severe penalties for aiding, advising, or sheltering a runaway apprentice.

NEWS TRAVELS

In 1843, H.H. Kellogg, then president of Knox College in Galesburg, attended the World Anti-Slavery Convention in London. He traveled East by way of the Illinois and Ohio Rivers. Before embarking from Peoria, newspaper editor Samuel Davis gave him pamphlets entitled, "Free Discussion Suppressed in Peoria" to distribute during his journey. When he reached the upper Ohio River, he was joined by another delegate to the convention, Jonathan Blanchard pastor of a Cincinnati church which had been at the center of anti-slavery activity. The two men gained great respect of each other. When Kellogg resigned from Knox College, he suggested that Blanchard would be his sucessor. Blanchard was visiting Illinois at the time because he had been invited to become president of Mission Institute in Quincy, and was asked to come to Galesburg. Blanchard's reputation as an opponent to slavery became known well beyond that college town as a result of his travels and his speeches which were then reprinted in the *Western Citizen*. After serving as president of Knox, Blanchard pastored the Galesburg First Church. In 1859 to 1960, he became the president of Wheaton College changing the school's name from Illinois Institute and continuing his anti-slavery crusade.

Ministers who were anti-slavery agents, and former slaves came to Illinois to report on Candian settlements of freedmen. Black newspaper publisher Mary Ann Shadd journeyed to Geneva, Illinois to seek subscribers to her *Provincial Freedman*.

40. Did all anti-slavery workers have the same views?

No. Some, such as William Lloyd Garrison, believed in full immediate emancipation.

Others, like Benjamin Lundy of McNabb, with whom Garrison had worked, recommended a more gradual emancipation.

Some anti-slavery workers actually helped slaves, while others thought it was a noble idea but did not become personally involved.

Some had more interest in denying the slaveholders their free laborers than in improving the status of the Negro.

Some proposed resettling free black people in Africa, but most blacks felt that they had contributed far too much to the building of America to leave it.

Some, like Allan Pinkerton of Dundee, taught slaves a trade and paid them for their work. This provided them with additional skills with which to earn a living and savings with which to establish farms or businesses.

ALLAN PINKERTON'S COOPER SHOP
Courtesy of The DuSable Museum of AfricanAmericanHistory

41. How did abolitionists exchange their views?

Although we think stagecoach and canal boat travel was slow, it is amazing how much communication and visiting took place between abolitionists from within and outside the state.

In 1837, amid threats from pro-slavery forces in Missouri, Elijah Lovejoy summoned Illinois anti-slavery workers to Alton. His murder prompted more people to take a stand against slavery and for freedom of the press.

At the first anniversary meeting of the Illinois Anti-Slavery Society (Farmington 1838), Benjamin Lundy, G.W. Gale, Edward Beecher, Jeremiah Porter, and Dr. David Nelson (who, like Lovejoy, had been driven from Missouri) were in attendance. Benjamin Lundy's travels were extensive and remarkable. His newspaper, The *Genius of Universal Emancipation*, (which later became the *Western Citizen* and still later, the *Chicago Tribune*) was a forum for anti-slavery workers.

Frederick Douglass, John Jones, Allan Pinkerton, and John Brown conferred at John and Mary Jones's home. Allan Pinlerton and John Brown held a secret meeting in Henry O. Wagoner's mill.

SMUGGLING ANTI-SLAVERY LITERATURE
Courtesy of The DuSable Museum of AfricanAmericanHistory

42. Were there antislavery newspapers?

Yes. Within the state of Illinois:

~ Lovejoy's *The Observer*

~ Lundy's *Genius of Universal Emancipation*, became the *Western Citizen*, which became Joseph Medill's *Chicago Tribune* ("a great thunder against slavery.")

~ The *Illinoisian* is sometimes referred to as an anti-slavery paper.

~ *Alton Telegraph*

~ *Illinois Intelligencer*

~ Hooper Warren's *Spectator*

~ *Western Christian* published in Elgin

~ Augustine A. Smith, the first president of North Central College spoke out against slavery in the *Evangelical Messenger*

HOOPER WARREN

Outside of Illinois:

~ Lovejoy's *St. Louis Observer*

~ Garrison's *Liberator*

~ Frederick Douglass' *North Star*

~ James G. Birney's *Philanthropist*

~ *Freedom's Journal* edited by John Russwurm and Rev. Samuel Cornish

~ William Cullen Bryant's *N.Y. Evening Post*

~ Oliver Johnson's *National Anti-Slavery Standard*

~ *The Pennsylvania Freedman*

~ George Moses Horton's *Hope of Liberty*

~ *The Mystery*, founded by Dr. Martin R. Delaney

~ Horace Greenley's *Tribune*

~ Publications of the American Missionary Association.

MARTIN R. DELANEY

In Canada:

~ *Provincial Freedman*, published by Mary Ann Shadd Cary

~ Henry Bibb's *Voice of the Fugitive*

Alton, IL — like Quincy, Chester and Cairo — was a Mississippi River city at which fugitive slaves entered Illinois. It is near St. Louis which was a busy slave market. Elijah Lovejoy, editor of *The Observer*, was forced to leave St. Louis because of his anti-slavery views. This is his Alton home (bottom) and printing office (top) in 1837.

43. What other things were people who objected to slavery known for?

Look in your encyclopedia and books listed in the back of this book and on the Internet to learn other accomplishments of:

~ Benjamin Bannaker, builder of the first clock in America, surveyor of Washington, D. C., and correspondent of Thomas Jefferson regarding the issue of slavery. (Correspondence can be seen at the Library of Congress.)

~ Lucy Stone, Susan B. Anthony, Sojourner Truth, Abby Kelly, Frederick Douglass, and Lucretia Mott, advocates of women's suffrage.

~ John Greenleaf Whittier, Henry Wadsworth Longfellow, Ralph Waldo Emerson, and Walt Whitman, noted poets who wrote against slavery. Joseph T. Murray, Thomas A. Edison's first partner, was an UGRR conductor who worked in partnership with John Greenleaf Whittier.

~ Hiram R. Revels, student at Knox, and later U. S. Senator from Mississippi.

~ Charles Sumner, the U. S. Senator who succeeded Daniel Webster, supporter of the Fugitive Slave Act.

PRISCILLA HOLLYHOCKS

Hollyhocks are tall stately plants with beautiful bell-shaped flowers. Once their seeds are planted they grow and bloom year after year. They became a symbol of hope to a young enslaved black woman named Priscilla.

Priscilla's story began in Georgia. She and other slaves met Brizilla (Basil) Silkwood of Mulkeytown, Illinois, when he visited the plantation. She was sold when the slaveholder died soon after Silkwood's visit. She was purchased by a Cherokee chief living on a near by reservation in the Great Smokey Mountains.

Before leaving the plantation Priscilla gathered some hollyhock seeds to take with her and plant around the chief's cabin. In 1838 many Cherokees were forced off their reservations in southeast and marched through winter weather and over rocky terrain to the Indian Territory (Oklahoma). The long, grueling march, known as The Trail of Tears, passed through Jonesboro, Illinois. Once again Priscilla had tucked hollyhock seeds in her pocket before leaving home.

Brizilla Silkwood happened to be in Jonesboro on business. He was standing outside the hotel when Priscilla passed. They recognized each other. Reportedly Silkwood purchased her from the chief for $1000. He took her back to his home in Mulkeytown. She planted hollyhocks there. They bloomed and beautified the log cabin beside the Shawneetown-Kaskaskia Trail from that time on. They were named Priscilla Hollyhocks in her honor.

The Cherokee reached Oklahoma in 1838. One hundred and twelve years later, seeds were sent to the daughter of the last Cherokee chief. Since then, Priscilla Hollyhocks have bloomed around the homes of descendants of Priscilla's fellow travelers on the Trail of Tears.

Priscilla lived at the Silkwood home until her death in 1892. She is buried in the family plot in Reed Cemetery beside Basil Silkwood and his wife. She was given freedom papers by Silkwood, which are recorded in the Franklin County clerk's office in Benton.

~ Harriet Tubman, who became a nurse and spy during the Civil War. She planned and led a military expedition in Port Royale, SC, with the aid of Col. James Montgomery, which freed 700 slaves in one night.

U.S. Senator Hiram R. Revels and the clock which his predecessor, Senator Jefferson Davis gave him. *Courtesy of Susan Woodson.*

~ Patrick Henry, who said of slavery, "I will not, I cannot, justify it."

~ Frederick Douglass, editor of the *North Star,* one of 40 black newspapers in the period between 1827 and 1865.

~ John Russwurm and Salmon P. Chase, Thaddeus Stevens, and William H. Seward, who devoted much time and effort to defending fugitive slaves.

~ Sarah Parker Redmond, physician.

~ Illinois resident Israel Blodgett and Jonathan B. Turner, whose metal plows broke the prairie.

~ Senator Cassius Clay, abolitionist from Kentucky.

~ Dr. Martin R. Delaney, a major in the Union Army.

~ Mary Ann Shadd Cary was a recruiter for the Union Army.

~ Thomas Jefferson was a slaveholder, yet his original version of the Declaration of Independence included a paragraph condemning slavery. He declared, "I tremble for my country when I reflect that God is just, that his justice cannot sleep forever."

OWEN LOVEJOY

A very special ceremony took place in Princeton on Sunday September 14, 1997. There were speeches, music and the unveiling of a plaque designating the Owen Lovejoy Homestead as a National Historic Landmark. This designation means that the site not only has local or regional significance. It is a confirmation of national significance.

In his lifetime, Owen Lovejoy did not limit his life and work to one locale or region. He was in Alton when his brother Elijah was murdered, and vowed never to forsake the anti-slavery cause.

He and another brother named Joseph wrote a book to inform the public about the details of Elijah's death. Former President John Quincy Adams wrote the introduction and the American Anti-Slavery Society helped publish it. It told how some respected Alton citizens, including two members of Elijah Lovejoy's church, had murdered him.

In 1839, Owen Lovejoy moved to Princeton to become minister of the Hampshire Colony Congregational Church. Lovejoy and other Illinois Congregationalists had such strong abhorrence of slavery that they ruled that their association "ought to receive no minister to its fellowship who does not rank slave holding with other heinous sins." Lovejoy was so outspoken against slavery that he made enemies among pro-slavery townspeople, but he continued to express his views.

Owen Lovejoy took a leadership role in organizing new congregational churches and spreading anti-slavery sentiment.

He married a widow who was a member of his church. Their home and that of John Howard Bryant became Underground Railroad stations in Princeton.

A secret door usually hidden behind a bedroom dresser opened onto a large closet. It was an ideal hiding place for weary Underground Railroad passengers. At one time, Lovejoy was indicted for "harboring, feeding and clothing two slaves." Lovejoy's lawyer was able to cite an Illinois law that led to a not guilty verdict.

The most famous episode at the Lovejoy house had to do with a young man named John Bowen. Bowen was intelligent and industrious. One day while he was at work two slavecatchers drew their pistols, tied his hands, and led him into town like a horse.

A neighbor notified Lovejoy who swore out a warrant for John Bowen and his captors. The warrant was served and the three men were taken to the court house. A crowd which included pro-slavery and anti-slavery sympathizers gathered.

The day on which the Owen Lovejoy Homestead in Princeton, Illinois received National Historic Landmark status.

Lovejoy had hoped the judge would release John Bowen, and detain his captors long enough for him to escape. Instead there was bedlam in the courtroom and Bowen's ropes were cut. He and Owen Lovejoy reached the Lovejoy's home before the crowd. A decoy horseback rider dashed out of the yard. That rider was chased but it wasn't Bowen. Soon afterwards two people rode away from the house in a carriage. One of them was Bowen in disguise.

In addition to operating an Underground Railroad station, Owen Lovejoy became active in anti-slavery politics. He was urged to run for office and lost four times then won on his fifth attempt.

He may have met Frederick Douglass at a national political meeting. He invited Douglass to come to

~ John Quincy Adams, former President, who felt that the gag rule in Congress denied freedom of speech and petition to abolitionists and all other citizens. He vowed to end slavery. Earlier, he had defended and won the case for the Africans of the *Amistad* slave ship revolt. Quincy, Illinois is named in honor of him.

~ Eliza Chappel Porter, first public school teacher in Chicago.

~ Alexander Hamilton, who urged black participation in the American Revolutionary War. Five thousand black men served.

~ William Wells Brown, a former slave who became a novelist and historian.

~ John Wentworth, mayor of Chicago.

~ President James Madison, who encouraged Congress to devise "further means of suppressing the evil" (that is, the slave trade).

Professor Jonathan B. Turner was noted for bringing Osage orange trees to this area and editing a newspaper. He and a number of other Jacksonville residents were involved in the UGRR; although sources disagree on the extent of Turner's participation.

OWEN LOVEJOY (CONT.)

speak in Princeton, Sycamore, Chicago and other Illinois towns against the Fugitive Slave Act and Black Codes. Lovejoy scholar Rev. William Moore believes that a statement Douglass made indicating that it was not possible for free and enslaved people to live in harmony foreshadowed Lincoln's famous "House Divided" speech.

In 1855 Lovejoy was elected to represent Bureau Country in the Illinois House of Representatives. It's probable that Lovejoy and Lincoln had the same Springfield barber, a black Haitian man by

the name of William de Fleurville. It's known they worked together in later years when Lincoln went to Washington as President and Lovejoy served in U.S. Congress. Both belonged to the newly formed Republican Party which opposed the views of the U.S. Senator Stephen A. Douglas on States' Rights.

Lovejoy took particular pride in promoting the legislation which recognized Haiti as an independent country, establishment of a Department of Agriculture, freeing slaves in Washington, D.C., and arming former slaves to fight for the Union.

44. What events between the American Revolution and Civil War had significant effect on Illinois and its UGRR operations?

1776   Declaration of Independence: "All men are created equal" American Revolution. A few masters promised freedom to slaves who fought side by side with them. Some kept their promises; others sent their slaves to fight. Prior to this, the French surrendered Canada and Illinois Country to the British.

1778   George Rogers Clark secured Illinois for Virginia from Britain.

1779   Jean Baptiste Point DuSable established a trading post at Chicago where the Chicago River and Lake Michigan meet. He was captured by the British while en route to deliver supplies to Clark. His strategic site was the inland port that Britain, France, and Spain had all sought.

1784   Virginia ceded its western lands to the United States government.

1787   The Continental Congress passed Ordinance which forbade slavery in any part of the "Northwest Territory."

Free African Society was formed.

1789   Constitution of the United States took effect March 4. When the Constitution was being written, framers Patrick Henry and Thomas Jefferson urged the Continental Congress to stop the importation of slaves.

1793   First Fugitive Slave Law was signed by President George Washington. Personal Liberty laws allowed anti-slavery sympathizers to take cases up to Supreme Court.

Eli Whitney patented cotton gin with the input of an enslaved African. The Constitution included a provision providing for an end to the importation of slaves in 1808. The cotton gin, created a greater need for slaves, and slave trade continued illegally.

In 1793 Upper Canada provided for freedom of all slave children at age 25, and the British Emancipation Act of 1835 forbade all slavery in the Empire.

TOUSSAINT L'OUVERTURE

1795   Treaty of Greenville. More than 25,000 square miles of Indian lands were ceded to the United States government following the Battle of Fallen Timbers.

1800   Congress created the Indiana Territory (which included Illinois) from the Northwest Territory.

1803   Louisiana Purchase. Toussaint L'Ouverture's successful Haitian revolt led Napoleon to give up his plans to establish an empire in the Western Hemisphere and to sell the Louisiana Purchase to the United States for less than $20 per square acre.

The governing council of the Indiana Territory drew up a "slave code," a system of long-term indentures which were virtually slavery.

1804   Lewis and Clark expedition. After exploration of the West most participants in the expedition received land and money in appreciation for their pioneering efforts. The exception to this was York, the enslaved black man who made major contributions to the success of the expedition. He was denied land, money, and his freedom and beaten when he requested it.

1807   British Parliament abolished the slave trade.

Congress barred further importation of any new slaves into United States territory. This law was to become effective on January 1, 1808. There were one million slaves in the country. Illegal importation continued and slaveholders increased slavebreeding practices.

1809   Illinois Territory was organized by Act of Congress.

1810   James Madison told Congress that the laws of humanity and the country were being violated by those Americans who carried on trade in enslaved Africans.

1811   William Henry Harrison defeated the Shawnee Prophet, Chief Tecumseh's twin brother, for whom Prophetstown in Illinois was named.

1813   Preemption Act for Illinois was passed by Congress.

Further migration of black people into Illinois territory was prohibited, indentures were allowed and all black people who already lived in the territory were required to register with the clerk of the court of common pleas of the county in which they lived.

1814   The Illinois territorial legislature authorized the use of slaves in the salt works.

1816   American Colonization Society was organized in Hall of the U.S. House of Representatives.

1818   Illinois became the 21st state. It adopted a constitution, which prohibited slavery, but permitted an indentured system.

1819   The Illinois state legislature passes a series of restrictive "black laws" known as the Black Codes.

1821   Benjamin Lundy began publishing *Genius of Universal Emancipation* in Mt. Pleasant, Ohio.

1822   The issue of whether to legalize slavery dominated Illinois politics. In 1823 the legislature passed a bill which authorized a constitutional convention to allow slavery. In 1824 the voters rejected the convention proposal.

1827   In New York, Samuel Cornish and John B. Russwurm published *Freedom's Journal*, the first black newspaper in the United States.

There were 136 abolition societies in the United States; 106 were in slave holding states. Many of these were formed as a result of Lundy's efforts.

1829   David Walker's *Appeal* is published. It was widely distributed and alarmed slaveholders.

Slavery was abolished in Mexico by presidential proclamation on September 15, 1829.

1830   Richard Allen chaired first National Negro Convention in Philadelphia.

1831   When the Fox and Sauk, led by Chief Black Hawk, returned from their winter hunt, they found their village on the Rock River occupied by white squatters. They retired across the Mississippi River to Iowa.

William Lloyd Garrison founded the *Liberator* abolitionist newspaper in Boston.

Nat Turner believed he was destined to lead slaves out of bondage. He led revolt in Southampton County, Virginia.

1832   Blackhawk's followers, consisting mostly of women and children, returned to Illinois to visit the Winnebagos and raise a corn crop. The Illinois militia was called to pursue the Indians. Atrocities were committed by both sides. At Bad Ax, Wisconsin, the Indians retreated to the Mississippi River, where many were slaughtered.

WILLIAM LLOYD GARRISON

South Carolina threatened secession over tariff policies.

The New England Anti-Slavery Society was formed.

1833   The Chippewa, Ottawa, and Potawatomi lands were surrendered between Lake Michigan and the Mississippi. As many as six thousand Potawatomi gathered in Chicago. They were satisfied with their ancestral homelands here and did not wish to be forced to move with the Sioux west of the Mississippi. After nine days, government orders were issued that treaty must be signed at once. A diorama of this event is at Illinois State Historical Society.

The American Anti-Slavery Society was formed by black and white abolitionists.

BLACKHAWK,
THE SAC CHIEFTAIN

The Philadelphia Female Anti-Slavery Society was formed by an interracial group of women.

1833   The United States Government opens land parcels to European settlers, though some had already occupied land.

Putnam County Anti-Slavery Society was established. It was the first society in Illinois and one of the few in the Midwest.

1834   English Parliament abolished slavery in the British Empire.

1835   North Carolina joined other southern states in denying the right to vote for black people and the teaching of free or enslaved blacks.

The last of the Potawatomi leave their Illinois lands and move to reservations along the Missouri River.

1837   In January the Illinois General Assembly adopted resolutions which condemned abolition societies and approved the U.S. constitutional section of slavery holding states. Lincoln was one of the members of the Illinois House of Representatives to protest against the sanctity of slavery section.

The U.S. House of Representatives adopted a "gag rule" forbidding congressional action on anti-slavery material.

On October 26 the first meeting of Illinois Anti-Slavery Society was called by Elijah Lovejoy. On November 8, he was killed defending his printing press.

Black men joined white men in the right to vote in Canada. Neither black nor white women had this right in Canada or the United States.

1838   Benjamin Lundy, editor of the *Genius of Universal Emancipation*, joined his

135

family in Putnam County. Illinois Anti-Slavery Society made the *Genius* its official publication.

1839 On August 23, Benjamin Lundy died at age 50. He was buried in the Friends Cemetery near McNabb.

The slave ship *Amistad* was seized by kidnapped Mende Africans under the leadership of a man named Cinque. The mutiny occurred off Cuba; the Africans demanded of the ship's crew that they be returned to Africa. The crew deceived their captors by sailing east by day then changing course at night.

1840 World Anti-Slavery Convention was held in London. Hiram Kellogg and Jonathan Blanchard were in attendance.

The Liberty Party is founded. Black abolitionists Samuel Ringgold Ward and Henry Highland Garnet are among leading supporters of this anti-slavery political party. It urged boycotts of slave-produced crops and products.

Former President of the United States John Quincy Adams argued the *Amistad* case before the United States Supreme Court. He won the case. Cinque and his followers returned to Africa.

1841 Liberty Party was formed to oppose slavery with the ballot. Frederick Douglass began abolitionist speeches. Slaves sailed slave ship to freedom in Bahamas.

1842 In Putnam County the first Illinois Anti-Slavery Society for women was formed.

George Latimier, father of the inventor Lewis Howard Latimer, was arrested in Boston as a runaway after escaping from slavery. This is the first of several famous fugitive slave cases.

William Lloyd Garrison and other white and black Boston abolitionists worked diligently for George Latimer's release. Frederick Douglass' first writings appeared in print while he was working to free George Latimer. "The Singing Hutchinsons," direct descendants of the first governor of Massachusetts rallied support for Latimer through their music. Three other prominent citizens started a newspaper called the *Latimer Journal.* George Latimer was released after a black minister by the name of Rev. Samuel Caldwell, acted on behalf of some of his church members and purchased his freedom for $400. John Greenleaf Whittier immortalized the Latimer case in his poem "Virginia to Massachusetts."

1843 Sojourner Truth began her abolitionist career.

1844   Texas was annexed by the United States. This is considered a defeat for anti-slavery forces.

        The Liberty Party received 62,324 votes (almost as many as received in 1840). By 1846, the Liberty Party held the balance of power in 13 counties of northern Illinois.

1846   Wilmont Proviso proposed the banning slavery from the territories that could be acquired from Mexico as a result of the Mexican War.

1847   In Rochester, New York, Frederick Douglass founded the *North Star* abolitionist paper. He operated an Underground Railroad station in his home.

        The Illinois Constitution of 1848 banned slavery.

        The Illinois Constitutional convention adopted a proposal excluding immigration of free Negroes to Illinois. Voters approved this provision and the constitution which denied rights of suffrage and militia service to free Negroes.

1848   The Illinois Michigan Canal was opened. It was a festival day all along the route.

1850   Congress passed the second Fugitive Slave act as a result of the efforts of Illinois Senator Stephen A. Douglas. This law was part of the Compromise of 1850 and much harsher than the earlier law passed in 1793.

1852   Harriet Beecher Stowe published <u>Uncle Tom's Cabin</u>.

1853   National Convention of Colored People was held in Rochester, New York.

        The Illinois legislature made it a crime to bring a free black person into the state.

1854   The Kansas-Nebraska Act was directly contrary to Missouri Compromise of 1820. It led to the admission of two territories to the Union without slavery restrictions. Senator Stephen A. Douglas was for this. Lincoln opposed it.

1855   Massachusetts Senator Charles Sumner was severely beaten with a cane on the floor of the U.S. Senate by a southern senator after speaking out against the Kansas-Nebraska Bill.

1857   Dred Scott Decision was handed down. Illinois was one of the states where Dred Scott lived. When taken to Missouri as a slave, he brought suit, claiming he should be freed after having lived in free states. A Missouri court agreed, but the state supreme court reversed the decision. This was followed by many years of appeals and reversals. The case eventually reached the U.S. Supreme Court. The Supreme Court ruled against Dred Scott. Abraham Lincoln denounced the Court's decision.

John Brown (L) and Dred Scott (R), two men whose sense of right
and wrong altered the course of American history.

1858   The Lincoln-Douglas debates were held.

1859   John Brown attacked Harpers Ferry.

1861   Abraham Lincoln became President of United States. The Civil War began
        before Lincoln took over office. Lincoln called for 75,000 troops and large
        numbers of black and white men volunteered.

        Southern troops fired on Fort Sumter, a United States military post in
        Charleston, South Carolina.

1862   Congress passed bill to accept Negroes for military service. Lincoln issued pre-
        liminary Emancipation Proclamation.

1863   Robert Smalls, a Negro pilot, sailed the *Planter,* a Confederate gunboat, out of
        Charleston Harbor and turned it over to the U.S. Navy.

        Prior to 22 May 1863 when the federal government first recognized black men
        as persons, it was unlawful for a black person to use weapons for any purpose
        in the United States. The first authorized Federal soldiers trained at Camp
        William Penn in LaMott, Pennsylvania.

        The Twenty-Ninth U.S. Colored Infantry was the first full Civil War regiment
        composed almost entirely Illinois men. Many of the men had fled from slav-
        ery in bordering slave states. Governor Yates was authorized to raise the regi-
        ment on September 24, 1863. It was officially sworn into United States service
        April 24, 1864.

        Abraham Lincoln signed the *Emancipation Proclamation.*

CHARLES SUMNER
Champion of the fugitive slave from
the Senate of the United States.

ROBERT SMALLS
Captured *The Planter*, a Confederate
gunboat in Charleston harbor.

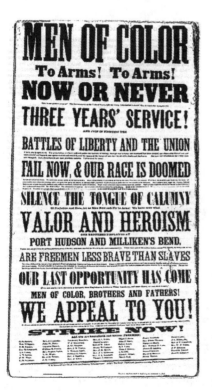

This was one of the huge recruiting
posters for U.S. Colored Troops (USCT),
the first authorized Federal soldiers
trained at Camp William Penn to fight
and destroy slavery and such
Constitutional provisions as the 3/5 rule.
Lucretia Mott, Harriet Tubman, Edward
M. Davis, Frederick Douglass and other
leaders in the antislavery movement
passed through the still standing gates of
Camp William Penn to address the
troops.

Courtesy Camp William Penn Museum,
LaMotte, PA 19027

139

45. Why did the Underground Railroad stop operating?

Slavery ended, though some vestiges remained. Significant dates and factors were:

1863   The *Emancipation Proclamation* was issued.

1865   The Civil War ended.

The Thirteenth Amendment was ratified. It abolished slavery throughout all the United States and areas subject to its jurisdiction.

THE 13TH AMENDMENT TO THE CONSTITUTION OF THE UNITED STATES

Section 1.

Neither slavery nor involuntary servitude, except as a punishment for crime whereof the party shall have been duly convicted, shall exist within the United States, or any place subject to their jurisdiction.

Section 2.

Congress shall have power to enforce this article by appropriate legislation.

1868   The Fourteenth Amendment was ratified. It granted black men the rights of citizenship.

THE 14TH AMENDMENT TO THE CONSTITUTION OF THE UNITED STATES

Section 1.
All persons born or naturalized in the United States and subject to the jurisdiction thereof, are citizens of the United States and of the State wherein they reside. No State shall make or enforce any law which shall abridge the privileges or immunities of citizens of the United States; nor shall any State deprive any person of life, liberty, or property, without due process of law; nor deny any person within its jurisdiction the equal protection of the laws

Section 2.
Representatives shall be apportioned among the several States according to their respective numbers, counting the whole number of persons in each State, excluding Indians not taxed. But when the right to vote at any election for the choice of electors for President and Vice President of the United States, Representatives in Congress, the Executive and Judicial officers of a State, or the members of the Legislature thereof, is denied to any of the male inhabitants of such State being twenty-one yeas of age, and citizens of the United States, or in any way abridged, except for participation in rebellion, or other crime, the

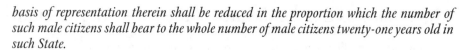

basis of representation therein shall be reduced in the proportion which the number of such male citizens shall bear to the whole number of male citizens twenty-one years old in such State.

Section 3.

No person shall be a Senator or Representative in Congress, or elector of President and Vice President, or hold any office, civil or military, under the United States, or under any State, who, having taken an oath, as a member of Congress, or as an officer of the United States, or as a member of any State legislature, or as an executive or judicial officer of any State, to support the Constitution of the United States, shall have engaged in insurrection or rebellion against the same, or given aid or comfort to the enemies hereof. But Congress may by a vote of two-thirds of each House, remove such disability

Section 4.

The validity of the public debt of the United States, authorized by law, including debts incurred for payment of pensions and bounties for services in suppressing insurrection or rebellion, shall not be questioned. But neither the United States nor any State shall assume or pay any debt or obligation incurred in aid of insurrection or rebellion against the United States, or any claim for the loss or emancipation of any slave; but all such debts, obligations and claims shall be held illegal and void.

Section 5

The Congress shall have power to enforce, by appropriate legislation, the provisions of this article.

1870   The Fifteenth Amendment was ratified. It granted black men the right to vote. Prior to that, only white men had the right to vote. The Fifteenth Amendment followed the example of the original Constitution in that it limited the franchise to men.

THE 15TH AMENDMENT TO THE CONSTITUTION OF THE UNITED STATES

Section 1.

The right of citizens of the United State to vote shall not be denied or abridged by the United States or by any State on account of race, color, or previous condition of servitude.

Section 2.

The Congress shall have power to enforce this article by appropriate legislation.

46. What was the significance of the Fifteenth Amendment?

As stated earlier, former slaves yearned for the opportunity to vote and have a voice in decisions that affected their lives. When the opportunity came after almost 250 years of enslavement, they valued it. Demonstrating a lack of resentment for their previous condition, they worked cooperatively with white men to heal the wounds of the Civil War.

One of the first priorities of the early black Congressmen was to join with Radical Republicans to grant amnesty to Confederates, they passed a Civil Rights bill which banned discrimination in public places and on transportation. Other black elected officials filled responsible positions in the southern Reconstruction government, and helped rewrite state constitutions to improve the quality of life for every citizen in the state. Taxation was made fairer, judicial systems improved, and, of utmost importance to the freedmen who had risked much to learn to read and write, free public education was provided to all children. Many of these laws were ignored or repealed after the Reconstruction Period. Others continued to be valued and upheld.

47. Who was the U.S. President when slavery ended?

Abraham Lincoln wrote and issued the *Emancipation Proclamation* on January 1, 1863. Although it didn't automatically free all slaves, it became a symbol of emancipation, and Lincoln became known as the Great Emancipator.

Andrew Johnson was President of the United States at the time the 13th Amendment went into effect.

PRESIDENT LINCOLN IS CHEERED IN RICHMOND APRIL 4, 1865

Perhaps the outstanding portrait of Abraham Lincoln. It was taken by pioneer photographer T. Painter Pearson shortly after a Lincoln-Douglas debate in 1858, but not found until more than 100 years later. *Courtesy of Richard Crabb.*

The Emancipation Proclamation

By the President of the United States of America

A Proclamation

Whereas on the 22nd day of September, A. D. 1862, a proclamation was issued by the President of the United States, containing, among other things, the following, to wit:

"That on the 1st day of January, A. D. 1863, all persons held as slaves within any State or designated part of a State the people whereof shall then be in rebellion against the United States shall be then, thenceforward, and forever free; and the executive government of the United States, including the military and naval authority thereof, will recognize and maintain the freedom of such persons and will do no act or acts to repress such persons, or any of them, in any efforts they may make for their actual freedom.

"That the executive will on the 1st day of January aforesaid, by proclamation, designate the States

143

and parts of States, if any, in which the people thereof, respectively, shall then be in rebellion against the United States; and the fact that any State or the people thereof shall on that day be in good faith represented in the Congress of the United States by members chosen thereto at elections wherein a majority of the qualified voters of such States shall have participated shall, in the absence of strong countervailing testimony, be deemed conclusive evidence that such State and the people thereof are not then in rebellion against the United States."

Now, therefore, I, Abraham Lincoln, President of the United States, by virtue of the power in me vested as Commander-In-Chief of the Army and Navy of the United States in time of actual armed rebellion against the authority and government of the United States, and as a fit and necessary war measure for suppressing said rebellion, do, on this 1st day of January, A. D. 1863, and in accordance with my purpose so to do, publicly proclaimed for the full period of one hundred days from the first day above mentioned, order and designate as the States and parts of States wherein the people thereof, respectively, are this day in rebellion against the United States the following, to wit:

Arkansas, Texas, Louisiana (except the parishes of St. Bernard, Palquemines, Jefferson, St. John, St. Charles, St. James, Ascension, Assumption, Terrebonne, Lafourche, St. Mary, St. Martin, and Orleans, including the city of New Orleans), Mississippi, Alabama, Florida, Georgia, South Carolina, North Carolina, and Virginia (except the forty-eight counties designated as WestVirginia, and also the counties of Berkeley, Accomac, Northhampton, Elizabeth City, York, Princess Anne, and Norfolk, including the cities of Norfolk and Portsmouth), and which excepted parts are for the present left precisely as if this proclamation were not issued.

And by virtue of the power and for the purpose aforesaid, I do order and declare that all persons held as slaves within said designated States and parts of States are, and henceforward shall be, free; and that the Executive Government of the United States, including the military and naval authorities thereof, will recognize and maintain the freedom of said persons.

And I hereby enjoin upon the people so declared to be free to abstain from all violence, unless in necessary self-defence; and I recommend to them that, in all case when allowed, they labor faithfully for reasonable wages.

And I further declare and make known that such persons of suitable condition will be received into the armed service of the United States to garrison forts, positions, stations, and other places, and to man vessels of all sorts in said service.

And upon this act, sincerely believed to be an act of justice, warranted by the Constitution upon military necessity, I invoke the considerate judgment of mankind and the gracious favor of Almighty God.

48. What were Lincoln's views on slavery?

This statement is often quoted to describe Abraham Lincoln's views. "As I would not be a slave, so I would not be a master. This expresses my idea of democracy—whatever differs from this, to the extent of the difference, is no democracy." Actually Lincoln's opinions and actions changed over time.

Abraham Lincoln argued two slavery-related cases. The first was *Bailey v. Cromwell*. In 1841 the Circuit Court of Tazewell County ruled in favor of the holder of a note given for the services of an indentured servant girl, "Nance." On an appeal, Lincoln obtained a decision from the Supreme Court of Illinois upholding the doctrine that the girl was free under the Ordinance of 1787, and the State Constitution. The note given to the person who claimed to be her owner was void.

In 1847 Lincoln accepted the defense of a Kentucky slaveholder. That case became known as the Matson Slave Case.

It grew out of the following situation. Each spring Robert Matson brought slaves from his Kentucky plantation to farm land and otherwise maintain the property he had bought in Coles County, Illinois. After the harvest each fall, he would return all but one of these enslaved workers to Kentucky.

The worker whom Matson left in Illinois was the overseer, Anthony Bryant. Since Bryant was a permanent resident of Illinois he became technically a free man. He learned to read and became a minister.

Black and white U.S. troops fight and die side by side.
Courtesy of DuSable Museum of African AmericanHistory

Civil War reunion held in Wheaton, Illinois almost 50 years after the war. Note the interracial makeup of the group.

In spring of 1847, a housekeeper named Mary Corbin accompanied Matson. That year his group of enslaved workers included Anthony Bryant's wife and her four children. The two women did not get along well.

Mary Corbin threatened to have Matson send Jane Bryant and her children back to Kentucky to be sold to work in the cotton fields of the Deep South.

The reunited Bryant family was panic stricken. Anthony Bryant rushed to the town of Oakland, Illinois. He enlisted the aid of the local innkeeper, Gideon M. Ashmore, and a young doctor Hiram Rutherford. They both believed that Jane Bryant had become free by coming to Illinois.

Bryant brought his family to the inn. Matson tried to persuade the family to voluntarily return to his farm. When they refused he engaged the legal services of Usher F. Linder.

Linder based his case on Illinois Black Laws. With the help of the justice of peace he had the family arrested and taken from the inn. They were lodged in the Charleston, Illinois jail for 48 days as runaway slaves.

Ashmore and Rutherford sued for a writ of habeas corpus demanding that the family be freed. The case generated so much interest that it attracted people from a distance.

Abraham Lincoln traveled from Springfield to Charleston. He was asked by representatives of both Robert Matson and the Bryant family to be counsel for their clients. He had agreed to represent Matson before he was contacted on behalf of the Bryants.

Two other lawyers, Orlando Ficklin and Charles Constable represented the Bryants. Although he did not refer to the *Bailey v. Cromwell* case, Mr. Ficklin used the very same argument against Mr. Linder and Mr. Lincoln that Lincoln had used some years earlier when he had successfully defended the enslaved woman named Nance. The argument was the Ordinance of 1787 and the Constitution of Illinois prohibited slavery.

Much of the case hinged on whether Jane Bryant and her children had the status of residents of the state or of seasonal workers. The court decision went against Lincoln's client. In fact, Robert Matson reportedly returned to Kentucky without paying Lincoln his fee.

Jane Bryant and her children were released from imprisonment. The judge stated, "...and they shall remain free an discharged from all servitude whatever to any person or persons, henceforth and forever."

The principle established by this case was that in the State of Illinois a person was free regardless of color, and it was illegal to sell a free person.

Many things influenced Abraham Lincoln's views on slavery. As a boy in Kentucky, he was aware of pro-slavery sentiment, however, his father's minister spoke out against slavery. While on board a river steamer from Kentucky in 1841, Lincoln saw a coffle of slaves. Seeing the slaves shackled together with irons, he brooded they were "like so many fish on a trot-line". Years later, in a letter to a Kentucky friend, Lincoln said that sight of coffled slaves "was a constant torment to him."

He opposed the extension of slavery into new territories and objected to the Dred Scott Decision. These views of Lincoln's were opposite those of Illinois Senator Stephen A. Douglas.

Yet, in the Illinois State legislature and in his first year as President, Lincoln expressed the view that neither the President nor the Congress had power under the Constitution to interfere with the institution of slavery in the states where it existed.

During the 1858 Lincoln-Douglas debate in Alton, Lincoln stated his support of the Fugitive Slave Act of 1850. Douglas observed that Lincoln made different statements in different parts of the state. Douglas said that Lincoln was "jet black in the North, a decent mulatto in the center, and almost all white in the South."

In the Ottawa debate Lincoln said, " ... in the right to eat bread, without leave of anybody else, which his own hand earns, he is my equal and the equal of Judge Douglas, and the equal of every living man," but before making these remarks he made a statement that reflected a more conservative view on social equality of the races.

Most of the black people Lincoln had met at the time of the Lincoln-Douglas debates had not had an opportunity to develop their full potential. He had not yet met and conferred with a black man of Frederick Douglass' stature.

Early in the Civil War, when Union generals Fremont and Hunter issued proclamations freeing the slaves of persons supporting the Confederacy, Lincoln overruled them. This bitterly disappointed his abolitionist friends.

Illinois Senator Lyman Trumbull and Massachusetts Senator Charles Sumner spearheaded emancipation legislation in the Thirty-seventh Congress. On June 19, 1862, President Lincoln signed a bill that abolished slavery in the territories. On July 12 Congress passed a confiscation bill which stated that all slaves of disloyal masters were free if they reached Union held territory. This legislation and the increasing numbers of enslaved Africans reaching Union lines was a turning point in the war.

Many abolitionists were hopeful that Lincoln would issue an emancipation proclamation in August. They were again disappointed when he did not.

Anti-slavery delegations and newspaper editors urged Lincoln to proclaim emancipation. In August of 1862, Lincoln wrote the editor of the *New York Tribune* stating his "paramount object in this struggle is to save the Union, and is not either to save or destroy slavery."

By this time though, Lincoln had decided on his course of action. He realized that enslaved Africans were a great potential source of much needed military manpower for the Union side. In early 1863 President Lincoln was faced with a military and manpower crisis. The Union had experienced severe losses, the length of time for which many regiments had enlisted was about to expire, and it would take months before a new conscription act could bring in new recruits. Lincoln believed with repeated Northern victories, France and England would be less likely to recognize the Confederacy. It was at this point that he began to word the document that was to become the *Emancipation Proclamation*.

This man's name was Gordon. Beaten on Christmas day, 1862 he escaped from his master in Mississippi and joined the Union Army in Baton Rouge, LA.

Close to 200,000 African Americans served in the Union Army. Black regiments fought valiantly. Secretary of War Edwin M. Stanton informed President Lincoln that:

"At Milliken's Bend, at Port Hudson, Morris Island and other battle fields, they (black military men) have proved themselves to be among the bravest, performing deeds of daring and shedding their blood with heroism unsurpassed."

Lincoln wrote a letter in September of 1864 telling about the performance of the 150,000 blacks then serving. He declared that they were a crucial "physical force ... keep it, and you can save the Union. Throw it away, and the Union goes with it." Historian Ronald Takaki summarized the results, "In other words, black men in blue made the difference in determining that this 'government of the people, for the people,' did 'not perish from the earth.'"

The death toll among the black soldiers was particularly great. One third of these men who pledged "to fight and die for the Union" were listed as missing or dead. Veterans of the U.S. Colored Troops are buried in towns around the state of Illinois. They include Batavia, Belvidere, Aurora, Lake View, and Lake Forest. In recent years, Captain Ernest A. Griffin learned that his grandfather, Pvt. Charles H. Griffin, had enlisted at Camp Douglas in 1864. The Griffin Funeral Home is located on the western edge of the site of Camp Douglas. Ernest Griffin honored both the Union and Confederate soldiers in Douglas Plaza and exhibited photographs, a map of the camp, and artifacts inside the building.

Ford Douglass was a black man who served with a white regiment. He had lived and worked in Ontario, Canada where he had helped Mary Ann Shadd Cary edit the *Provincial Freedman* newspaper. He was a recruiter for the 29th U.S. Colored Infantry.

FREDERICK DOUGLASS AND HARRIET BEECHER STOWE
The words of Frederick Douglass and Harriet Beecher Stowe made much of the American public aware of the horrors of slavery.

49. Who were some of the abolitionists Lincoln knew?

Congressman Farnsworth of St. Charles, Illinois was elected in 1860. When the war started, he resigned to return home and raise a Calvary. The regiment strongly opposed slavery. Farnsworth states publicly that "if by shedding his blood on the banks of the Potomac, he could secure the liberty of every bondsman in America, that same blood would flow freely." Lincoln referred to this unit as "Farnsworth's Big Abolition Regiment." Reportedly when Lincoln met Harriet Beecher Stowe at the White House, he greeted her as "the little lady who started the Civil War." Her book, *Uncle Tom's Cabin*, had done much to make the larger public aware of the institution of slavery. Having witnessed the sale of slaves in Maysville, Kentucky, she was inspired to write her book after the enactment of the Fugitive Slave Act of 1850. Her home was an UGRR station.

In the autumn of 1864 antislavery lecturer and abolitionist Sojourner Truth visited Lincoln in the White House. Although she was unable to read, she kept up with Lincoln's views and actions by having her grandson read the papers to her. She told Lincoln, "I never heard of you until you were talked of for President." Lincoln smiled and said, "Well I've heard of you years before I even thought of being President. Your name is well known in the Middle West."

At one time, both Lincoln and Allan Pinkerton worked for the Illinois Central Railroad. Lincoln was a lawyer, and Pinkerton, a detective. Their employer was a Mr. McClellan who was to become General McClellan in the Civil War. A photograph of the three men hangs in the Dundee Historical Museum.

HARVEY B. HURD

Judge Samuel Lockwood of Batavia gave the bar exam to both Lincoln and Stephen A. Douglas. At that time, the examination was less formal than the bar exam of today. It's said that as Lincoln and Lockwood strolled around the yard, Lockwood asked legal questions of Lincoln. Lincoln answered satisfactorily and became a lawyer.

Williamson Durley of Hennipen received a letter in which Lincoln explained his views on slavery. Mr. Durley's descendants gave the letter to the Illinois State Historical Society.

In 1862 the Union Leaguers of America organized in Pekin for the sole purpose of preserving the Union. Many more chapters were formed in the North and some in the South. The founders were staunch supporters of the principles that the Union stood for. Many undoubtedly knew Lincoln. Some were possibly involved in the UGRR. After the Civil War, some of the founders of the Union Leaguers of America were also founders of the Union League Club in 1879.

Lincoln knew Chicago abolitionist, Dr. C.V. Dyer. He appointed Dr. Dyer to be a judge on an international slave trade commission. The commission was charged with deciding the fate of captured slave ships and their cargoes of human beings.

Judge Hurd of Northwestern University Law School knew both Lincoln and John Brown. Of his friendship with John Brown, Judge Hurd's grandson, author James Ayars, shared a story that has been passed down in the family: Brown needed a new suit. He would have been recognized if he'd gone to be fitted, so the judge, who was the same size, went to be measured in his place.

READING THE EMANCIPATION PROCLAMATION

50. How is Emancipation Day commemorated?

Black and white people who had worked and sacrificed to end slavery met in churches and meeting halls throughout the Northern states to rejoice and give thanks for the *Emancipation Proclamation*. Large crowds gathered on New Year's Eve anticipating this momentous announcement at midnight on the morning of January 1, 1863.

In Chicago African Americans prayed all night and waited for the dawn—the dawn of freedom. Since then churches everywhere have followed their example and held Night Watch Services.

There was a huge gathering at the Tremont Temple in Boston. Frederick Douglass, William Lloyd Garrison, Charles B. Ray, Harriet Beecher Stowe, and William Wells Brown were among these awaiting the news.

Historian Lerone Bennett, Jr. describes the moment when the announcement came across the telegraph wires, "Suddenly, everyone was on his feet shouting, laughing and weeping." Church bells rang. People joined hands to pray for the New Age the Proclamation ushered in.

Upon careful examination of the document, Frederick Douglass and others that had worked for freedom were disappointed to see that the Emancipation Proclaimation promised freedom to only a portion of the slaves in states that would refuse to abide by President Lincoln's directives, and that it did not abolish slavery in the Border states. However, they were pleased to see that it did include a policy of inviting newly freed men to join the Union army and navy. (Frederick Douglass had encouraged President Lincoln to give black men the opportunity to participate in the fight for freedom.) The freedmen responded in large numbers.

January 1st became a day of annual celebration and solemn commemoration by African Americans, particularly along the Atlantic seacoast. Other dates were celebrated elsewhere.

News of freedom reached different cities and states at different times. And Emancipation Day was celebrated on the anniversary of when the good news arrived.

August 8th is Emancipation Day in the southern Illinois, Paducah, Kentucky area. There are several possible explanations for the selection of an August date:

~ The harvest would be in (most blacks were farmers) and this would be a rest period before time to prepare for winter. The weather was still warm enough to have picnics, revival meetings, and reunions.

~ It is the same date that the slaves of Santo Domingo were freed in the Caribbean.

~ Perhaps it was August before the word reached Paducah.

Black people in Paducah still set aside each August 8th as a very special day. People there have memorial services to commemorate the occasion. Families hold reunions. There's a parade. Big bands entertain during dancing, singing, and the homecoming picnic. In the early days, excursion trains and river steamers brought thousands of people. In 1905, two thousand came by train from Memphis, Tennessee.

An 1882 observance was held in Elizabethtown, Hardin County, Illinois. Local black and white citizens cooperated. The barbecuing began before daybreak. In the afternoon, people all gathered to visit and feast on. A fiddler supplied music, and square dancing was the order of the day. In 1940, a Negro man of more than eighty, reflected about the first celebration he'd attended almost sixty years before. This was a most cherished memory.

Emancipation Day celebrations were held in Metropolis, Brookport, Carbondale, and Elgin in Illinois, and Paducah and McCraken counties in Kentucky.

A guiding spirit in Elizabethtown was Moses Barker; in Carbondale, Frank B. Johnson; and in Elgin, Mrs. Mary Wheeler. In some communities, observances were discontinued after their organizers died.

It was June 19, 1865 before slaves in eastern Texas learned about the *Emancipation Proclamation* and that the Civil War had ended. That was their Freedom Day, which has continued to the present as Juneteenth. It is now celebrated in cities and towns across the United States.

FIRST SUNDAY MORNING AFTER EMANCIPATION
Courtesy of DuSable Museum of African American History

TAKE A LITTLE TOUR

Slavery was the main topic of the famous Lincoln-Douglas Debates. The Debates took place in seven Illinois cities during the summer and autumn of 1858. The statue of Lincoln and Douglas stands in Washington park in Quincy to commemorate the debate in that city. The statue shown on the opposite page was erected in honor of the Quincy Debate. *Courtesy of Judy Taylor and the Quincy Historical Society.*

TAKE A LITTLE TOUR

In 1858, slavery was the foremost issue in the campaign. The candidates for Senate were Abraham Lincoln and Stephen A. Douglas. Douglas was already in the Senate and running for re-election. Lincoln, a lawyer, was running for Douglas's seat. Douglas wished to allow slavery to be extended into Nebraska. Lincoln was against the extension of slavery into new territory. He challenged Douglas to debate this before the people of Illinois.

The debate generated great excitement. Since most present day communications had not been invented these debates provided the public with a rare opportunity to learn what these two candidates stood for. Newspapers were other major sources of information, but reading about the debates wasn't as exciting as going to one.

The first debate was held at Ottawa, August 21, 1858. Lincoln told the cheering crowd,

"There is no reason in the world why the Negro is not entitled to all the natural rights enumerated in the Declaration of Independence, the right to life, liberty, and the pursuit of happiness. I hold that he is as entitled to these as the white man."

Lincoln's statement encouraged his abolitionist friends. Lincoln did not win the Senatorial election that year, but became President in 1860.

Douglas defended his own position. He was elected to serve another term in the Senate. The remaining debates were held in Freeport, Galesburg, Quincy, Alton, Charleston and Jonesboro. People traveled long distances to see and hear the Lincoln-Douglas debates. They came by riverboat, on foot, on wagons, on horseback, trains, and on canal boat drawn by mules walking on towpaths beside the canals. They wanted to witness what is still considered by many historians to be the most significant political events ever to take place. Politicians still use the same debate technique.

Look at the map of the debate locations. The circles show the area within a 100-mile radius of each of those cities.

How long do you imagine it would have taken to go 100 miles back in 1858?

~ On foot?
~ On horseback?
~ On a canalboat pulled by mules walking on the towpath?
~ In a wagon?
It will take you a much shorter time now, won't it? Find the debate location nearest where you live. Take a little tour with your class, your family, or your club group.

You can make the round trip in less than one day!

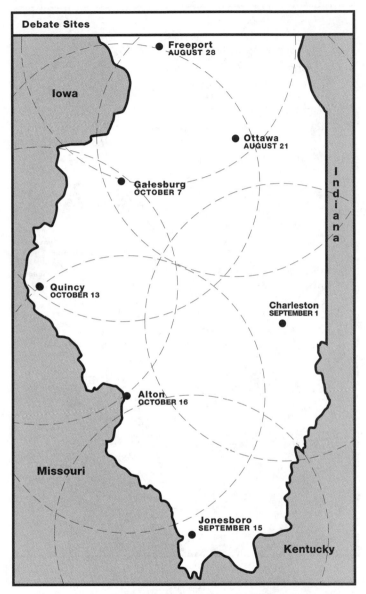

Debate Sites

Iowa

● **Freeport**
AUGUST 28

● **Ottawa**
AUGUST 21

● **Galesburg**
OCTOBER 7

I n d i a n a

● **Quincy**
OCTOBER 13

Charleston
SEPTEMBER 1
●

● **Alton**
OCTOBER 16

Missouri

Jonesboro
SEPTEMBER 15
●

Kentucky

Sites of the Lincoln-Douglas Debates in 1858. Circles show the area
within a 100 mile radius of each site. Which is nearest your home?

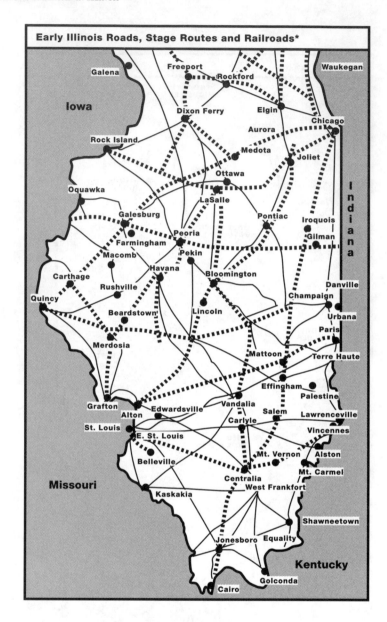

Early Illinois Roads, Stage Routes and Railroads*

LEGEND
— Roads and Stagecoach routes in use in 1837
||| Railroads between 1850 and 1860
* This is a composite map based on information from a number of sources. Positioning of towns and railroads are approximate.

Old map of Illinois with town and county names.

The early roads were Indian trails and buffalo traces. In wet weather they became impassable. Stagecoach and other travel were often bogged down. Later, bumpy plank toll roads were built. You would not have found land travel very comfortable.

There are, however, old trains and boat rides you can still enjoy. In Union, Illinois, you can ride on old trains. Tour boats on the Chicago River go past the location of the DuSables' homestead in Chicago. In Peoria and St. Charles, paddleboats ply the Illinois and Fox rivers in summer. Vacation cruises can be taken on the *River Queen* and *Mississippi Queen,* which can be boarded at Cairo.

Elsewhere in the state, you can follow the Illinois Prairie Path and imagine what plants and animals you would have seen during the time of the Underground Railroad. If you're a hiker (or bicycle rider), you can take the river trail to the nineteen canyons at Starved Rock. In the Mattiessen State Park, you'll see a face possibly carved into the rock by a former slave.

When you drive on the Stevenson Expressway into Chicago, you are on the old Illinois and Michigan Canal right of way. The Illinois State Park across the Illinois River from Marseilles is less than a mile from the historic canal. You can visit the Illinois and Michigan Museum in Lockport.

Near Princeton and Chatham there are covered bridges. Can you imagine riding through one in a farm wagon more than 100 years ago?

Toll ferryboats operate just south of Golden Eagle, at Batchtown and at Hamburg. At Kampsville and Grafton free ferries operate. These are all in the vicinity of Kampsville where archeologists have unearthed remarkable records of early Indian civilization in Illinois.

Style of passenger car most frequently used during the decade from 1840 to 1850. The windows of this vehicle were not raised, but the entire panels were dropped bodily down into the sides of the car.

Something else of interest at Grafton:

~ This area is known for its exceptionally fine stone. The school that Dr. Hamilton built at Otterville is of Grafton stone. The monument dedicated to Dr. Hamilton by freedman George Washington stands in front of the school building.

~ There's a state park nearby.

~ The story of the Piasa bird had its origin here. The great Piasa bird lived in a great cave. It terrorized the Illinois Indians, capturing their children in its talons.

PIASA ROCK

In 1673, Father Jacques Marquette described the painting of this bird on limestone bluffs overlooking the Mississippi. The story of how this bird was killed begins with Outoga, the Illinois chief. He was old and concerned about the harm the bird would bring to his people. He went to the highest bluff and communed with the Great Spirit. He came away with a plan to offer himself as prey. One hundred of his most fearless braves tipped their arrows into the poison of copperhead snakes, and shot the bird. Outoga was gravely injured, but the bird was killed. Through loving care, the chief regained his health. There was much rejoicing. The next morning, Terahionanaka, the arrow maker, painted the Piasa bird on the highest bluff. From then on, whenever Indians went down the river they each fired an arrow at the picture, in tribute to Outaga's great feat.

WHERE WERE THE UNDERGROUND RAILROAD ROUTES?

Most Illinois routes linked cities along the Mississippi River with Chicago, the city that had its beginnings when Jean Baptiste Point DuSable established his trading post where the Chicago River met Lake Michigan. This is how today's big city looked in the 1850's.

Where were the Underground Railroad Routes?

Most often passengers entered Illinois at a point along the Mississippi or Ohio Rivers. They arrived after having:

~ Successfully planned and made an escape from the place where they had been enslaved,

~ Survived all the dangers of being hunted and hungry as they traveled through a slave state,

~ Found their way to a river that bordered Illinois, and,

~ Discovered a method of making a safe crossing.

The following pages show the basic direction of routes through Illinois. They were subject to infinite variations. They often merged sometimes on a regular basis and sometimes on a situation-by-situation basis. When danger was near, routes zigzagged—and on occasion doubled back southward to outwit pursuers.

Here's a glimpse of how the "operations" were carried out:

> In Quincy, the line started at the sawmill of John and William Van Dorn. This sawmill was located on the (Mississippi) riverfront between Delaware and Ohio streets. The Van Dorns were assisted by Dr. David Nelson and Dr. Richard Eells. They took the slaves to St. Mary's Prairie and then on to Petti Johnson in Hancock County. There the slaves were hidden in a large cellar with a trap door. They found refuge in McDonough County with the Allison or Blazer families, perhaps hiding in Billy Allison's attic. Their next stop was with Dobbins in Fulton County. From there they went to Galesburg. Several branches ran north from Galesburg. In 1840, Rev. John Cross surveyed the stations of the "railroad" between Quincy and Chicago. This was essentially the same route later followed by the Chicago Burlington and Quincy Railroad.

Galesburg was a connecting point for many routes. One ran through Smithfield and London Mills; another through Mendon, Carthage, LaHarpe, Roseville; and yet another through Jerseyville, Waverly, Jacksonville, and Springfield. A 1910 article in the *Quincy Journal* indicates that there were routes from Galesburg to Rock Island, Freeport, and Indiana. Wilbur Siebert's book identifies routes leading to Galesburg from Quaker settlements in Iowa and from Galesburg northward toward the Rock River. The map in the back of this book lists specific place names and shows how many of the routes converged. It also shows how many routes led to Chicago.

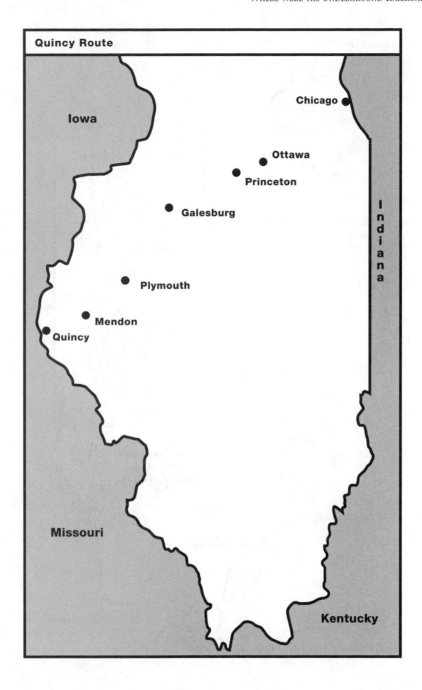

165

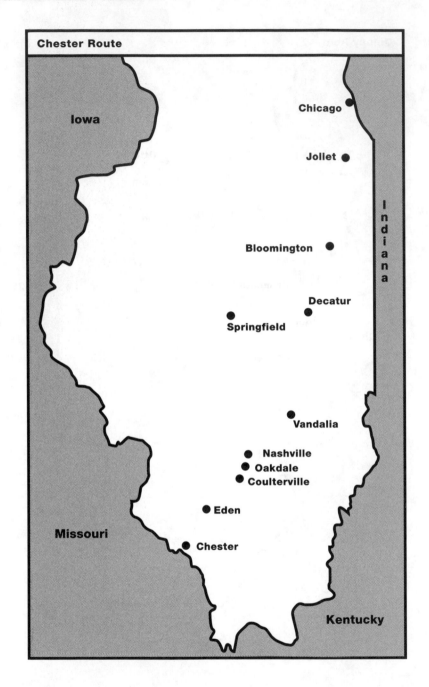

Chester Route

Iowa

Chicago

Jollet

Indiana

Bloomington

Decatur

Springfield

Vandalia

Nashville

Oakdale

Coulterville

Eden

Missouri

Chester

Kentucky

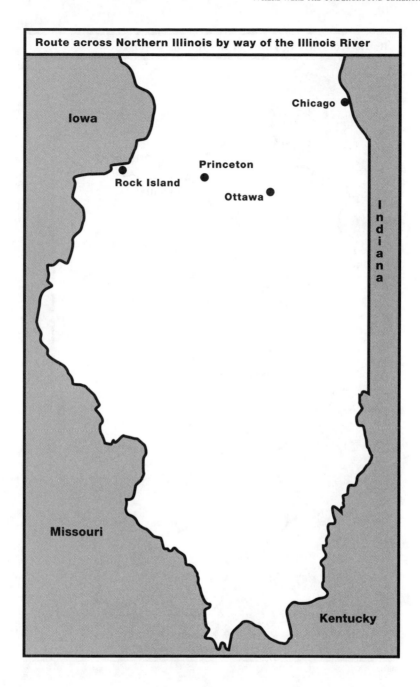

Route across Northern Illinois by way of the Illinois River

Iowa

Chicago

Princeton

Rock Island

Ottawa

Indiana

Missouri

Kentucky

167

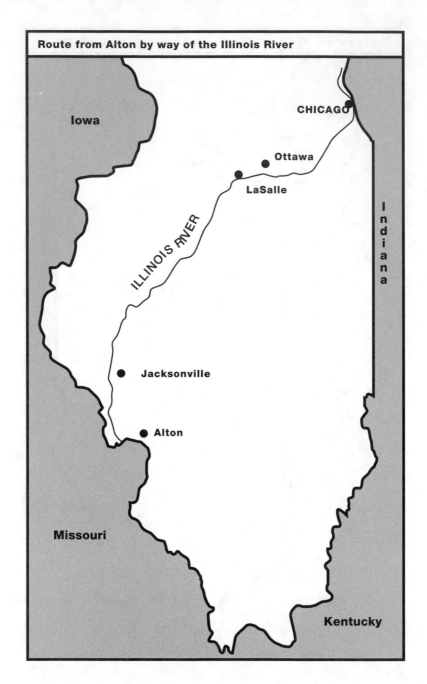

Route from Alton by way of the Illinois River

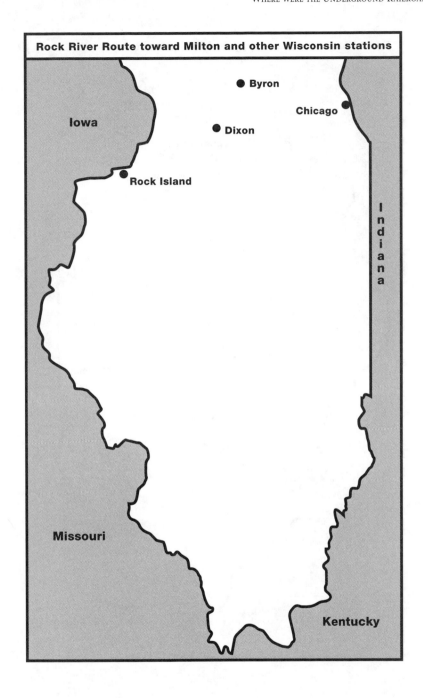

Rock River Route toward Milton and other Wisconsin stations

Iowa

● Byron

● Dixon

Chicago ●

● Rock Island

Indiana

Missouri

Kentucky

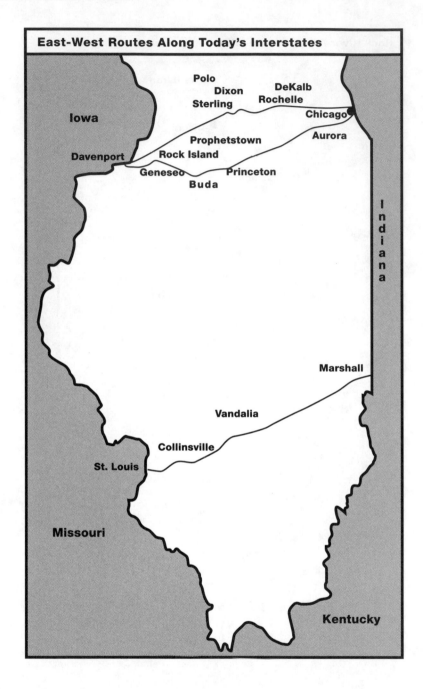

East-West Routes Along Today's Interstates

Iowa

Polo

Dixon

DeKalb

Sterling

Rochelle

Chicago

Davenport

Prophetstown

Aurora

Rock Island

Geneseo

Princeton

Buda

Indiana

Marshall

Vandalia

Collinsville

St. Louis

Missouri

Kentucky

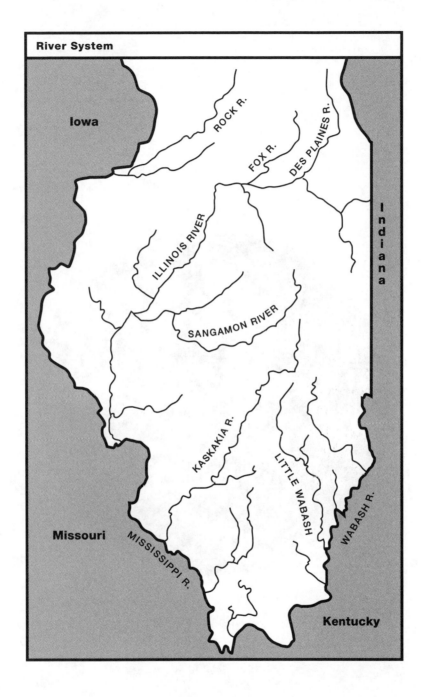

River System

Iowa

ROCK R.

FOX R.

DES PLAINES R.

Indiana

ILLINOIS RIVER

SANGAMON RIVER

KASKAKIA R.

LITTLE WABASH

WABASH R.

Missouri

MISSISSIPPI R.

Kentucky

FIND YOUR CLOSEST STATION

If you are anywhere in Illinois, you're not too far from a place where the Underground Railroad operated. Reportedly Jonathan Blanchard operated an Underground Railroad station in his home pictured here. There may have been stations in your own hometown or in a town nearby. Check with libraries and historical societies then do your research. *Courtesy of Wheaton College Archives*

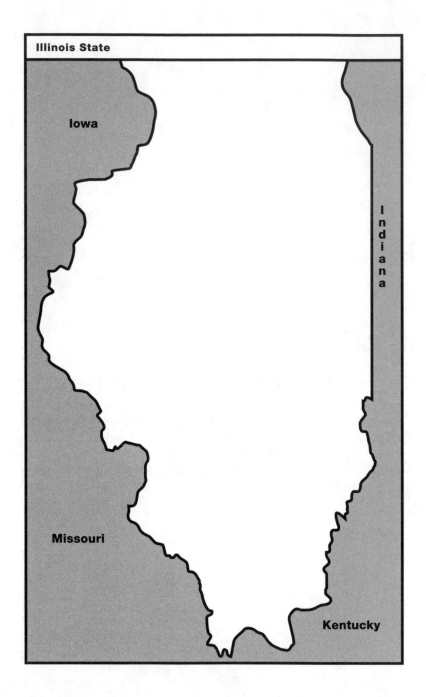

Illinois State

Iowa

Indiana

Missouri

Kentucky

Fill in the Illinois map on the opposite page by writing in as many of the following place names as you can. These locations have been listed in at least one source as having been the site of Underground Railroad or other antislavery activities. Some cities and towns have disappeared or changed names since the 1800's.

Sketch in the Illinois rivers, the I & M canal, Indian trails, early roads, stagecoach and railroad lines. What new insights does this give you?

ADAMS	CARTHAGE	EPPARD'S PLACE
ALBANY	CASS	ERIE
ALEDO	CENTRALIA	EVANSTON
ALTON	CHANDLERVILLE	FARMINGTON
AMBOY	CHATHAM	FLORID
ANDOVER	CHENOA	FRANKFORT STATION
AUGUSTANA	CHERRY GROVE	FREEDON
AURORA	CHESTER	FREEPORT
BATAVIA	CHICAGO	FULTON CITY
BAYNE'S PLACE	CIRCLEVILLE	GAGE'S LAKE
BELLEVILLE	CRETE	GALESBURG
BELVIDERE	CROW CREEK	GARY'S MILL
BERLIN	(in Richland Twsp.)	GENESEE GROVE
BERNADOTTE	CUBA	GENESCO
BIMBAY	DECATUR	GENEVA
BIRGE'S PLACE	DEERFIELD	GENOA
BLOOMINGTON	DEKALB	GLEN ELLYN
BLUE ISLAND	DEVALAN	GLENCOE
BRADFORD	DEVIL'S POINT	GLENWOOD
BRIGHTON	DEWITT'S	GRAND DETOUR
BRIMFIELD	DIXON	GRANVILLE
BROAD OAKS	DOLTON	GREENVILLE
BRUCE	DOVER	HAVANA
BUFFALO GROVE	DOWNERS GROVE	HAZELTON
BYRON	DUNDEE	HENNIPEN
CAIRO	DWIGHT	HILLSDALE
CAMBRIDGE	EAGLE POINT	HINSDALE
CANTON	EDEN	HOLLAND'S PLACE
CARLINVILLE	ELGIN	INDUSTRY TOWNSHIP
CARLYLE	ELKHORN	JACKSONVILLE
CARNAHAN'S	ELMIRA	JERSEYVILLE
CARROLLTON	ELWOOD	JOLIET

KEWANEE

KNOXVILLE

LAHARPE

LAMOILLE

LASALLE

LAWN RIDGE

LEBANON

LEE CENTER

LEXINGTON

LOMBARD

LOVEJOY

LOW MOOR

LOWELL

LYNDON

LYNVILLE

LYONS

MACOMB

MAGNOLIA

MARENGO

MCCORY'S PLACE

MCHENRY

MCLAUGHLIN'S PLACE

MCLEAN

MENDON

MENDOTA

METAMORA

MITER'S PLACE

MOKENA

MOLINE

MONMOUTH

MORRIS

MT. MORRIS

MT. PALATINE

NAPERVILLE

NAUES

NEPOSET

NEW BOSTON

NEW HARMONY

NEW PHILADELPHIA

NEW WINDSOR

NORTHVILLE

OAKDALE

OAKBROOK

ODELL

ONTARIO

ONTARIOVILLE

OREGON

OSCEOLA

OTTAWA

PAW PAW

PAYSON

PEKIN

PEORIA

PERU

PLAINFIELD

PLATTVILLE

PLEASANT HILL

PLYMOUTH

POLO

PONTIAC

PONTOOSUC

PORT BYRON

PRAIRIE CENTER

PRAIRIEVILLE

PRINCETON

PROPHETSTOWN

PROIDENCE

QUINCY

RENO

RICHVIEW

RIVERDALE

RIVERSIDE

ROCHELLE

ROCHESTER

ROCK ISLAND

ROCKFORD

ROCKWOOD

ROUND PRAIRIE

ROCKY FORK

ROSEVILLE

SARDINIA

SENACHWINE

SILVER CREEK

SOMONAUK

SOUTH HOLLAND

SPARTA

SPRINGFIELD

ST. CHARLES

STERLING

STRAWN'S PLACE

SUGAR GROVE

SULLIVAN

TAMAROA

TEMPERANCE HILL

THORN CREEK WOODS

TOWANDA

TREMONT

TROY GROVE

UNION GROVE

URBANA

VANDALIA

VARNA

WARRENVILLE

WASHINGTON

WAUKEGAN

WAVERLY

WAYNE CENTER

WENONA

WETHERSFIELD

WHEATON

WHITE'S PLACE

WILMINGTON

WINCHESTER

WOODFORD

WORDEN

YORKVILLE

AURORA CONGREGATIONAL CHURCH

The historic Aurora Congregational Church building became an iron works before it was eventually demolished. Within its walls courageous antislavery speakers discussed the issues of the day including such nationally known orators as Frederick Douglass. On one such visit Douglass won General John Farnsworth over to the abolitionist cause. *Courtesy of the Aurora Historical Society*

BERNADOTTE COVERED BRIDGE

As much constant danger as they were in, and as desperately as they wanted freedom, UGRR passengers and conductors tried to avoid violence. They sought to outwit, rather than hurt, their pursuers. An event that took place here, on the old Bernadotte bridge, is one of the few instances in Illinois UGRR records where a slave hunter was killed in the attempt to capture a freedom seeking slave. *Courtesy of Mr. Curtis Strode*

LUCIUS READ HOUSE

The Lucius Read home is now the Byron Museum of History. Lucius Read, Rev. Gammell, and Jared Sanford transported slaves who had traveled from Sugar Grove (Lee County) to Buffalo Grove near Polo. Other stops en route to Chicago were Lynnville, Rochelle, and DeKalb County. The last load of thirteen passengers was brought to Read's by horse drawn bobsled late in 1862. *Courtesy of Byron Museum of History*

HENRY BERRY HOUSE

Here on a hilltop in Cuba, Illinois, Henry Berry operated an Underground Railroad station. He was not the only member of his family who was involved in this work. His brother, Thomas operated another station near Table Grove. *Courtesy of Virginia Ewing*

STAIRWAY IN THE BERRY HOUSE

This stairway led to a secret room-behind-a-room hiding place in the Henry Berry house. Passengers who stopped at this house might also travel through Industry or Vermont to Table Grove, Ipava or Bernadotte, Springfield, Boynton's near Fiatt, Canton, and an Indian trail in Orion Township, via London Mills or Delany, Harlan Barn, Galesburg. *Courtesy of Virginia Ewing*

STONE HOUSE IN DIXON FERRY

It is believed that this stone house near the Dixon Ferry was part of the Underground Railroad. It is across the Rock River from Grand DeTour. It was in an area called "the Kingdom." *Courtesy of the William Shaws*

STAGECOACH INN IN CHATHAM

This is the stagecoach inn between Waverly and Springfield. It is believed to have been an Underground Railroad station. *Courtesy of Opal A. Lee*

THE GRAUE MILL

If you go down to the basement of the Graue Mill and Museum in Oak Brook, you will find a plaque that tells how freedom seekers took many paths to reach it. Photos, films, historic documents, and an interpreter tell the story of the UGRR in general and of this specific site. Blacksmith John Coe, was the local conductor and two nearby businesses were reportedly Underground Railroad stations.

JESSE KELLOGG HOUSE

The home of Deacon Jesse Kellogg in Sycamore was an Underground Railroad station. A little room connected to an outside door by a narrow hall, and a secret dugout under a corncrib were two hiding places at this station. Deacon Kellogg was a prominent member of the Congregational church and community. *Courtesy of the Joiner History Room, DeKalb, Illinois*

DUNDEE STAGECOACH INN

The "Old Dundee House Hotel" was a stagecoach stop on the Frink and Walker route between Galena and Lake Michigan. It was also a safe house on the Underground Railroad. Slaves were hidden in a basement room with ventilation pipes leading in from the outside. The operator of this station was James Wardle, a foreman at the Allan Pinkerton cooper shop. *Courtesy of Dick DeVoss.*

OLD POLO HOME

In 1938, this Polo home, once a station of the underground railroad was torn down to make room for a filling station. The house was built in the 1850's by Samuel and Elizabeth Waterbury, who came form New York state and settled in Eagle Point towhship, then a part of Buffalo township, Ogle county. The cellar was divided into several sections with ceiling and sides plastered and whitewashed. A tunnel about three feet high led from the cellar to a barn.

PIERCE DOWNER HOUSE

Pierce Downer, for whom the village of Downers Grove is named, operated an Underground Railroad station here in his home. He built quite near Ogden Avenue which was a major thoroughfare for stagecoach and wagon traffic between southwestern Illinois and Chicago. *Courtesy of Arthur and Judith Frigo*

179

THOMAS FILER HOUSE

The Thomas Filer house, which stood at Crescent Boulevard and the east branch of the DuPage River in Glen Ellyn, had a tunnel which ran from the house to the barn. The walls were insulated with slew grass to muffle any sound. The UGRR next stop was about a mile east at Sheldon Peck's house in Lombard. *Courtesy the Glen Ellyn Historical Society*

LUTHER BIRGE HOUSE

Sometimes the placement of a house made it perfect for UGRR operations. This home was situated near a stream, a railroad, a road, and a wooded area. Reportedly it also had a tunnel opening in the basement and a ladder leading to the first floor. It was the home of Deacon Luther Birge in Farmington. *Courtesy of William DiVoice*

EVERETT HOUSE

This house once stood at 801 N. Twelfth in Quincy. It was thought to have had a tunnel running from its sub-basement to the Mississippi River. It had winding, short stairways with rooms on every level. Cubbyholes, hidden rooms, and trap doors were believed to have been used as UGRR hiding places. *Drawing by Dorothy Kennard*

MOTHER RUDD HOUSE

The Mother Rudd Home Museum served as a tavern and stagecoach stop. Built in the 1850's it was restored by the Village of Gurnee. Its barn was the hiding place used by escaping slaves. Although that structure no longer stands, its foundation still remains visible. *Courtesy Warren Township Historical Society of Gurnee, Illinois*

ASA TALCOTT HOUSE
The Asa Talcott house in Jacksonville is now the Barton W. Stone Christian Home. Talcott may have hidden freedom seekers in the front of this house built in the 1830's. He was one of the white abolitionists with whom black UGRR conductor, Ben Henderson, worked. Joseph and Horace Bancroff, J.W. Lathrop, and T.E. Eames were other workers. *Courtesy of Barton W. Stone Christian Home*

PUTNAM COUNTY CAVE
This cave on the banks of the Illinois River at Hennipan is rumored to have been the exit to an escape tunnel from the Putnam County Court House. A cave in Matthiesson State Park may have been occupied for years for someone sculpted an African face there around 1840. It and another nearby sculpture may have been used for communication between UGRR passengers and agents.

DAMON G. TUNNICLIFF HOUSE
Judge Damon G. Tunnicliff of Macomb built this Greek Revival home in the 1850's. The trap door, which led to an UGRR hiding place, still exists. Originally it was part of a brick summer kitchen. Judge Tunnicliff was a Lincoln supporter and undoubtedly entertained Lincoln in his home. At one time the west wing of the house was used as the McDonough County Court House. *Courtesy of Charles II. Weston*

GARFIELD FARM
This century old St. Charles building was purchased by the State of Illinois from private owners and was used as a farm cottage at the Illinois State Training School. It is reputed to have been a station on the UGRR. The building was razed in the 1940's. The present site serves the institution as a trailer park for employees. *Courtesty of Samuel Sublett*

181

| LAKE VIEW MONUMENT | PORT BYRON CONGREGATIONAL CHURCH |

LAKE VIEW MONUMENT

This monument honors the pioneer settlers and residents who lived in the Lake View (Carrier Mills) community between 1820-1920. The founding family was that of Zachariah and Lydia Taborn from Wake County, NC. The Taborn land grant was the basis of this all black community in Saline County. The front of the monument dedicated May 24, 1992, lists names of the pioneer families: Taborn, Allen, Blackwell, Cole, Evans, and Mitchell. Servicemen including Civil War veterans David Cole and Oliver Russell are listed on the back. Families who came between 1855-1920 are listed on either side. Farming and coal mining were the main occupations. *Courtesy Lina Witherspoon and Lucille Mooreland*

PORT BYRON CONGREGATIONAL CHURCH

During the UGRR era, Port Byron, was situated at the top of the Mississippi River rapids. It was known for its lumber mills. The stagecoach was ferried across the river here This was an ideal place for enslaved cargo handlers to jump ship when northbound steamboats stopped for cordwood. Members of the Port Byron Congregational Church opposed slavery. Although the church building was not an UGRR station, the old Methodist Church and two local homes were. One home near the river, is a private home. The other, the Olde Brick House is a bed and breakfast. At one point it was owned by industrialist Cyrus McCormick whose housekeeper reportedly operated an UGRR station in McCormick's absence. The next occupant was an abolitionist named Dr. "Billy" Lyford. *Courtesy of Marion Dugan*

ELIJAH DRESSER BARN

According to the Ogle County Bicentennial history, on Independence Day, 1848, appropriate to the date, a wagon containing three men and two women arrived in Lynnville, Ogle County. The Underground Railroad passengers were welcomed, fed, and guided to the next stop on their escape route.

TERWILLIGER HOUSE

Between Crystal Lake and McHenry, Samuel Terwilliger of Nuda Township, McHenry County, built this Greek Revival house on 160 acres he received from the government for serving in the militia. The house is listed on the National Register of Historic Places. It is believed that Terwillinger used the cupola as a lookout he was assisting UGRR passengers.

CHARLES HIBBARD

Charles Hibbard, one of Marengo's first storekeepers and nurserymen, built the Cupola House in 1846. It was long rumored to be an UGRR station. Legend has it that a lantern was placed in the window of the cupola when it was safe to stop there. In 1968 Francis Muzzy was rolling the front lawn and the roller fell through the ceililng of a secret room which could be entered from a concealed entrance near the front steps. The Cupola House was just down the street from the home of black Civil War nurse, Rachel Harris. *Courtesy the McHenry County Historical Society*

JUDSON GREEN HOUSE

Judson Green, a deacon in the Baptist church in Plainfield, operated a blacksmith shop next to his Greek Revival style home. There is reason to believe that he sheltered slaves at both locations. *Courtesy of Bonnie D. Latter*

SHELDON PECK HOUSE

This is the first house built in Lombard. It was built by artist, Sheldon Peck, and used as an UGRR station. Peck had studios in St. Louis and Chicago. He painted portraits of farm couples as he traveled between studios. On return trips from St. Louis, he transported enslaved Africans to his home and on to the Tremont House Hotel in Chicago

STONE BARN

If the stones in this barn could talk what do you think they would tell of the Underground Railroad operations in the Triumph-Mendota area?

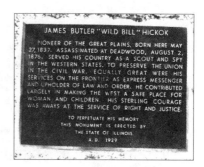

THE WILD BILL HICOCK PLAQUE

Wild Bill Hicock's father was an Underground Railroad conductor in Troy Grove. It was while helping his father in this work, that Wild Bill, who became a legend in the West, learned to handle horses. According to one account, shallow holes were dug under the floors of the Hicock house and Green Mountain Tavern to provide safe hiding places for UGRR passengers.

184

QUINN CHAPEL AFRICAN METHODIST EPIS-COPAL CHURCH

When Quinn Chapel was located in downtown Chicago where the Monadnock Building now stands, it was a very active Underground Railroad station. Many of its operators were men and women who had personally experienced enslavement. *Courtesy of Quinn Chapel A.M.E. Church*

STARVED ROCK MARKER

The marker in the yard of a large, four story stone building near Starved Rock. Reportedly it had an upstairs ballroom. According to the hard-to-read sign the structure was built as a hotel on the Peoria-Chicago stagecoach route, and Abraham Lincoln stayed there when he was a Springfield lawyer trying cases in Ottawa. The building was also believed to have been an Underground Railroad station..

JOHN FAIRBANK HOUSE

Like many houses of its period there is a stone basement in the John Fairbank house in Warrenville. The unusual feature of this basement is that one large stone had no mortar around it, and when removed led to an underground tunnel and cave in which archeologists found a number of items including bones of cooked meat and a stone marble of African or Native American origin. *Courtesy H.F. Hardy*

E. C. GUILD RESIDENCE

Dr. and Mrs. E.C. Guild hid slaves in their home in Wayne Center. A grandson, Judge William Guild, recalled seeing a journal in which his grandparents had made entries which mentioned their Underground Railroad activities. The next stop on this route was in Ontarioville (now named Hanover Park). *Courtesy of Judge William Guild*

185

HALFWAY HOUSE INN NEAR VARNA

This is the halfway house midway between Springfield and Chicago. It was built by Livingston Roberts. His home was said to be an Underground Railroad stop in the Varna area. Reportedly Lincoln stayed here many times.

STONE HOUSE

This stone house in back of the Halfway House predates the brick inn. It, and later, the Halfway House were on a road heavily trafficked by farmers taking their produce to markets in Chicago.

WHEATON COLLEGE

The original section of Blanchard Hall was an UGRR station. In the early days when the school was Illinois Institute, Professor Lucius Matlock forwarded UGRR passsengers to Thomas Filer in Glen Ellyn. Later when it was renamed Wheaton College, President Jonathan Blanchard continued UGRR operations. Former student Ezra Cook said "the fugitive slave law was nullified by a Higher Law."

TANNER BARN

In recent years, lightning struck the Tanner barn east of Byron. The stone walls—which had tunnels and caves built into them—were razed. This barn and the Lucius Read house in Byron are believed to have had features suggesting a possible network of tunnels beneath the city that linked them with another stone barn east of Byron. All three sites are near the Rock River.

PAW PAW POST OFFICE

This building was a stagecoach stop in Naperville. It has an inconspicuous trapdoor cut into in the floor of the parlor. It is possible that it, like the Castle Inn, the Hoffman House, and the stagecoach stops in Chatham and New Lenox, served as an Underground Railroad stop. It has been moved to Naper Settlement.

STEPHEN TOWNSEND HOUSE

This picture of the Stephen Townsend house appeared in the 1871 plat book. Stephen Townsend was a politically active abolitionist. Townsend, David West, Jesse Kellogg, William Nickerson, Curtis Smith, Dr. Page, and Judge Jesse Rose were all involved in Underground Railroad operations in DeKalb County.

HISTORIC BUREAU COUNTY HOUSE

This house on the "Old Chicago Road " in northeast Bureau County near LaMoille is not far from the Owen Lovejoy house, the best known of the Underground Railroad stations in the county. It, and the home of the brother of William Jennings Bryan, are believed to have been an Underground Railroad stations in and around Princeton. *Courtesy of Curtis Marcum.*

THE BLODGETT HOME

The Israel and Avis Blodgett home is now the location of the Downers Grove Historical Museum. This building was constructed on the foundation of Blodgett's earlier home. The earlier home which was relocated, was the site of a reunion of a husband and wife who had feared they had been permanently separated by the actions of a slaveholder.

TALL GRASSES

Natural hiding places like tall grasses, dense forests, ravines and caves were widely used by freedom seeking Underground Railroad passengers. Sometimes they were the only hiding places used by passengers. Sometimes passengers hid in cornfields, barns, or houses in addition to natural landscapes.

SCHRAM HOUSE

In 1850 John M. Schram, the operator of a large flour mill, built this stone house south of Pontoosuc on a hillside overlooking the Mississippi River. Three rooms built into the hill were called the "side basement." There were many opportunities for UGRR passengers reach and stop here. They might even have found transportation with customers who came from a distance and camped while waiting to have their grain ground. *Courtesy of Kim Weaver*

BEN HENDERSON'S GRAVE

Ben Henderson is buried in Jacksonville East Cemetery. He worked at Illinois College with Edward Beecher, associate of Elijah Lovejoy and brother of author Harriet Beecher Stowe. His grave is very near that of Rev. Andrew Jackson, pastor of Mount Emory Baptist Church which was founded in 1837 by seven former slaves. *Courtesy of Jack Barwick, A Place in Time*

OVERTON LOG CABIN

The building at the top center section of this photo is in the Spoon River Valley near Bernadotte. It is about where the Francis Overton log cabin stood. The cabin was an Underground Railroad station.

THEBES COURT HOUSE

Dred Scott, the enslaved black man who sued for his freedom after having been brought into Illinois, was held overnight in the Thebes Court House, not because he had done anything wrong, but because of the laws which were in effect at the time. This historic building still stands. Thebes is twenty miles north of Cairo. *Courtesy of Thebes Historical Society*

NEW BETHEL A. M. E. CHURCH

(FORMERLY THE ROCKY FORK A.M.E. CHURCH)

Erastus Green and George Hindman were founders of this historic pre-Civil War church. They are buried in the old graveyard beside this more recent church building. It is located in the Alton area where many UGRR passengers came ashore after escaping from slavery in Missouri. *Courtesy of New Bethel A.M.E. Church*

UNDERGROUND CHAMBERS/THE HALLIDAY HOTEL

The Halliday was an elegant Cairo hotel. During the Civil War General Grant's room overlooked the confluence of the Mississippi and Ohio rivers. Dungeon-like chambers beneath the Ohio River levee and near the Illinois Central railroad tracks were rumored to have been used as UGRR hiding places as well as for storage. In 1998 these chambers were excavated. The tunnel which connects the chambers may have led to the basement of the hotel. *Courtesy of Jim West.*

LIBERTY ISLAND

Before the Mississippi River changed its course, there was an island between the Allan Plantation in Missouri and a town called Liberty (now Rockwood) Illinois. In fall, when the water was low, UGRR passengers could walk across. At other times a person could ride across on horseback. A black man named George was the UGRR agent at the Allan Plantation. Ezekiel Barber, a white shoe cobbler in Rockwood took UGRR passengers whom George had sent, to a cave near the Harvey Clendin Farm in Chester. From there passengers hid at a tannery and/or the A.A. Burlingame house in Sparta.

This list is incomplete. During the years of research,
new locations were learned of continuously.

If you know of an UGRR site, check it out and contact

Newman Educational Publishing Company

P.O. Box 461

Glen Ellyn, IL 60138

www.UGRR-Illinois.com

Take a Walk
in Their Shoes

Imagine yourself living in the 1800's. Imagine the danger. And imagine the exhilarating feeling you'd get from each thing you did to outwit slavery.

Here are suggestions that groups and/or individuals can follow to vicariously relive those adventurous days. As you read this book, you'll think of other creative ways to "walk in the shoes" of UGRR participants. *Silhouette by Jean Kuhn.*

Science

Make terrariums:

Show a slave family escaping in this time of year. Change it to show other seasons by adding little artificial spring or summer flowers, snow, or leaves in autumn.

Or divide into four groups and let each group depict a season.

Make a cave by pressing rocks into the soil. Put in little plants to look like sheltering trees.

Make a miniature prairie with grasses to almost hide a horse and rider(s).

Make a terrarium showing extinct plants and animals (use models) that provided an ecological balance.

* * *

SLAVES ESCAPING BY BOAT (HARPERS WEEKLY, APR. 9, 1864)

Take two pie pans. Put 2" of water in each and partially freeze them. Put the pans side by side on a table. With your right hand, make your fingers move as if they are "walking" on the ice. Slide the palm of your left hand on the other pan of ice. Press just as hard with your left hand as you did with your right. Which ice breaks most easily? When the ice was thin slaves sometimes slithered across on their stomachs. This showed their understanding of the scientific principle.

* * *

Check to find out how scientists today can test to see how deep or dangerous a river or other body of water is. How do you suppose slaves tested?

* * *

Early tomorrow morning you can see the sun in the East. Which of your shoulders would be toward the East, when you face North? Knowing this, escaping slaves had a natural compass.

* * *

Next time you see moss on a tree, notice which side it's on. Can you find out why moss grows on the north side? Had you ever noticed this before?

* * *

It was safest to escape on a moonless night. How can you predict a moonless night? Can you figure out a way to predict this without using a calendar?

* * *

Look at the night sky. Do you see the Little Dipper? Which star is the North Star? It's almost directly above the North Pole. It served as a welcome guide for UGRR passengers. A dictionary or encyclopedia will have more about the constellations.

* * *

In the Lovejoy home in Princeton a moveable wall led from a bedroom to a secret hiding place in a closet on the other side of that wall. Can you make a model of a room with a moveable wall?

* * *

Write to the Morton Arboretum in Lisle, Illinois for information on how to help restore some of the Illinois prairie. They have literature that tells how to care for seeds, and how to grow some plants in your backyard.

* * *

Look up information about animals that are extinct. Museums such as the Field Museum in Chicago have skeletons or models of these animals. There is at least one buffalo herd in the state. Can you find out where it is?

Since most rivers flow south, UGRR passengers knew that they should walk in the opposite direction to go north.

The sloped sides and leafy foliage of ravines provided natural, protecting pathways. Just think how welcome a ravine would be if you'd travelled miles across the prairie without seeing a sheltering tree! Do you think you might find berry bushes or other edible plants in such a place?

Interpretive Reading

Compare what the following people wrote about slavery. All had very deep anti-slavery feelings. Notice their different ways of expressing themselves.

Phyllis Wheatley
William Wadsworth Longfellow
Frances Ellen Watkins Harper
William Lloyd Garrison
Sojourner Truth
John Greenleaf Whittier
Mary Brown Davis
Martin Delany

Angelina Grimke
Elijah Lovejoy
Mary Ann Shadd
Benjamin Lundy
Harriet Tubman
Frederick Douglass
Lucretia Mott
David Walker

What motivated these people to speak out? Read their works just as you think they might have.

* * *

A husband and father tells a journalist of his family's experience in and escape from slavery.

Imagine being a UGRR passenger who has been hidden on a Chicago bound Illinois Central train by B.G. Root in Tamaroa or George L. Burroughs in Cairo. You have somehow managed to learn how to write while you were enslaved, and have a pencil and paper tucked in with your belongings. Jot down your plans you have for your future in freedom.

Here are some little rhymes.

Read them and sway in a rhythmic way. Try doing choral speaking in a group. The whole group or individuals can pantomime the poems as they're recited. For example, when the lines say "You look and you listen," you could look all around in an exaggerated way and hold your hand up to your ear. When they say "Get up and go," you can pretend to tiptoe toward the window.

Pretend your family is planning
to escape from slavery.

You look and you listen
When you want to be free
You never know when
Escape will be.

You strain and you struggle
And finally get
To a wide, wide river
Don't fear getting wet,

You walk and you shiver
And you hide by day
Follow the North Star
To find your way.

You're happy and pleased
If you can find
A helping hand
And an open mind.

You hear that Canada
Is cold but free
So that's the place
Where you want to be.

Pretend your parents are black or white abolitionists.

You've gone to bed
The house is still
You hear a knock
At the windowsill.

Your dad or mom
Get up and go
They whisper "Friend"
By the window.

They open the door
And say, "Come in"
A shivering black family
Enters then.

Your parents say
"Stay here tonight"
We'll stand guard
So you can sleep tight.

You go to sleep —
Can't wait for day
You're hoping that
The kids can play.

The kids tell you.
About slavery
Wow! You find out
Why they want to be free.

Writing Activities

Pretend you escaped. Write a letter to initiate action to try to free the rest of your family.

* * *

Pretend you have some relatives who are slaveholders. Write them a letter telling why you have a different point of view.

* * *

In a poem, describe how it feels to be free, or how it feels to help someone make a daring escape.

* * *

Pretend you're an abolitionist. Write a skit in which you and your spouse discuss whether to tell your children of your UGRR activities. How will you tell them so they'll keep it a secret? Write a second skit. Have someone pretend to be your children asking questions about the UGRR.

* * *

It's dangerous but you must inform another UGRR agent that slave catchers are in the area. You want passengers to bypass his house and for him to let the next agent know the passengers will arrive early. How would you do this?

* * *

Write a coded newspaper advertisement. Then compare your ad with the political cartoon which appeared in the *Western Citizen.*

Enslaved Africans feeding escaping Union prisoners of war in their enslaver's barn. Pretend you are one of the soldiers. In your journal tell how you felt when you received this hospitality.

Pretend to be an abolitionist doing a highly dangerous thing: Write a diary or journal in which you describe your UGRR activities. William Still hid his in a Philadelphia cemetery. Where could you hide yours?

* * *

Pretend to be a slave who had tried to learn to write by copying sentences from the Bible. You've heard that other slaves have had their fingers cut-off for trying to write, yet you feel that writing is very important and you're determined to learn how. You could trace letters in the earth with your fingers or a twig then "erase" them by rubbing them with your hand, or you could dip your fingers in water, write words or letters on a surface that will dry off quickly.

* * *

Pretend you're writing an article for Benjamin Lundy's paper or the *Western Citizen*. How did the writing style in the old papers differ from today's style?

* * *

Find out what you can about printing processes today. Compare them with how Elijah Lovejoy or other printers set type in the 1800's.

* * *

Pretend this is 1850 and you are a reporter for one of the Chicago papers that is against the Fugitive Slave Act. How would you report the meeting of the Chicago Common Council where Senator Stephen A. Douglas explained his support of it and black and white residents voiced their objections?

Negro street patrols defy fugitive slave law at Haymarket Square
Courtesy of DuSable Museum of African American History

201

FRANCIS ELLEN WATKINS HARPER

Letter to John Brown's Wife

FARMER CENTRE, OHIO, Nov. 14th.

MY DEAR MADAM:—In an hour like this the common words of sympathy may seem like idle words, and yet I want to say something to you, the noble wife of the hero of the nineteenth century. Belonging to the race your dear husband reached forth his hand to assist, I need not tell you that my sympathies are with you. I thank you for the brave words you have spoken. A republic that produces such a wife and mother may hope for better days. Our heart may grow more hopeful for humanity when it sees the sublime sacrifice it is about to receive from his hands. Not in vain has your dear husband periled all, if the martyrdom of one hero is worth more than the life of a million cowards. From the prison comes forth a shout of triumph over that power whose ethics are robbery of the feeble and oppression of the weak, the trophies of whose chivalry are a plundered cradle and a scourged and bleeding woman. Dear sister, I thank you for the brave and noble words that you have spoken. Enclosed I send you a few dollars as a token of my gratitude, reverence and love.

Yours respectfully,   FRANCES ELLEN WATKINS.

Post Office address: care of William Still, 107 Fifth St., Philadelphia, Penn.

May God, our own God, sustain you in the hour of trial. If there is one thing on earth I can do for you or yours, let me be apprized. I am at your service.

* Mrs. Harper passed two weeks with Mrs. Brown at the house of the writer while she was awaiting the execution of her husband, and sympathized with her most deeply.

Drama

SITUATION 1:

Pretend to be a fugitive slave or, a free black or white abolitionist.
You're under pressure. For example, there are slave catchers in the area, or the news has leaked out that you are helping slaves escape.
Record your feelings, your conversations, or fears.

SITUATION 2:

Read the story of Henry "Box" Brown.
How do you think he and Smith worked out their scheme?
Role-play their conversations.
Can you provide sound effects for when Smith is nailing the crate? And for the ship caught in the storm?
Form a welcoming committee in Philadelphia. Will you need special lighting as members of the Vigilance Committee carefully pry the crate open? Show your amazement when Brown springs out of the box, introduces himself, and shakes hands with all the committee members. Demonstrate how the committee rejoices by singing his favorite hymn.

SITUATION 3:

Pretend you're an abolitionist. You want a house built with secret rooms. How can you find a carpenter who won't tell of your UGRR activities?

SITUATION 4:

Often someone in a group became ill or injured while making an escape.
The person might be carried by others in the party. If he or she could walk with assistance, he or she might use a walking stick. Sick or injured UGRR passengers would sometimes insist on being left behind rather than risk the safety of the entire group. Pretend you are a member of the group. What would you do if you were the injured person? If the injured person was your grandmother?
Other situations throughout the book will suggest your dramatic interpretations. If you film it, you will enjoy seeing yourself on film.

Music

Pretend you're being transported in a farm wagon or driving one. Or pretend you have hidden inside a boxcar on a fast moving freight train. You notice that the wheels make a rhythmic sound. Make up words to fit the rhythmic sound. Choose a theme like "no more slavery".

Pretend you're hiding in the woods waiting for night. Stand or sit in one place but move the rest of your body to try to keep warm.

Learn spirituals that were used to signal escape plans, "Get on Board Little Children," "Wade in the Water" and "Steal Away." Learn the song "Follow the Drinking Gourd". Decode their hidden meanings.

Compose a simple melody in a minor key (spirituals were written in minor key.) Write words that you feel are appropriate to go with your melody.

Learn songs that were sung in the churches of the abolitionists from New York and New England.

Though these would have been too large to be carried during an escape, today you can make African instruments as:

~ Drums
~ Rattles (made from dried gourds)
~ Xylophones, etc.
Plan background music for skits, films or interpretive readings.

Pretend the UGRR is still operating plan some catchy TV commercials advertising it.

A train entering the Chicago railway station of the Illinois Central and Michigan Central roads. Date, 1857.

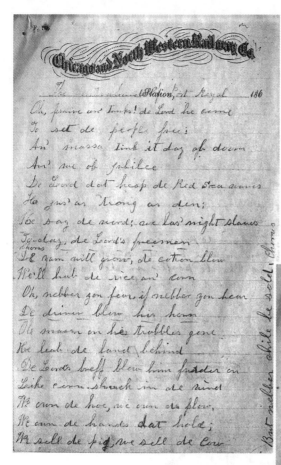

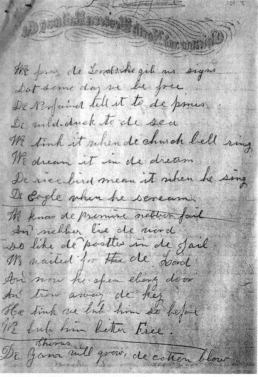

This "Contraband Song" was found in a sale of railroad memorabilia. *Courtesy of Keith Letsche.*

205

Social Studies

Pretend you're at an anti-slavery society meeting. Some members are abolitionists who feel slavery must be ended immediately. Others are abolitionists who feel there must be a period of preparation (in the South and North) for ending slavery. Some are for freeing slaves if they can be colonized in Liberia or Sierra Leone. Some are against the cruelties of slavery, but don't want to become actively involved with the UGRR. Another member feels slaveholders have an unfair economic advantage and he opposes slavery for this reason. Still another is an immigrant who has come to this country to avoid persecution and will feel uncomfortable as long as any of his fellowmen are in bondage. A former slave has come to the meeting to report on the Canadian settlement and schools. Think what points of view would be presented by each person during the meeting. Re-enact about 10 minutes of the meeting.

* * *

Plan an escape in winter, and one in summer based on weather conditions in your own home-town. What basic necessities would you need anytime of year? What would be the advantages or disadvantages of each season?

* * *

Pretend that you belong to a church that is soul-searching about slavery. Many members feel slavery is sacrilegious. There are, however, some pro-slavery members—some of whom make large financial contributions. How would you solve this dilemma?

Examples of devices used to shackle freedom seekers.
Courtesy of the Bob Jacobsen Museum.

If you have a camera, take pictures of natural hiding places nearby. How do you think they were used?

* * *

Pretend you are a farmer, a miller, an innkeeper, a barber, a deck hand, a cooper or a printer. How can you most effectively help abolitionist cause?

* * *

Use an opaque projector to greatly enlarge the UGRR map (or make a large freehand drawing). Work in groups to:

~ write in names of cities. These names can be color-coded to designated cities on different routes, cities that have county seats, and (after doing some personal research) cities with Quaker, Presbyterian, African Methodist, Congregationalist or Covenant churches.
~ draw in rivers with blue marking pen,
~ add roads, railroads, and ferry boat crossings,
~ make little 3-dimensional houses, bluffs, and caves along the rivers,
~ make human figures and farm wagons to move from place to place on map,
~ figure out a scale to show how many miles are represented in an inch on the map,
~ pretend to "walk" the (map) route from Chester, Alton, Rock Island or Quincy.

Use an overhead projector to make transparencies and overlays of routes, rivers, trails and roads.

Rigdom Washington Brown & Wright Washington Brown

These twin brothers escaped from a South Carolina plantation and hid in a swamp. They had been told that Yankees were monsters and were frightened when a soldier from the 52nd Illinois Volunteer Infantry Regiment discovered their hiding place. Two officers, one from Elgin and the other from Dundee brought the brothers to Illinois. Wright later moved for Chicago and Rigdom lived in Elgin for the rest of his life where he worked as a pressman for the *Advocate* and was a highly respected citizen. *Courtesy of Raleigh Sutton.*

Math

Look at the mileage distance on an Illinois road map.

~ How many miles would a fugitive have traveled between Chester, Quincy, Alton, or Rock Island to Chicago?

Look in the chapter where routes are listed. Figure their comparative length with this state.

~ Estimate how long one of these routes would take if covered in wagons traveling at night. Remember how bumpy early roads were.

~ Estimate the same route if covered on foot.

~ How would the seasons effect these travel times?

~ How long would these distances take now if you were in a car on a highway?

~ Would steam boat travel have been faster than wagon? If boat passage could be obtained, how many miles of the trip could have been traveled this way? The old stagecoaches stopped every 20 miles or so. How many stops would a stage coach make traveling between two points as Springfield and Chicago?

It took 6 or 7 days to ride from Randolph County to Chicago on horseback. The Illinois Central train took one day. Make a graph comparing these times.

If a slaveholder purchased a 10 year old boy for $200 or $300 and that child worked without pay for the next 60 years estimate what he would have earned in a lifetime as a free blacksmith, caterer, inn keeper or brick mason.

Sketch a farm wagon. Figure measurements for a regular farm wagon. How would you alter this if you were going to put a false bottom in it? How much space would you need to allow for runaways to hide inside of it?

* * *

The Fugitive Slave Law set fines at $1,000.00. What would that be equal to today?

* * *

Money was needed for train or boat passage. Try to find the cost of travel from Cairo to Chicago.

* * *

How much would four tickets cost?

* * *

How much did Frank McWorter pay for freedom of each member of his family?

* * *

A short while before the time of the second Fugitive Slave Law, the Government was selling land for $1.25 an acre. The law included a penalty of $1000.00. Find out how much an acre of land costs now. Do you think that $1,000.00 seemed like one million dollars back in 1850?

* * *

These fishing devices from Nigeria are an excellent example of how Africans traditionally combine beauty with practical function. Notice the tortoise shell hook on the bird shaped fishing pole. The intricately carved device has a rock at the bottom. The rock is used to knock the fish out. *Courtesy of the Pump House Museum and Art Gallery.*

Art

Take a box and:

~ make a farm wagon with a false bottom,
~ or make a barn with a secret hiding place inside,
~ make a house with a trap door to the basement or a little room hidden behind the fireplace.
~ make a diorama of a slave family crossing the Mississippi River,
~ make a diorama of a house sitting on a hill beside a river. Form the hill from clay or other material that you can make a tunnel in. Use a small cylinder for the tunnel (a can with both ends cut out will do). Show miniature people inside.

* * *

Make a cave out of paper maché.

* * *

Design a house with ingenious hiding places.

* * *

Draw a picture book that tells what UGRR people thought and did. Show silhouettes of people or wagons outlined against protective night sky.

* * *

Draw a story in sequence. Use frames like cartoonist use. Use "cartoon balloons" to show what your characters say and think.

* * *

Make a mobile that depicts a typical UGRR scene.

* * *

Make a little flipbook. Begin by putting 16 to 20 small pages together to form a booklet. Then choose a topic. For example you might show the beginning of a chase scene with one man running after another. Show a tree or building in the background. On each page after that make the men look as if they moved forward a bit. Draw the tree or building in the same spot as you drew it on the first page of the book. When you are all through with the book, hold it with your thumb then release the pages in such rapid succession that the men seem to be moving right before your eyes.

* * *

Draw a frieze, or backdrop for your creative dramatics.

211

Andrew P___t came to j___
in 1861 was cared for and
the underground passage,
him a job with David Plott___
village where he worked &
Afterwards emigrated to ___
Wis he settled up on Gov___

EXTRA, EXTRA
READ ALL ABOUT IT

This section includes the story of the Underground Railroad period as told in newspapers and other significant documents. Although some are aged and may be difficult to read, they are reprinted for their historic importance.

The fragment of the hand written note on the opposite page tells about a man named Andrew Pratt. He escaped from slavery, was imprisoned in Illinois under the Black Codes and eventually reached the Milton House in Wisconsin. *Courtesy of the Milton House Museum.*

Accounts of the Underground Railroad which appeared in the *Western Citizen*

From the Voice of Freedom.

MAN SELLING IN A FREE (!) STATE.

The Western Citizen, published at Chicago, Ill., gave some weeks ago the particulars of a man auction in that place, at which the sheriff sold for one month, to the highest bidder, a *free* colored man who had been found quietly at work in the field. His offence whereby he incurred such a penalty, was being at work without a slip of paper in his pocket, to certify that he was a human being, with a human being's natural and inalienable rights. As if Heaven's own broad seal—the image of God enstamped on man — were not evidence enough of his birthright to manhood and all things thereto belonging.

The Citizen states that a large company assembled to witness the novel spectacle, but were unwilling to bid. At length, to save the poor fellow from being committed to jail again, a man bid him off for a month for *twenty-five* cents.

Deeply as Chicago is disgraced by such a transaction, it should be recorded to the credit of the place, so far as it goes toward redeeming its credit, that the citizens generally regarded the whole scene with disgust. But if this is all which can be said for them, they will hardly stand clear of the disgrace, in the eyes of honest, right-thinking and right-feeling men. If they do nothing to wipe from their statutes the foul stain which is fixed there by a provision authorizing such scenes,—to arouse the public mind against it, and to form a public sentiment which will no longer tolerate either that or any other manifestation of the fiendish prejudice and horrible injustice which grind the helpless, free colored man to the dust, and rivet the chains on the slaves' galled limbs,— they are guilty of these very outrages upon humanity which so excite their disgust.

A late number of the Citizen announces that the poor man's '*free papers*' came on from Ohio a short time after the sale. His FREE PAPERS! think of that ye men of Vermont! A peice of paper needed to save a *man* from being esteemed a brute and treated accordingly! And that is a state called *free!* Shame on the legislation, the morality, the humanity of such a state! And shame on the morality, the humanity of any state or any people that does not cry aloud and unsparingly against such an abomination! Well does the Citizen exclaim! "what a strange fact is this, that a man's humanity must be committed to a fragment of paper certified to by a Justice of the Peace, and be subject to all the liabilities attached to the preservation of such an insignificant article! For some people to lose their free papers, is to lose their personal identity, and thus, instead of being men, protected by the dignity of their nature, they become mere things upon which the law lays its malignant grasp, and sells them off for money."

Maine Legislature.—On Wednesday the Senate of Maine was organized. On Friday the committee on the Governor's vote reported as follows;

Whole number of votes,	71,788
John Fairfield has	49,855
Edward Robinson (Whig)	26,745
James Appleton (Abo.)	5,080
Scattering,	108

"Man Selling in a Free State", *Western Citizen,* February 13, 1843.
Courtesy of The Chicago Historical Society

Communications.

FOR THE WESTERN CITIZEN

ANTI-SLAVERY HYMN.

1. Guide us, O thou great Jehovah;
   Save, oh, save our guilty land!
   Though our foe is proud and mighty,
   Bind him with thy powerful hand:
   See, he rages,
   Bind him with thy powerful hand.

2. Open thou the prison doors;
   Bid the bondman freely go;
   Let thine arm, revealed in power,
   Bear his cause triumphant through,
   Strong Deliverer,
   Bear his cause triumphant through.

3. While he treads the wheel of slavery,
   Bid his hopeless tears subside:
   Bear him through oppression's current;
   Land him safe on freedom's side:
   Songs of praises
   Freedom's friends will give to thee.   S.

IS ILLINOIS A FREE STATE?

MR EDITOR.—You will confer a favor on a numerous class of the inhabitants of this region, by giving an answer to the query stated in the caption at the head of this communication, through the columns of the Western Citizen. My reason for asking you to do so, are as follows:

When I became a resident of the State of Illinois, I believed that no involuntary servitude could be sustained by the laws thereof, otherwise than by conviction of crime. But the event of judicial action, in the circuit court of Randolph County, last April, has led me to doubt whether my belief has been correct. This must be so, otherwise the action of the court is corrupt, in a case of which I

[...] question stated, became a subject of [...] in this neighborhood, and was often made a subject of debate, which still led to more investigation; the result of which was a determination to have the question brought before the proper tribunals for adjudication, so soon as suitable opportunity offered. Not long since this opportunity was offered, in a case which occurred, respecting a colored woman, who had lived with Andrew Borders for some years, having a daughter, woman grown, living there also, and four other colored persons, all claimed by him as his slaves. These unfortunate beings were treated so inhumanly and were so badly provided for, as to excite the feelings and sympathies of the whole neighborhood, except the pro-slavery minions who are often worse than the slaveholder [...] was made as to the terms on [...] they were held; but as one waited on another, the inquiry progressed [...] feelings of the people [...] circumstance which took place in [...] family, as which the colored woman named Sarah, was cruelly beaten, and badly wounded in her arm. Fearing her life was in danger

true to the scent of human flesh, as a blood hound, would find her and force her to return, she fled where she could remain with greater secrecy. Borders, with his mean and generous accomplices, soon became very noisy in blaming the neighbors for secreting his slave. For some time he bantered and bullied through the neighborhood, manifesting the true spirit of a slave holder, used to tyranize over his defenceless slaves. The people, who believed he had no legal claim to his negroes, did not wish to be insulted and trampled upon by this petty tyrant, they entered suit in her name for assault and battery, and sued for the time she had lived with him and determined to await the issue. The design of the people, however, was not her case alone, but through it to reach the case of all others held in slavery in the state. A society was formed, assuming the name of the "Friends of National Liberty." The ablest council was employed, and the case came up before judge Brown in Kaskaskia, last [...] Politics and council agreed

are valid. Assuming the ground that the ordinance of Congress is a compact and not a law, and the people of Illinois were one party in the compact, and they agreed to have these indentures held valid, and asked Congress to allow that it should be so. Congress being the other party in the compact, admitted the state into the Union, with that provision in its constitution, and thereby confirmed the same. The case is appealed to the Supreme Court, to sit at Springfield next December. The friends of the oppressed are very anxious that the case have a full and able investigation before that court, and that the talents of the best lawyers should be enlisted on the side of the oppressed. The ablest council that can be procured in these parts will be employed on the opposite side. We hope that abolitionists of the North will solicit the aid of gentlemen of the bar, friendly to the cause of freedom and human rights; that this great question, the result of which will affect some hundreds of wretched creatures now held in slavery in this state, may not be lost for want of sufficient advocacy.

[...] neys, council will [...] given productive of much good to the poor slave, and which may materially affect the issue of the case. I hope therefore, that you will invite arguments on this important question, and let them appear in your columns, that our state may have the foul blot of slavery wiped from the statute book, which justly denominated black [...] As intend being a reader of your paper, whatever arguments are brought forward on the subject, will come under my investigation. I trust true friend of the slave will not be silent.

The cruel treatment which the rest of Borders colored people received, excited them to seek safety by flight. They escaped and traveled North, leaving Borders to search the corn-fields and thickets, which he

search the corn-fields and thickets, which he did painfully, for more than a month. When he heard of them 300 miles North. These are the same we see noticed in the 8th No. of your paper. On investigation it was found he had no indenture, nor legal claim to one of them, and yet claimed them with as much audacity as though they had been really secured to him by law. One had served him until she was thirteen years over age, the other had served him one year over age, yet they never received any thing like wages.   HUMERTAS.

Eden, Randolph Co., Ill., Oct. 15, 1842.

RHODE ISLAND CONTROVERSY.

"Christian Investigathor, No. 5: Whitesboro, N. Y., September, 1842."

"The Rights and the Wrongs of Rhode Island: comprising views of Liberty and Law, of Religion and Rights, as exhibited in the recent and existing difficulties in that State. By William Goodell. Press of the Oneida Institute." P. 120, 8vo.

For sale by the Author, at 25 cents per single copy, $2.50 per dozen, or $18.75 per hundred.

Remittances may be forwarded by postmasters, according to law.

Through the social nature God has given him, man every where is bound to his fellow man. He cannot, if he would, sunder this relationship. He may disregard the obligations Heaven thus imposes on him, but he is unable to shield himself from participating in the bliss or woe which is his brother's portion. The blood which he suffers to be shed unheeded cries to God from the ground, and the sentence goes forth, "a fugitive and a vagabond shalt thou be in the earth." The evils which flow from the ignorance and wretchedness of others, find a thousand avenues to his own fireside. The slavery of the black man is subversive of the white man's liberty. The oppression of the poor in England extorts groans from their brethren in America. "And whether one member suffer, all the members suffer with it; or one member be honored, all the members rejoice with it." Thus "the Rhode Island controversy is no mere local concernment. It touches vitally, and harshly, the great interests of liberty and law, of religion and rights, not only in Rhode Island, but in the whole country." The same power which has placed its iron heel on the neck of popular sovereignty in that State, will, if unresisted, sooner or later trample in the dust popular sovereignty in Illinois.

Whatever may be "the rights and the wrongs" of either party in the Rhode Island controversy, it is incontrovertible, that the only legitimate sovereignty of that State, or of any other on the globe, is vested in the people. This authority is not acquired by mutual consent, neither is it derived from parliaments—it is a God-given prerogative. The thing cannot be, therefore, that the majority of a people are insurgents, rebels, or traitors. To deny the right of the people to govern, is to controvert all government authority [...]

"Is Illinois a Free State?", Western Citizen, October 23, 1842.
Courtesy of The Chicago Historical Society

SLAVERY AS IT IS.

Many of our readers will recognize an old acquaintance in the subject of the following sketch. She passed through the State of Illinois on her way to freedom. The Grand Jury of La Salle County attempted to indict some of the citizens of that county for giving food to that poor and dependent aged woman. They failed through an iniquitous portion of our iniquitous slave code—that the testimony of colored persons shall not be admitted against white persons.

From the Signal of Liberty.

A BAPTIST FUGITIVE.

AGNES, aged sixty-two years, was born in Prince Edwards, Virginia. She was raised—(the word is a very expressive one, for we cannot say of a slave that she was educated, or brought up,) on a plantation where there were about 60 slaves. She was employed in spinning cotton and wool. When she was thirty-one years of age, her master, whose name was Henry Holland, became much embarrassed in his circumstances, on account of large sums lost by betting on horses. In consequence, her five children, the oldest about twelve years of age, were taken away by the sheriff, and sold successively at public auction to pay her master's debts. She has never seen them nor heard from them, save only she has heard that two of them were taken by the purchaser to Alabama.

Agnes was a member of the Baptist Church in Virginia nine years, and attended meetings of that denomination frequently. Her mistress was also a Baptist. After the death of her old master the slaves were divided among the heirs, and she fell to the portion of one of his sons. Some years since, he removed to Missouri, in hopes of bettering his condition. But he had the misfortune to have his bedding and clothing completely wet on the passage, and upon opening them in Missouri, they were nearly spoiled. In order to replace them, he was obliged to make large purchases of a merchant in St. Louis. He was unable to meet his obligations as they became due, and the sheriff was directed by the creditor to attach property and sell it. Agnes was taken on execution and sold at public auction, at Keesville, for two hundred dollars, to a man named Herrinan. This was about two years since. Her new master was poor, having only one other slave, a female, and about sixty acres of land, on which he raised chiefly corn and tobacco. He did not work himself owing to some bodily infirmity. He was mean niggardly and cruel. Here Agnes suffered much for want of food and clothing. The

other slave was kept chiefly in the house, while she was sent into the field to plough and hoe corn. Her ordinary day's work was to plough 2000 hills of corn with a horse, and hoe them the next day. When she failed to accomplish her task, she was beaten by her master. Having come in at noon for dinner, she was often obliged to go back to her work almost as hungry as she came. The rest of the family dined first, and she had only that left. Her master promised her that if they had a good crop of corn she should have plenty of corn bread to eat; but after the crop was raised, there was no difference in her treatment. On one or two occasions, where the neighbors had taken pity on her, and mended a pair of shoes and given them to her, her master took them away, and wore them himself, saying she did not need them. This treatment seemed the more grievous to her, as in Virginia she had never wanted for necessary food and clothing. During the two years she lived with this man she attended meeting only twice. Every Sunday she was compelled to work in the field, in the barn, or in the house. Her condition was so intolerable, that she could not endure it and ran away, and was absent several weeks. After her return she was rigorously treated, and closely watched. Sometime in November last, just at night, her mistress bade her make a good fire, and she would get supper. Presently some of the house logs were on fire, and Herrinan had much trouble to extinguish it, and became very angry with her for making so great a fire. He sent her to the barn to get some corn to feed the horse, and hearing his loud and angry tones, she was afraid to come into the house, and hid behind the fence. This awakened his suspicion that she had ran away, and he came out and looked for her. He then ran down to a near neighbor's house, to get his dogs, declaring he would have her in ten minutes. She had hid herself behind an old chimney, waiting for an opportunity to get into the house, unperceived, and get her clothes, as she was very thinly dressed. Herrinan soon returned with the dogs, and after searching for her near the house, he left for the woods in that direction he supposed she had escaped. Despairing of obtaining her clothes, she entered the woods in an opposite direction. The night was very dark and rainy, and after walk-

ing about all night, she was much alarmed to find herself close to Herrinan's fence. She ran into the woods as fast as possible, and in the course of the day she heard the dogs approaching. Worn down with fatigue, faint and hungry, she could go no farther; and having done all she could, she thought she must submit to her fate. As a last resort, however she crawled in between two old logs, and covered herself, as well as she could, with leaves. The dogs soon came on in full career, and passed a few paces from her. Two men on horseback followed close behind, and one of them dashed his horse over the logs under which she lay so near that the horses feet parted the bushes that concealed her from view. Agnes said it seemed to her that her heart beat so loud that they must hear it, and thus discover her. But they were soon out of sight and she once more renewed her exertions. She wandered about in the woods, having no particular object in view, except to avoid being caught by her master, subsisting on buds, and on winter grapes which she could find. On one occasion she obtained three turnips from a farmer's field, which lasted her for a fortnight.

For three weeks she lived in continual fear of the dogs which she could occasionally hear, and of which she was very apprehensive, as she knew her master would search for her thoroughly. These dogs when young, are trained to hunt colored people, by making the slaves run, and then putting the dogs on the pursuit. Having once found the track of an individual, they will follow it by the scent, distinguishing it from the track of any other person. Agnes adopted various methods to baffle them. She went around several times in a circle. She rubbed the soles of her shoes with garlics, and on one occasion stood in a creek two days. After she had been out some time, she concluded to follow the north star, as she knew it would lead her to the free States.

She was in the woods three months, without having entered a house. By this time the weather had become inclement—her clothes were in rags, and sometimes were frozen stiff, so as to clatter against her ancles as she walked—her shoes were worn out and the snow had fallen ancle deep, and she could endure her sufferings no longer. Having procured a staff, she went to a house and appeared before the inmates as a broken down, decrepid old woman, seeking her children. They took pity on her, and gave her something to eat. On inquiry, she found she was distant about a hundred miles from her master, and fifty miles from St. Louis. Thus she

"A Baptist Fugitive", *Western Citizen,* August 12, 1842. *Courtesy of The Chicago Historical Society* traveled from house to house and where she thought it would answer, she made them acquainted with her real history. She crossed the Mississippi at Quincy, and is now in Canada, in hope of living her few remaining years in *freedom*. This is her *only* object. She has no friends or acquaintance there. Her children she will never see again. She has no relatives except in Virginia. He must be base in heart, who will endeavor to disturb the remnant of her days.

We would say one word to our *Christian* readers. Agnes related these things to us, and feelingly expressed the consolations she had experienced in all her affliction, from the consideration that Christ was her friend and Savior, and having gone to prepare a place for her, he will yet come and receive her to himself. We have reason to believe that Agnes is beloved of God, and has been " translated into the kingdom of His dear Son," and " made a partaker of the divine nature." Why, then, we ask, is this aged, helpless, homeless, childless, friendless individual—who has wronged no one, but has received wrong through all her life: why is she hunted like a partridge on the mountains, and chased by dogs and more ferocious men, from hill to hill, and town to town, while guiltless of crime? One prominent reason is because ministers and deacons and elders and private church members, who do these things, and maintain that the institution of manstealing with all its effects, is an ordinance of heaven, and a practical blessing, are in fellowship with us, and are invited to fill our pulpits, and to surround the Table of the Lord, and we thus countenance this great iniquity. It was only last year that Elder Davis, a Baptist clergyman, went through the North, publicly maintaining that manstealing and all its accursed concomitants, as they exist at the South, are in accordance with the will of God. And he went home to his fellow manstealers, boasting how well he had been received at the North! Now Christian, your master, Christ, came to set the captive free. Will you not be co-worker together with him, and by your prayers, your exertions and your votes, manifest to all that you have sworn ETERNAL HATRED to the whole manstealing system, and

while *you* live, no consistent effort of yours, as a Christian or a citizen, shall be wanting for its everlasting overthrow:

Communications.

FOR THE WESTERN CITIZEN.

THE CAUSE OF THE OPPRESSED.

The cause of the oppressed has been to me, from my early childhood, a subject of deep interest. In the nursery I learned to sympathize with the despised slave, and the sable matron who watched over my tottering infancy, instilled into my young mind that the most favorable lot of the negro was a hard one. As I ripened into womanhood, I felt that each one of that unhappy race (but more especially the females) was the subject of very great injustice, cruelty, and oppression. My mind was often led to the inquiry, Is there no remedy? Can nothing be done to remove the curse from our land? Must we live for ever beneath the withering, blighting influence of this simoom, which wafts its poison over my " Father land." Colonization seemed to move on leaden wings ; conscience would whisper *immediate emancipation*; but that appeared to me *then*, surrounded as I was by the noxious atmosphere of slavery, perilous in the extreme. I could not believe that the African, or rather the descendant of the African, and the white man, could dwell together in the same land, and on the same footing, without murder, rapine, and every abomination. But, thank heaven, I have received light on that subject ; my views have been enlarged; prejudice has been removed, (for it is only prejudice that causes many really good people to start at the bare mention of immediate emancipation) and I believe that the simultaneous abolition of slavery in the different states is not only entirely practicable, but perfectly consistent with the safety, happiness, and prosperity of the inhabitants of these States.

Who can look at the progress of good order, morality, and religion in those islands where the system of immediate emancipation has been adopted, and remain skeptical with regard to this fact? What has been done in the West India Islands can be done in our own country, and *must* be done at no distant day, or the now fettered slave will himself throw off the yoke of oppression, and obtain that freedom which is now fraudulently, cruelly withheld from him. Heaven avert such an alternative from our land! But, at the same time, I would invoke high heaven to remove this plague-spot from us as a nation, and reserve from moral and physical degradation the thousands of helpless victims who are now sacrificed at the shrine of southern cupidity. To the

attainment of this object, I rejoice to know that men and women of ardent piety, talents, and influence are devoting their powers ; and I also rejoice that Illinois has again unfurled the banner of liberty, and re-established a press, which, I trust, will send such an influence, that every man, woman and child in the State will learn to " *obey the law of God rather than man.*"

Mr. Editor, I send you these imperfect remarks as preliminary to something further on the subject of slavery. Should you deem them worthy a place in your paper, they may perhaps do some little good as coming from one who was born and reared in those regions of our land where the black man, because of his *sable color*, is regarded as a THING ; an article of traffic, to be bought and sold ; a beast of burden, intended by the great Creator to be subject to all the whims and caprices of those more favored ones who are so happy as to have a fairer complexion.

Many facts calculated to expose the horrors of slavery are vivid to my recollection, which I will hereafter send, if you think they will, in the most humble way, aid the cause of humanity. To this cause, I purpose, by the grace of God, to devote my powers ; my time, as far as practicable ; my prayers ; my all : and in this cause I hope and believe the " Western Citizen" will become a powerful and valuable auxiliary.

M. B. D.

Peoria, July 1, 1842.

FOR THE WESTERN CITIZEN.

ORGANIZATION IN KANE COUNTY.

Pursuant to previous call, signed by forty-one individuals of Kane county, for the purpose of forming an Anti-Slavery Society, a meeting was held at the Presbyterian Church in Batavia, on Thursday, the 14th of July, 1842.

The Convention was organized by electing Reuben Beach Chairman, and Lucien Farnam Secretary.

The meeting was opened with prayer by Rev. C. Cook. The following resolutions were moved, and after a free discussion, were adopted, viz.

"The Cause of the Oppressed", *Western Citizen,* August 12, 1842.
Note Mary Brown Davis' initials. *Courtesy of The Chicago Historical Society.*

THE FUGITIVES IN KNOX COUNTY.

Mr. Editor:—In a former communication respecting the family which was imprisoned in Knox Co. jail, under the black code of Illinois, and who were taken at the time of the "Farmington row," I erroneously gave the name of their former master as a Mr. Boggs, of Randolph Co. I had been informed that such was his name. I have since learned that his name is Andrew Borders, of Randolph Co., the same against whom a suit is now pending in behalf of a colored woman named Sarah, before the Supreme Court of this State, which is particularly noticed by your correspondent "Honestas" in the Citizen of Oct. 29th. One of those who were imprisoned at Knoxville is the daughter of Sarah. The six weeks for which they were imprisoned expired on or about the 17th of October, at which time they were offered to be hired out for one month. But bidders were scarce. The month soon passed away, and again, on the 10th of November, they were offered by our sheriff at the door of the court-house. But bidders were still wanting. I have understood that only two of the five were bidden upon, and these only to the amount of fifty cents each. On Thursday, the 24th inst., Andrew Borders and his son again made their appearance at Knoxville.—For the three little children he now institutes an entirely new claim from that which he instituted before. He now demands them as indented apprentices under the poor laws, and exhibited indentures executed in 1839 and 1841, by two justices of the peace in and for Randolph Co. This claim being perfectly satisfactory to the sheriff, he delivered over the children to Mr. Borders. The friends of humanity, unwilling that Borders should succeed in carrying off his victims, and [...] been given for his appearance at the Circuit Court, Borders was informed by the counsel who had been employed to conduct this case, that if he had such indentures and would exhibit them, and if they contained probable evidence of correctness, he would not be troubled farther till the session of the Circuit Court. He however declined exhibiting his papers, and immediately left town for Knoxville, intending, as we supposed, to start off with the children, whom he had kept in confinement all day in our county jail, under circumstances of slaveholding barbarity.—Another warrant was immediately issued against Borders and his son for the imprisonment of the children on Friday, and an officer dispatched in pursuit, who returned by 9 o'clock on Friday evening with his prisoners.

They had their examination on Saturday. At this examination Borders exhibited his indentures; but the opinion of the magistrate was unfavorable to their validity, and both men were ordered to give bail for their appearance at the Circuit Court. This they at first refused to do, and they were delivered into the hand of the sheriff to be committed. Subsequently, however, they gave bail and were discharged. This closed the week. It was reported that they would now stay and spend another week and bring the people of Galesburg to Knoxville to answer for their misdemeanors. This, however, was probably a feint to conceal their operations; for we are now upon the third day of the week, and no arrests have been made. But where are the children? Nothing has been heard of them since Friday night, and the probability is that some one was employed after the arrest of Borders and his son to take them off. Their friends are on the look-out for them; and if any trace of their steps can be had, they will be followed, and whoever has taken them off will be held to answer for it. But I fear they will not be found. Truly, on the side of the oppressor there is power. But who can describe the anguish of the poor mother robbed of her little ones! True, she might have gone with them; but she did not believe that the hard-hearted men would take away those little children at this inclement season without her, nor did she suppose that her presence could prevent their sufferings.

We offered to give Borders security for their appearance on the first day of court if he would leave them; but no inducement we could offer would prevail on him to relax his hold. It was our intention to keep an eye upon their movements, and as often as they attempted to go away with the children, to arrest them. But they have probably, through the assistance of those who ought to befriend the helpless, defeated us for the present. No effort or expense has been or will be spared to have justice done to the poor; and the suits, both in behalf of the people and the children, will be prosecuted so far as the law will enable us to go. May the Savior of the poor take care of them,

In haste, yours, &c., H. H. K.
Galesburg, Nov. 29, 1842.

A SHORT REMINISCENCE.

When I was quite a little girl I used often to spend a week or two in the family of a near relation, who was a very lovely woman, and remarkably kind to her slaves. Her husband was a gentleman, as far as the world could see, but a tyrant in his family, very ambitious and very avaricious. Among the slaves on the plantation was a woman to whom the mistress was very much attached. She had one child, a little female babe, when it pleased God to release her from her earthly bondage, and take her to the land of eternal rest. With her dying breath she implored her mistress to take care of the little one, and use all her influence to keep her always with her, and never let her be sold. The mistress religiously observed this promise, (or, I should say, observed it as far as one whose mind was dark as to equal rights would do,) brought her up well, taught her many useful things, and kept her usually in the room with herself. This girl was about my age, and was generally a playmate for me. When I was visiting at my cousin's house, at the time of which I am speaking,

THE FUGITIVES IN KNOX COUNTY.

Mr. Editor:—In a former communication respecting the family which was imprisoned in Knox Co. jail, under the black code of Illinois, and who were taken at the time of the "Farmington row," I erroneously gave the name of their former master as a Mr. Boggs, of Randolph Co. I had been informed that such was his name. I have since learned that his name is Andrew Borders, of Randolph Co., the same against whom a suit is now pending in behalf of a colored woman named Sarah, before the Supreme Court of this State, which is particularly noticed by your correspondent "Honestas" in the Citizen of Oct. 29th. One of those who were imprisoned at Knoxville is the daughter of Sarah. The six weeks for which they were imprisoned expired on or about the 17th of October, at which time they were offered to be hired out for one month. But bidders were scarce. The month soon passed away, and again, on the 10th of November, they were offered by our sheriff at the door of the court-house. But bidders were still wanting. I have understood that only two of the five were bidden upon, and these only to the amount of fifty cents each. On Thursday, the 24th inst., Andrew Borders and his son again made their appearance at Knoxville.—For the three little children he now institutes an entirely new claim from that which he instituted before. He now demands them as indented apprentices under the poor laws, and exhibited indentures executed in 1839 and 1841, by two justices of the peace in and for Randolph Co. This claim being perfectly satisfactory to the sheriff, he delivered over the children to Mr. Borders. The friends of humanity, unwilling that Borders should succeed in carrying off his victims, and

"Fugitives in Knox County", *Western Citizen,* December 23, 1842.
Courtesy of The Chicago Historical Society.

The Underground Railroad.

[From the Polo Press]

My attention was recently called to an article in the Press in reference to the "Underground Railroad," and I thought I would give a short history of the last trip I made with "Uncle Sol," as we familiarly called Mr. Shaver. I had been over the same route before with Deacon Perkins and Schuyler Lunt.

The year I do not remember, but think it was earlier than '55. On the 3d of July "Uncle Sol" called at my house in Old Town and asked me to go with him to Byron. He had a four horse team and quite a load of passengers, consisting of a man, his wife and two children, and his father-in-law and mother-in-law. "Uncle Sol" had been to Newton Barber's store, in Old Town, and bought a couple of yards of factory with a red edge for a flag. He cut a pole in the grove and hoisted the flag, saying he had understood they had threatened at Mt. Morris to take up any who went through there on the "Underground R. R." and he was going to go through with his flag flying.

Our principal passenger was a young man of good build, looking strong and determined. He was well armed, and no doubt would have defended his wife and children to the last. He had escaped from slavery some years before, and lived in Canada. Freedom was so sweet to him that he resolved to risk liberty and perhaps life in securing his wife and children from bondage. It was "liberty or death" with him, as I think likely the man Mr. Petrie spoke of would have found out if he had come on.

On his way back to Missouri, the escaped slave met friends in Iowa who agreed to help him, promising to meet him at a certain stream with a covered wagon. When he reached Missouri he hid in the brush till he had an opportunity to see his wife without fear of detection. He hid in the brush by day and consulted with his friends by night until they had their plans formed.

Quite a number of them escaped at night, but were followed in the morning. Their pursuers on horseback with dogs captured part of them and the others had a narrow escape. When they reached the stream where the covered wagon was waiting, instead of crossing they went into the water, walked up stream for some distance, and landed on the same side, thus eluding the scent of the dogs. The pursuers soon caught sight of the wagon, and, supposing the fugitives were on board gave chase. The driver in the wagon understood the situation, and kept his horses at full speed, so his followers were led several miles out of their way before they discovered their mistake. No doubt they were greatly chagrined at finding an empty wagon. The fugitives made the most of their time and finally reached Buffalo Grove.

We passed through Mt. Morris as stated by brother Petrie, with flag flying, reaching Byron on the third of July. "Uncle Sol" went to the tavern and I stayed at Rev. George Gammel's. In the morning the tavern keeper threatened to take up our load. This made "Uncle Sol" pretty wrathy, and some high words passed between the two men.

The Byron folks had made arrangements for a picnic on an Island in Rock River, and agreed to pay our expenses if we would take the fugitives on, so we forded the river below Byron, stopped opposite Byron to give three cheers, then drove on to "Kill Buck." There we found a tent where the people had met to celebrate the Fourth. "Uncle Sol" told the driver to drive right up to the tent. When we reached it we heard the words, 'We hold these truths to be self-evident, that all men are equal; that they are endowed by their Creator with certain unalienable rights; that among these are life, liberty and the pursuit of happiness.' One of the managers came out, and with tears in his eyes asked us to stop and celebrate with them. We concluded not to stay, so they directed us to their lunch baskets telling us to help ourselves. Towards evening we reached South Grove. Mr. Shaver seemed acquainted there. We had supper at the tavern, but when we offered to pay for it the woman said she "could not think of charging anything."

"Uncle Sol" asked the Justice of the Peace, Mr. Byers, to take the fugitives on, but he said, holding the office he did, he could not do it, but, he added "I will pay you twenty-five cents a head for all you bring." Mr. Byers' daughter was going to a party that evening, and when she saw the four horse team and flag, hurried to get ready, supposing it was her company coming. Her mistake gave the old gentleman a hearty laugh.

A few miles beyond South Grove we came to a settlement of Wesleyans, a place called Brush Point. Here we found true anti-slavery men, loving freedom for others as well as for themselves. We spent the evening very pleasantly, the people of the settlement coming together for a general good time. The next morning we left for home, and at the same time the fugitives left for Canada. On our way home we spent the first night with Deacon Lewis, across the river from Byron. Soon after we forded the river, we met John Ankeny going toward Byron. "Uncle Sol" was acquainted with him and told him that we talked of running a line of stages from Buffalo Grove to Byron, and asked him to name some good house at Mt. Morris where they could put up. Mr. A. thought it a good idea and named one or two places, but when "Uncle Sol" spoke of it as the "Underground R. R." he called to his horse, "Get up!" and drove on without another word. We reached home that evening, having been gone four days.

"Uncle Sol" was reputed to be skeptical, perhaps he was, but the last time I saw him he grasped my hand, and, speaking of the war, then in progress, said, "I tell you, the Almighty has a hand in this."

J. C.

"The Underground Railroad", *Sycamore True Republication*, March 12, 1884.

Excerpts from the letter a self-emancipated slave wrote to a slaveholder who had invited him to "come back home" at the end of the Civil War. *Reprinted from The Freedmen's Book, compiled by Lydia Maria Child.*

To my old Master, Colonel P.H. Anderson, Big Spring, Tennessee.

Sir.

I got your letter and was glad to find that you had not forgotten Jourdan, and that you wanted me to come back and live with you again, promising to do better for me than anybody else can. I have often felt uneasy about you. I thought the Yankees would have hung you long before this, for harboring Rebs they found at your house. I suppose they never heard about your going to Colonel Martin's to kill the Union soldier that was left by his company in their stable. Although you shot at me twice before I left you, I did not want to hear of your being hurt, and am glad you are still living. It would do me good to go back to the dear old home again, and see Miss Mary and Miss Martha and Allen, Esther, Green, and Lee. Give my love to them all, and tell them I hope we will meet in the better world, if not this. I would have gone back to see you all when I was working in the Nashville Hospital, but one of the neighbors told me that Henry intended to shoot me if he ever got a chance.

I want to know particularly what the good chance is you propose to give me. I am doing tolerably well here. I get twenty-five dollars a month; with victuals and clothing, have a comfortable home for Mandy,—the folks call her Mrs. Anderson,—and the children—Milly, Jane, and Grundy—go to school and are learning well ... Now if you will write and say what wages you will give me, I will be better able to decide whether it would be to my advantage to move back again.

As to my freedom, which you say I can have, there is nothing to be gained on that score, as I got my free papers in 1864 from the Provost-Marshal-General of the Department of Nashville. Mandy says she would be afraid to go back without some proof that you were disposed to treat us justly and kindly; and we have concluded to test your sincerity by asking you to send us our wages for the time we served you. This will make us forget and forgive old scores, and rely on your justice and friendship in the future. I served you faithfully for thirty-two years, and Mandy twenty years. At twenty-five dollars a month for me, and two dollars a week for Mandy, our earnings would amount to eleven thousand six hundred and eighty dollars. Add to this the interest for the time our wages have been kept back, and deduct what you paid for our clothing, and three doctor's visits to me, and pulling a tooth for Mandy, and the balance will show what we are in justice entitled to. Please send the money by Adam's Express, in care of V. Winters, Esq., Dayton, Ohio. If you fail to pay us for faithful labors in the past, we can have little faith in your promises in the future. We trust the good Maker has opened your eyes to the wrongs which you and your fathers have done to me and my fathers, in making us toil for you for generations without recompense ... Surely there will be a day of reckoning for those who defraud the laborer of his hire.

In answering this letter, please state if there would be any safety for my Milly and Jane, who are now grown up, and both good-looking girls. You know how it was with poor Matilda and Catherine. I would rather stay here and starve—and die, if it came to that—than have my girls brought to shame by the violence and wickedness of their young masters. You will also please state if there has been any schools opened for the colored children in your neighborhood. The great desire of my life now is to give my children an education, and have them form virtuous habits.

Say howdy to George Carter, and thank him for taking the pistol from you when you were shooting at me.

From your old servant,
Jourdan Anderson

Deed of Emancipation — Pate and others
By John Maxey, planter of
Powhatan County, Va.

To all to whom these presents shall come

Know ye that I John Maxey of Powhatan County do believe that all men are by nature equally free and independent. Therefore from a clear conviction of the injustice and criminality of depriving my fellow creatures of their natural right do hereby set free the following persons (Viz) Pate to be free the 25th of Dec. 1789. Aggy to be free the 25th of Dec. 1794. Judith to be free December 1790. Jacob to be free Dec 25 1798. Nancy to be free 25th December 1799. Sampson to be free 25th Dec. 1800. Hannah and yet to be free 25th Dec. 1801. Suckey to be free Dec 25 1803. Jouls to be free Dec 25 1804. Sylvia to be free 25th Dec. 1805. William to be free Dec 25 1805. Cate to be free the 25th Dec. 1807. Pat & Milly to be free 25th Dec. 1808. Zacharia to be free 25th Dec. 1809. I do hereby

2.

relinquish all right title I claim to the said people after they arrive to the dates above hereunto set my hand and affixed my seal this 18th day of Dec. 1788.

John Maxey (Seal)

At a court held for Powhatan County at Scottville on Thursday the eighteenth day of December 1788 This Deed of Emancipation from John Maxey to sundry slaves within named was presented in court and acknowledged by the said John Maxey and ordered to be recorded.

Powhatan Clerks Office.
Jan 2nd 1815

Teste
Als. Crump

EMANCIPATION PAPERS
(RECOPIED/HANDWRITTEN)
Courtesy of Ruth Mulholland

221

Regular monthly meeting. Dea. Bon
ner mo~~deratory~~.
On motion of Robt. Pollock, seconded
by Wm. Kerr _ it was voted that
James Bonner be restored to the
privileges of the church.
                    James M. Dodge

At a special meeting of the 1st. Cong.
Chh. of Milburn, held on the 2d day of
Dec. 1859, after spending an hour in
prayer with particular reference to the
tragedy to be acted this day at Charles-
town, Va. the following preamble and
resolutions were adopted.
Whereas, the slaveholders of this country are making desperate efforts
to extend and perpetuate the system
of slavery which now exists
in nearly one half of the States
and exerts a baleful influence upon
the prosperity of the nation; and
are using the most base and unjus-
tifiable means to accomplish their
ends_ repudiating the doctrine of
our fathers, that all men are created free and equal;- disregard-
ing the most sacred compromises
of the and agreements of the patriots who founded the government;
and have revived the infamous slave
trade in defiance of the government,
and the laws of the land; and
are this day imbruing their hands
in the blood of a christian patriot,
who, inspired by the spirit of our
fathers, sought the liberty of the oppressed and enslaved. Therefore
Resolved, That ~~we will~~ do good to

henceforth, we will redouble our efforts for the abolition of slavery, by all means justified by the word of God and a good conscience.

Resolved, That we will do good to those who have escaped from bondage as we have opportunity, by supplying their present wants and aiding them in their flight.

Resolved, That in future we will devote special attention to the subject of emancipation on the 2nd. of Dec, annually, in grateful remembrance of John Brown, who fell a sacrifice to slaveholding vengeance, for his efforts peacefully to liberate the down-trodden slaves of Virginia.

James M. Dodge Clk.

1860
Jan'y 2. Annual meeting of the Church.
Pastor Moderator.
Treasurer reported; received $6.36
            paid debt & expenses   4.66
                Associa― tax   1.00
            leaving in the Treasury   70

R. Pollock
J. M. Dodge   } were chosen business
Dea. Wm. Bonner   Committee.
& Alex. Watson
R. Pollock was chosen Clerk.

James M. Dodge.

Courtesy of Millburn Congregational Church

FROM THE PASTORS

In the 1840s and 1850s Congregational-ists and Presbyterians in Chicago were working very closely with black abolition-ists, men and women, in Chicago. It was an exciting and dangerous time for all.

JOHN and MARY JONES were leaders in the African-American community of the city which grew from 33 in 1833 to 145 in 1845. By 1850 of the 23,047 Chicagoans, 378 were colored. These men and women, early black settlers, were free (often of mixed black and white ancestry) and from the East and upper South, drawn to Chicago by economic opportunity and a reputation for racial tolerance.

John Jones came to Chicago at age 23 in 1845. He brought his wife, Mary Richardson Jones, a free African-American from Tenn-essee. Jones was born in North Carolina, son of a free mulatto mother and a father of German ancestry. He was a skilled tail-or and established his own business in his home at 119 Dearborn Street, catering to a white clientele. According to Olivia Mahon-ey in her article, "Black Abolitionists in Illinois," in the 1991 Summer issue of the Magazine of the Chicago Historical Society, Mr. Jones' business prospered as he invest-ed in real estate and by 1860 he was one of the wealthiest black Americans.

But soon after he settled in Chicago, Jones became good friends with abolitionist Charles Dyer, Lemuel C. P. Freer, Zebina Eastman, Philo Carpenter, Jeremiah Porter and all their wives--Presbyterians and Con-gregationalists. Dyer and Freer taught John Jones to read and write. In 1847 Jones join-ed the Illinois Constitutional Convention's debate about whether free African-Americans should be allowed to immigrate into Illin-ois. Many delegates feared that an influx would "degrade white labor" and "antagonize white citizens."

In September, 1847, Jones had already published articles refuting this position in the abolitionist Chicago Tribune, later reprinted in Zebina Eastman's The Western Citizen. Jones said that blacks were citi-zens entitled to all rights, arguing that the founding fathers hadn't inserted the word "white" into the definition of free citizens. The ideals of the 18th century Enlightenment, the standards of republican government, and black service in the Revol-ution, Mahoney reports, were sufficient grounds for recognizing black citizenship.

But the Constitutional Convention includ ed the anti-immigration provision, called the Black Codes. Though John Jones lost that "round," he kept working against the codes until they were repealed in 1865.

John Jones helped establish the Olivet Baptist Church. According to their daught-er, Favinia Jones Lee, both her parents provided a place for fugitive slaves and opened their home to abolitionist meetings. They sent "hundreds of fugitives to Canada ..." and their home was "a haven for escap-ed slaves" and whites alike. Frederick Doug lass and John Brown were guests, even though Jones did not think Brown's plan for Harper's Ferry was helpful.

After the Civil War John Jones was a Commissioner on the Cook County Board, one of the first African-Americans to win elective office in the North.

+

Abram T. Hall was a free black from Pennsylvania who also came to Chicago in 1845 at age 23. He was a barber. Hall helped organize Quinn Chapel.

Emma J. Atkinson came with her hus-band Isaac Atkinson to Chicago in 1847. She and three other women, whose names we do not yet know, worked at Quinn Chapel to provide food, clothing and shelter to runaway slaves. They were called "The Big Four".

Quinn Chapel, which was the first black church in Chicago, located on the east side of Wells Street near Washing-ton Street, drew more than 300 black Chicagoans on September 30, 1850. They gathered to protest the Fugitive Slave Act, federal legislation which provided a more effective method of returning fugitive slaves to their owners. Among the speakers that day were John Jones, Henry O. Wagoner and William Johnson, all black Chicago abolitionists.

+

This group formed a vigilance commit-tee consisting of a black police force of 7 divisions (each with six persons to patrol the city each night to watch for slave catchers).

It formed a Correspondence Committee (similar to the one formed during the American Revolution) called the Liberty Association.

And of course they stepped up the work of the Underground Railroad. White abolitionists worked with John Jones, Lewis Isbell, a barber from Kentucky; William Johnson, a barber of Chicago; and William Styles, a tailor.

They met at the office of The West-

Courtesy of The Spire, *DeKalb Congregational Church*

ern Citizen as the Committee for the Relief of Fugitives in Canada. One report said the committee had collected "about $150 and 15 barrels of flour, 1 barrel of clothing, 9 boxes of clothing, 1 sack clothing and 13 bags of flour and meal" for fugitives escaping to Canada by way of Chicago.

+

Two of these black abolitionists, Abram T. Hall and John Jones, were selected as delegates to the National Colored Convention in Cleveland. Olivia Mahoney points out that there was a series of Conventions from 1830 to 1855 of free black men. At Cleveland the 65 black artisans, merchants, laborers and professionals elected Frederick Doublass president and John Jones vice-president.

+

There are a number of stories of harrowing escapes of slaves through the Chicago Underground Railroad, worth retelling in which these individuals were central players.

+

White Congregational and Presbyterian abolitionists worked closely, learned greatly from these black abolitionists. As Mahoney concludes, black leaders had accomplished alot. Although they were not able to abolish the Illinois Black Laws until the Civil War was over, they put the issues of slavery and black citizenship rights at the front of state and national politics. "And even though denied full access, they had proven themselves to be effective participants in American politics."

Photographs are of JOHN and MARY JONES.

Rev. Bill + Rev. Jane Ann

WHAT'S HAPPENING!

WEDDING ANNOUNCEMENT:

The Montana Grill on Flathead Lake in Montana was the site of the wedding of Peter C. Rolfing to Tamara Chappell on February 13, 1993. Peter is the son of Verle and Mary Bogue of Pebble Beach, California, and the late James E. Rolfing. Tamara is the daughter of Avonne Chappell of Carmel, California, and the late William Chappell.
The couple will reside in Montana.

PARISH NEWS:

Anne Marie Moss is training for VISTA in Austin, Texas and has been assigned to work with the Literacy Program in Albuqurque, New Mexico.
Gladys Simon enjoyed a visit from her daughter who lives with her family in France and who gave her a birthday dinner party with French cuisine.
Marjorie Vonderheide assisted while her daughter-in-law set up a Gift Shop in Florida.
Dewey Yaeger writes from Central National Bank of Mattoon where he is President and CEO: "We truly appreciated your kind send off on our final Sunday in DeKalb. We have many pleasant memories from our 7½ years there and will be looking for opportunities for return visits. Best wishes to you and the Church Family."
Phyllis Kelley presented information about the leading "Conductor" on the Underground Railroad" in DeKalb County at the Rockford Historical Society.
Jayne Schafer visited A Japanese family in Tokyo and daughter Denise.
Isabel and Francis Cash have returned from San Diego.
Lois and Bob Meissner returned from Honduras and Lois showed slides at Shabonna Church. Barbara Skelley represented our church at the installation of the Rev. David D. Wernecke at Shabonna U.C.C. March 7th. David graduated from Elmhurst College, worked in the public sector, completed seminary at Dubuque Theological Seminary in Iowa. He married Karen Habeck in 1991.
Everett Cutsinger spent many hours of last week painting areas around the elevator and Church Secretary Carol Sievert's new Church Office.

CHURCH ORGAN IS NOW BEING REPAIRED:

Tuesday morning Howell Organ professionals from Dixon, IL., brought our new electronic panels made in England and shipped here over the past three months. How fortunate we were; for that night the whole shop in Dixon burned to the ground. Lost in the fire was a $250,000 organ almost prepared for installation in a Peoria church. We are most grateful to have been spared. March 7th worship was led by piano only. We hope for the organ Mar. 21.

Courtesy of The Spire, *DeKalb Congregational Church*

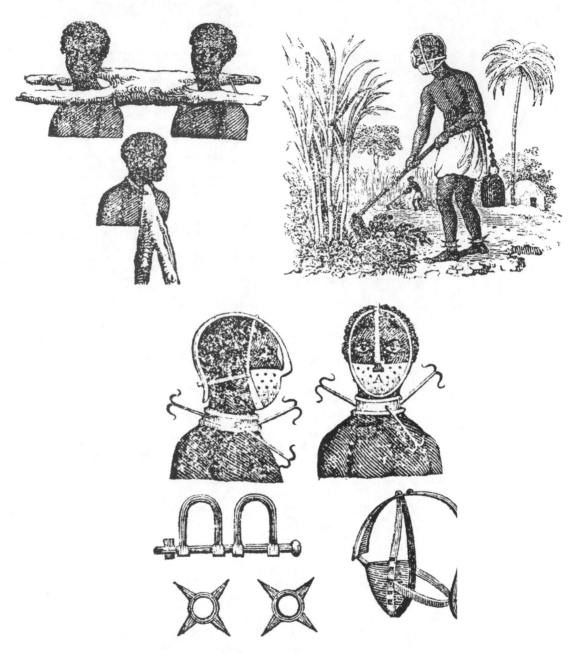

SLAVE RESTRAINTS
Head frames and log yokes were methods of control common in the West Indies and used to some extent in North America.

The Under Ground RR was established from St Louis - through Alton Farming-
settlement (west of Springfield) Woodrow settlement on sand Prairie- Deacon Strut
Washington Metamora & vicinity Crow Creek so on to Ottoway - + ___ ____
The express was run generally after dark - at one time there were 15 passengers —
some times only one - At one time, a man his wife & child with another men were
pursued from Springfield, as a large reward was offered for their capture. The
woman & child came from Tremont to my house in the evening & stated, that the two
men were coming on foot. but they did not arrive; so my Brothers took the
& child in a wagon for Washington prairie & got the hunter from Springfield
get Ed Tinney at Tremont (who afterwards was a rebel General in Kentucky) to help him
as my Brothers were driving along. two men sprang out in front with guns
and commanded a halt, they took the captives to Pekin and down the river
to St Louis and sold them, as they got more money than the reward offered
The two men soon arrived and finding his wife & child were in despair, the men
were guarded and our houses watched, so I kept them secreted for more than a
week & found the roads guarded north of us. I went to Peoria to consult
with the friends. what was best to be done. I proposed to take the fugitives on
horse back to the Peoria Lake opposite Main Sts. the river being high extending
into the woods. Mr Adams & Babcock were to take a skiff and row to where
we signaled them. Accordingly we met and they were taken across into Peoria and
so transferred on the Farmington line and were safely taken through to where
_____ __ __ __ "

ZEBINA EASTMAN LETTER

Although very few written accounts of UGRR activities were recorded (since those activities were in violation of the Fugitive Slave Law), this excerpt of a letter from J.H. Roberts to
Zebina Eastman provides insights into Illinois UGRR Activities. Other Chicago Historical
Society manuscripts include the Constitution John Brown wrote in anticipation of a government of freedmen in Canada and a letter signed by Frederick Douglass.

Courtesy of The Chicago Historical Society

Courtesy of Beverly Gray.

Courtesy of Beverly Gray.

GENIUS OF UNIVERSAL EMANCIPATION

THE GENIUS OF Universal Emancipation.

EDITED BY BENJAMIN LUNDY.

SATURDAY, JANUARY 5, 1828.

REMARKS, OCCASIONAL.

MEMORIAL TO CONGRESS.

CARTERS AND DRAYMEN.

THE "CLOVEN FOOT" VISIBLE.

WORSE AND WORSE!

Courtesy of Beverly Gray.

230

GENIUS OF UNIVERSAL EMANCIPATION

Literary Department.

"Various, that the mind
Of desultory man, studious of change,
And pleased with novelty, may be indulged."

In the following sentimental effusion, we recognize the
ardent & further esteemed and welcome correspondent. It
ould be exceedingly gratifying to hear from him more
requently.—G. U. Emen.

FOR THE GENIUS OF UNIVERSAL EMANCIPATION.

REFLECTIONS.

My heart is a desert, most dreary and lone,
And the joys of my bosom are vanish'd and flown;
Fate presses me down while a suppl'ant I bow,
And the year marks of anguish corrode on my brow.
From the womb to the grave must my spirit be chain'd,
To misery's car, then eternally pained;
With the cursed to rove, with the cursed to grieve,
Unworthy of pardon, unknown to reprieve!
I sub't the dire blessings omnipotence sends
Deprives me of fortune, divests me of friends;
Tears all that is pleasant away from my heart,
And bids every vision that's blissful depart;
Plants thorns in my bosom, surrounds me with care,
And sinks me still deeper in gloom and despair;—
Why then was I born! is it mercy that gave,
This being to torture? relentless to save!
Can it be! can it be, that His terrible wrath,
Pursues me through life and consumes me in death?
O, no! for the blood of Redemption is giv'n,
To cleanse my pollutions and fit me for heav'n!—
Tho' my sins are as scarlet, or crimson their dye,
My head a full fountain whose gush is the eye;
That Being who first from confusion refin'd
This chaos of matter, and lighted the mind,
With a spark of his own living essence, can give
To my soul a pure lustre, and cause me to live
In peace and contentment while tenanted here,
Seal up the full fountain, and "dry the big tear."
He is not that tyrant which Priestcraft assigns,
Who torture on torture with anguish refines;—
But a God ever gracious, unchangeably pure,
Whose laws formed on justice forever endure;
To spirit and matter alike they extend,
And perfect, like him, they accomplish their end.
Sin pregnant with sorrow, peace still follows good,
The essence and fruit of that mystical blood,
Which thro' righteousness saves and thro' evil con-
demns,
And marks us as foes to our God or as friends,—
How great is His glory! how poor is that life,
Which leads us to wander, thro' darkness and strife,
When fill'd with amazement and comfortless driv'n,
We break every chord that would bind us to heaven.
His love will pursue us, O! bless'd be his name,
His mercy and kindness are ever the same.
. . . . peace offerings or lambs,
Angle rivers of oil, or the . . . .
The skin of the death-stricken animals bleed;
To gorge like a vampire, o'er sated, with food;
His ways are not carnal, His spirit shall teach,
What a gold grasping Priesthood would tremble to
preach;
The fire of His love shall consume every name,
And blast on their brow's the wreath'd laurels of fame,
No matter what cloak for their deeds they may claim,
Be it pray'r, be it tribute, alike 'tis in vain;
The soul must be bow'd, 'tis the law of our Lord,
Let mortals not shrink at His heart-searching word;
Unseen is their tribute, unheard are their pray'rs.
O! let me be humble and contrite of heart,
And like Mary, endeavour to choose the good part,
Then when life ebbs away and my spirit is gone,
'Twill unite with its God, and our spirits be one.   P.

From Mrs. Colvin's Messenger.

O! smile to those that smile to thee;
For there is nought on earth so sweet
As, when the heart is full of glee,
A look of kindred glee to meet.
The evening star that shines alone
Can scarcely thro' the shades be known,
But when her sisters all arise
How brilliant are the midnight skies!   G. H. B.
[City N.Y.

ON SEEING A FLAKE OF SNOW FALL AND MELT ON A
LADY'S BOSOM.

The envious snow comes down in haste,
To prove thy breast less fair;—
It grieves to see itself surpassed,
And melts into a tear.

THE TWINS.

"I tell it to you as it was told to me."

In the autumn of 1826 I had occasion to visit
the town of N—— beautifully situated on the
western bank of the Connecticut river. My business led me to the house of B—— a lawyer of
three score and ten, who was resting from the labors and enjoying the fruits of a life strenuously
and successfully devoted to his profession. His
drawing room was richly furnished and decorated
with several valuable paintings. There was one
among them that particularly attracted my attention. It represented a mother with two beautiful
children, one in either arm, a light well thrown
over the group, and one of the children pressing its
lips to the cheek of the mother.—"That," said I,
pointing to the picture, "is very beautiful—pray,
sir, what is the subject?" "It is a mother and her
twins," said he; "the picture in itself is deemed a
fine one, but I value it more for the recollections
which are associated with it." I turned my eye
upon B——; he looked communicative and I asked
him for the story. "Sit down," said he, "and I
will tell it." We accordingly sat down and he
gave me the following narrative:

During the period of the war of the revolution,
there resided in the western part of Massachusetts
a farmer by the name of Stedman. He was a man
of substance, descended from a very respectable
family, well educated, distinguished for great firm-
ness of character in general, and alike remarkable
for inflexible integrity and stedfast loyalty to his
king. Such was the reputation he sustained, that
even when the most violent antipathies against
royalism swayed the community, it was still admitted on all hands that farmer Stedman, though a to-
ry, was honest in his opinions, and firmly believed
them to be right.

The period came when Burgoyne was advanc-
ing from the north. It was a time of great anxie-
ty with both the friends and foes of the revolution,
and one which called forth their highest exertions.
The patriotic militia flocked to the standard of
Gates and Stark, while many of the tories resorted to
the quarters of Burgoyne and Baum. Among the latter was Stedman. He had no sooner decided it to
be his duty than he took a kind farewell of his wife
and children, a twin boy and girl; a long embrace,
then mounted his horse and departed. He joined
himself to the unfortunate expedition of Baum, and
was taken with other prisoners of war by the victo-
rious Stark. He made no attempt to conceal his
name or character, which were both soon discovered, and he was accordingly committed to prison
as a traitor. The jail in which he was confined,
was in the western part of Massachusetts, and
nearly in a ruinous condition. The farmer was
one night waked from his sleep by several persons
in his room. "Come," said they, "you can now
regain your liberty: we have made a breach in the
prison through which you can escape." To their
astonishment Stedman utterly refused to leave his
prison. In vain they expostulated with him; in
vain they represented to him that his life was at
stake. His reply was, that he was a true man, and
a servant of King George, and that he would not
creep out of a hole at night, and sneak away from
the rebels, to save his neck from the gallows.
Finding it altogether fruitless to attempt to move
him, his friends left him with some expressions of
spleen.

The time at length arrived for the trial of the
prisoner. The distance to the place where the
court was sitting at that time was about sixty miles.
Stedman remarked to the Sheriff, who came
to attend him, that it would save some expense and
inconvenience, if he could be permitted to go alone
and on foot. "And suppose," said the sheriff,
"you should prefer your safety to your honor, and
leave me to seek you in the British camp." "I had
thought," said the farmer reddening with indigna-

tion, "that I was speaking to one who knew me.
I do know you indeed," said the sheriff; "I
spoke but in jest; you shall have your way. Go
and on the third day, I shall expect to see you at
I——." The farmer departed, and at the appointed time he placed himself in the hands of the
sheriff.   (Conclusion next week.)

AFFECTING ACCOUNT OF TWO MEN WHO WENT INTO
THE CELEBRATED MAMMOTH CAVE, ABOUT TEN
MILES IN LENGTH, IN GREEN COUNTY, KY. WITH
THE INTENTION OF EXPLORING IT.

The men, after having provided themselves with
a lantern, food and refreshments for one or two
days' journey, entered the cave and commenced
their subterranean tour. As they walked on from
one apartment to another, viewing, in astonishment,
the wonders of this stupendous cavern, they often
came to large and almost fathomless pits, which
they passed with much difficulty, by crawling on
their hands and knees. They proceeded in this
way, walking and crawling for about a day, and in
the mean time had passed a number of these pits.
They had just passed one of them, when, by some
fatal accident, their light was extinguished. One
of them, in the agony of despair, appeared to lose
his reason—became bewildered—whirled round,
exclaiming, Lord have mercy on us, and fell—and,
in falling, plunged headlong into the pit they had
just passed. His companion listened, and heard
him distinctly strike on the bottom and groan. He'd
called to him, but received no answer—he called
again, but all was silent as the tomb. I thought,
said he, had I but fallen with him, it must have been
a happy circumstance, for to attempt to find the
mouth of the cave, and pass the many dangerous
places they had met with in entering, must, he con-
ceived, be impossible. He thought, therefore, of
dying only by starvation. He concluded, however,
to make an attempt to get out; he could but die,
he thought, by sharing the fate of his companion,
and this would sooner put an end to his sufferings.
He set out, crawling on his hands and knees, and
proceeded safely in this way about a day, when he
again yielded to his feelings, and burst into tears.
This alone, he said, relieved his agony. He set
out again, but with little hope of ever arriving at
the mouth of the cave, and continued winding his
way in midnight darkness about a day longer. As
they entered the cave, they observed that it branch-
ed . . . various directions, and he concluded that
he had taken the wrong one, and was as far, or farther from the entrance than when he set out. The
possibility again occurred to him of finding the way
out; and once more he summoned his remaining
strength, and commenced groping his way through
the dreary cavern; and on the morning of the third
day, when nature was nearly exhausted, and all
hope had fled, he thought he perceived the dawn of
daylight; and, on suddenly turning a corner, the
morning star shone full in his face. His feelings,
he said, must be imagined, for they could not be
described.—Zion's Herald.

TERMS OF SUBSCRIPTION,

TO THE
GENIUS OF UNIVERSAL EMANCIPATION.

The price of subscription is THREE DOLLARS per annum,
payable within six months of the time of subscribing—but a
full receipt will be given, if TWO DOLLARS AND FIFTY CENTS
be paid in advance.

Subscriptions will not be received for less time than a
year, out of the city of Baltimore; and the money must always be paid in advance by distant subscribers, unless they
communicate their names through the medium of an authorized Agent. The difficulty in collecting small sums, at
a distance, renders a strict adherence to this rule indispen-
sably necessary.

Subscribers will not be at liberty to withdraw their names
if they are in arrears.

The postage must be paid on all letters and communications received by the editor, through the Post-Office.

Address   BENJAMIN LUNDY, Editor,
South-East corner of Market and Gay Streets, Baltimore.

Courtesy of Beverly Gray.

ST. CHARLES CHRONICLE

Family gives society memento

BY VICTORIA PIERCE
Staff Writer

At first glance it looks like any other ordinary chair, but this bent wood rocking chair has more years of history behind it than most people could remember.

The chair, which was recently given to the St. Charles Historical Society by owner Shirley Coleman, was carried from a southern plantation to Moline, Ill. on the underground railroad during the Civil War.

Coleman's grandmother Matilda Harris was responsible for bringing the chair. Coleman

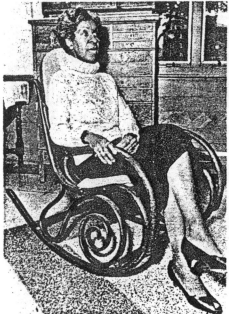

Chronicle photo by Bob Gerrard

Yvonne Luckett Almo sits in the 'slave chair' which was donated to the St. Charles Historical Society by her cousin, Shirley Harris Coleman.

said her family used to call it "the slave chair."

Coleman's father brought the chair to St. Charles after his mother's death. The chair was kept on the back porch for many years, until her Uncle William Luckett refinished the chair to what it looks like now.

"It really was a beat up old thing," Coleman said. "There's a place on one of the arms where you could get a splinter if you weren't careful. If you look you can still see it."

The chair was originally held together with wooden pegs and had a wicker back and seat, she said.

Luckett, who was a local artist, covered the back and sides and nailed the chair back to its original sturdiness. It now leans slightly to the left from so many years of use.

Coleman's house also has a lot of history behind it. It is one of the latest St. Charles homes to be awarded a landmark plaque by the St. Charles Historical Society.

Coleman's great-great-grandmother, Joanna Garner moved to St. Charles after traveling up from the south about 120 years ago.

Coleman is the fifth generation of the family to live in the house on South Sixth Street.

"They are one of the oldest continuous families living in St. Charles," said Barbara Martin, curator of the St. Charles Historical Society museum.

Joanna Garner worked for a family in St. Charles and was given the entire block with a small two-room house in repayment for her services to the family.

Over the years the house has had many "room additions and decor rearrangements," including a basement that was dug later, Coleman said. The original two-room structure is now in the middle of the current house.

Coleman said she was "very thrilled" to hear her house had been chosen as a St. Charles landmark and said she hopes the house stays in the family for many more generations in the future.

Courtesy of St. Charles Chronicle.

Sycamore True Republican

DECEMBER 8, 1909.

NEAR CENTENARIAN

Helped Organize Republican Party In DeKalb County.

DISTINGUISHED PIONEER

Death Of William A. Nickerson Closes Career Of Last Of Prominent Leaders In This County Before The Civil War.— Important History.

The following important facts in the history of DeKalb county and interesting story of the life of William A. Nickerson, who was from 1846 to 1864 one of the most prominent citizens of DeKalb county, are here for the first time published.

This last survivor of all the group who were prominent before the Civil war in DeKalb county, this pioneer of two states, political and moral reformer, minister of the gospel and public man during most of his mature years, died at the home of his son in Grand Traverse county, Mich., last Wednesday, December 1, 1909, at the great age of 98 years.

Just three weeks before his death, at the request of L. M. Gross of Sycamore, his grand-daughter wrote his biography as he dictated it to her, at which time he gave promise of rounding out a full century of life.

William Nickerson spoke on many subjects including the U.G.R.R.

I came in 1845 from a short distance north of Elmira, N. Y., to Illinois with a horse team and covered wagon, accompanied by three neighbors—Mr Crawford, Mr. Wilder and Mr. Hatch. Five weeks and three days were required to make the journey to the Fox river in Illinois. The traveling was so bad in places, especially in Michigan, that we were able to go only from four to seven miles a day.

On reaching Illinois I had only about $25 left, but found new friends who gave me work. I visited Chicago twice to find land, expecting to build a boarding house there, but my wife was opposed. On one visit to Chicago I met Mr. William Rowen, who told me there was still public land in DeKalb county, just west of Kane county, where I had located. I visited DeKalb county and decided to locate there. I had very little money, but without asking for it, Joshua Townsend (great grandfather of Frederick B. Townsend, the Sycamore banker), came and offered to lend me money to pay for my first 40 acres. This was in 1846, for I had remained one year in Kane county working by the day. This first land I acquired was the 40 acres constituting the north portion of M. Ault's farm in Mayfield township. I lived here about ten years, and then bought land cornering this on the southeast, and afterwards sold it to Mrs. Mary Gross, grandmother of L. M. Gross.

Although I was poor, I was known as an Anti-Slavery man, and I assisted

There was an incident of another character which was amusing. Mr. Cross, another underground railway man, was suspected of carrying negroes by the sheriff and he was arrested. The road over which he must travel with his prisoner was through a Quaker settlement, and he was sure he would have trouble with the Quakers if they knew he had John Cross in custody. Cross told him that he (the sheriff) might lie down in the wagon and he would drive through the settlement and there would be no suspicion on the part of the Quakers that he (Cross) had been arrested. He did so, covered up, and Mr. Cross drove slowly through the Quaker town. The sheriff delivered Mr. Cross to jail, but they failed to prove anything against him.

One more incident of another character. I was home one cold wintry night when the prairie winds were howling. I was reading and heard a timid knock at the door. I went and opened it, and there stood a woman—a mulatto with a little girl. As she stood there she asked: "Do Mr. Nickerson live here?" I said "Yes." She said: "I was told that you were a friend of the colored people." I answered "Yes, walk in." It was very cold, but the man who brought her had driven off immediately. I told the Townsends of what I had and that she was an excellent cook, so said the certificate that she had with her. We made up our minds that the cold winter was a hard time to send that woman on to Canada and thought to try to find a home for her. We went to Sycamore and found a home for her in Dr. Page's cellar kitchen. She remained there four months and then we sent her on her way to Canada.

One thing more, I would say: Some of the lake captains were very

Chicago

OLUME XIV.　　　　　　　　　　　　　　　　　　CHICAGO, TH

THE ARREST OF THE HARRIS FAMILY.

A Card from U. S. Marshal Jones.

FURTHER COMMENTS ON THE CASE.

To the Public.

CHICAGO, April 9, 1861.

I had not designed replying to the statements contained in the Chicago TRIBUNE, in relation to the arrest of the fugitives in this city on Wednesday last ; but so much has been said and so many false statements made and repeated, that I feel it due to the public and to myself that a correct statement of facts should be made.

The duty of a Marshal is suggested by the language of his official oath, which is as follows. "I do solemnly swear that I will *faithfully execute all lawful precepts* directed to the Marshal of the Northern District of Illinois under the authority of the United States, and true returns make and in all things well and truly and without malice or *partiality* perform the duties of the office of Marshal of the Northern District of Illinois during my continuance in said office and take only my lawful fees, so help me God." The law makes it as much the duty of the Marshal to execute a warrant for the arrest of a fugitive slave as it makes it his duty to execute any other process, and having sworn to execute the law in good faith, I saw no other alternative when the warrant was placed in my hands but to execute it. The warrant was carefully examined by one eminently qualified to judge of its legality, and I was told by persons in whose judgment I placed implicit confidence, what my duty clearly was, and that anything short of its faithful execution would be a palpable violation of my oath. I knew too that if I succeeded in getting the fugitives into my custody, the law made me responsible for the full value of such fugitives in the State from which they escaped, in the event of their escape, whether with or without my assent. I also believed (a belief justified by the result, in as much as a mob of several hundred negroes *did assemble* immediately after the arrest) that the arrest could not be made publicly, without the certainty of a serious risk and probable loss of life. I therefore decided to have the arrests made early in the morning, before there were many persons on the street. The arrests were made at a few minutes past six o'clock, in broad daylight, and at half-past six the train started for Springfield (stopping out of the city limits two hours and a half, awaiting for the regular morning train down to take them forward). The warrant described the fugitives so minutely that it was impossible to mistake them. The claimants brought letters from citizens of St. Louis of the highest respectability, among others one from O. D. Filley, late Mayor, indorsing him as a man of high moral character, and one whose statements were entitled to the utmost confidence. The TRIBUNE'S statement that the fugitives were "aroused from a state of somnolence" *is not true.* They were all up and dressed, with the exception of one of the children, which was but partially dressed.

No such language was used towards the woman as is attributed to one of the party making the arrest. The statement that " the United States Marshal, Jones, was the while frowning down the efforts of a grizzly headed colored person to get out of a bed room, against the door of which the majesty of the law, in the shape of Mr. Jones, had placed its back, with a revolver at the key hole should the grizzly colored person prove obstreperous," is utterly false. I was not present at the arrest, did not go near the house where the fugitives were and did not see them or any of them, until they got out of the omnibus at the depot. The statement that I "took none but pro-slavery Democrats into my office, to one of whom I had already given, probably with reference to such affairs as this, a regular Deputyship," is utterly untrue. The only Deputy I have appointed is as sound a Republican as any in the country. He supported Scott in 1852 ; published a Republican paper and supported Fremont in 1856, and was heartily a Lincoln man in 1860, and never voted a Democratic ticket in his life.

In regard to the statement that "other tools of like antecedents and sympathies were chosen, and their hard heartedness tested, as the man tries the steel on which he is to rely," I have only to say that I did not know one of the men selected by my Deputy to assist him in the arrest—had no conversation with any of them on the subject, nor do I now know what their political sentiments are.

Allusion is twice made in the TRIBUNE'S article to the probability of my being rewarded by a service of plate from the "nigger drivers." In the same issue is a notice of a silver pitcher on exhibition on Clark street, marked "Mrs. J. R. Jones," but the writer of the article carefully avoids giving any of the circumstances connected with the pitcher, leaving its readers to infer that the reward above referred to had already been received. I shall be pardoned for saying that the Pitcher alluded to was presented to my wife by the Merchants' Association of Chicago, as a return for the zeal which it was supposed I had manifested in looking after their interests during the past winter at Springfield—the presentation of which I knew nothing of until I reached home on Sunday last.

The statement that I " hired the wretch Hayes to betray his colored brethren" is utterly false. Neither my deputy nor myself ever saw or heard of the man Hayes, until we saw his name connected with the matter in the TRIBUNE ; we had nothing whatever to do with him, directly or indirectly. The statement that " the fatalities that were inflicted upon the whole family, dragged, bound and gagged, and half naked down stairs, the oaths and curses and show of revolvers with which the tools of Marshal Jones did his bidding," &c., &c., is utterly false and without a semblance of truth. There was no more violence used than was absolutely necessary to make the arrest. No revolver was displayed or seen in the transaction, and no one gagged.

Neither my deputy nor myself ever heard of the $200 reward referred to until we saw it in the TRIBUNE. I have only to add, in conclusion, that being first fully convinced that my oath required that I should execute the warrant in good faith, painful as the duty was, I sought to do it in such a manner as to avoid any scenes of lawless violence, and the more than probable loss of life in the event of a riot—and the riot itself—which would have been inevitable had the arrest been made at any other time or in any other manner. I very much doubt if any of those persons who are now so ready to censure me for a faithful discharge of an exceedingly unpleasant duty, have really any more sympathy for the negroes, or will do more to relieve their sufferings, than myself ; or that they are at heart more thoroughly opposed to slavery than am. The difference between them and myself is that I have taken a solemn oath to execute the law, while they have not. If for a faithful discharge of my duty I am to be condemned, then I am prepared to take the consequences.

J. R. JONES, U. S. Marthal.

The story of abudction of the Harris family was a front page article the day before Fort Sumpter. *(Chicago Tribune)*

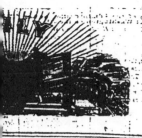

Tribune.

AY, APRIL 11, 1861. NUMBER 243.

COMMENTS.

We give place, and have given a careful perusal to the above Card of United States Marshal Jones, It is no wonder that he desires to free himself from the just odium that would necessarily attach to an officer in his position, were our recent strictures on his course in the arrest of the Harris family true. "Now the question is how far this letter of Marshal Jones is to be taken as a defence."

And we do not see that the features of the affair, whereof we complained are relieved a single whit by the careful special pleadings of Mr. Jones. The earlier statement in our first notice, quoted at length above, as to Mr. Jones' being present at the time of the arrest, was fully and distinctly withdrawn in our next issue, but the further and indisputable fact remains, on the best of evidence, that *some person calling himself U. S. Marshal Jones* did play the part at the bed-room door, and that one of the inmates of the room, a colored woman, was so frightened by the violence of the persons making the arrest that she leaped from the upper window to the ground, so severely injuring herself that she is still under physicians care.

We censured Marshal Jones severely, but reluctantly, for the spirit and mode of this arrest, we do so still. We called it an outrage not so far from the atrocity and severity of the law itself, precisely as we might, without questioning the laws for collection of debt, censure a sharp constable for over and inhuman zeal in the discharge of his duty.

Marshal Jones says he was not there, but he was not far off, for he states that he met the party at the depot. He denies that he knows any of the men who aided in making the arrest, and we are bound to believe him; but not to excuse him. A man is responsible for the acts of his Deputy. It was Marshal Jones' business to know who was aiding in this arrest, and how it was accomplished. We tell him it was done inhumanly, and see nothing in his letter to disprove it, for the *strongest point Mr. Jones makes is lack of all personal knowledge of the matter*.

This omnibus is driven to the door in the grey of the morning. The household within doors are silent. The wretch Hayes whom Marshal Jones does not dare to say was not hired, had left the bolt drawn and six armed men pass up stairs. One or two persons, neighbors, whose testimony we have, hear outcries and a scuffle. The children are brought down, and placed in the omnibus, then a stout colored man is dragged down, manacled, and his elbows tied behind his back. He is only half dressed, and the woman is brought down wrapped in a quilt for decency's sake. And this was precisely the form of arrest. Mr. Jones may make what fine point he pleases as to the actual state of "somnolence" of the party captured. There was certainly a somnolence to all ordinary calls to humanity on the part of the captors.

One of the Police Commissioners has since the arrest, questioned the Federal officers somewhat closely as to "who the men were who were stars" at the time of this capture. He was told they were none of the city police, and the inference is left that stars were illegally worn by the pimps and bullies who were making up a reputation for Marshal Jones without his knowledge, as it appears from his card. Mr. Jones vouches for his Deputy's Republicanism. It will strike the minds of many of our citizens as a novelty, and we are sorry to be convinced. But there the matter of disproving the Tribune's statement ends, for there is no question that this Deputy sought men who were "found off the goose," and sound Democrats.

The reference to Mr. Jones' connection with this arrest, and the suggestion of a possible reward in plate, was in type before a city notice was made of an elegant article of plate, made to order by one of our jewelers, and inscribed "Mrs. J. E. Jones." No one could think that plate could be made to order and inscribed, in the interim of one night and forty hours since the Harris affair, and there was no such imputation.

We leave this matter, and Marshal Jones' connection with an arrest we trust will be without a parallel in the future, as it has none in the past history of Fugitive Slave processes in this city.

It was with reluctance that we found ourselves called to review and comment upon one of the earliest official acts of our new United States Marshal. The personal relations between Mr. Jones and one of the editors of this paper run through years of kindly intercourse, and we had hastened in these columns to congratulate and welcome him to his new post. It was unlooked for, and unwelcome to us, to be forced to censure him; and we are willing to accept the most charitable construction to be derived from his letter above given—that, with a determination to perform his duty, in the very place where his reputation for humanity was at stake, as a man and an officer, he gave over the whole into the hands and conduct of men with neither humanity nor reputation, forgetting that although ignorant of what they might do, he was none the less accountable. Had Marshal Jones sought his advisers and assistants from men "thoroughly opposed to slavery" as he claims to be himself, the law, odious as it is, might have been vindicated, and a gross outrage spared this community.

Astounding Developments—Slave Stealing and Negro Hunting.

Some weeks since, a man, a stranger, came to a respectable colored woman, for fifteen years resident in this city, a Mrs. Johnson. He introduced himself by saying that he was a friend of the colored race. He had learned that Mrs. Johnson had a daughter in slavery in Missouri. This started the old colored woman's confidence only slowly, and it was not until the second visit that he made much headway with his errand. Finally, however, he persuaded her of his good intention, his experience and ability in this particular line, and she agreed with him that he was to receive from her $150, for services and expenses in running off this daughter and her family, a husband and three children. Mrs. Johnson mortgaged her little home for a part of this sum.

This family was the Harris family, and they arrived in due time, and were closely sheltered here. Their new found friend and rescuer stuck closely to them, bade them keep the house of the mother and never be seen out of doors, and they followed his instructions.

Meanwhile this identical man, after a trip to St. Louis, came back, and was closeted again and again with Federal officers in this city. They used a room at the Tremont House for this purpose; and when the scheme was carefully ripened, the string was pulled, the game bagged, and the very party who stole the slaves in Missouri and was paid one hundred and fifty dollars by the mother of the woman for so doing, is equally officious in sending them back, and so shares in the reward offered by the master.

There is reason to believe that the scoundrel is one of a regularly organised gang in St. Louis and Chicago who make a business of running off and then returning slaves, by the shuttle-like process, making a very good thing of it. The principal operators are ex-policemen, and policemen high in favor at St. Louis.

Y. A. U. S.—All members will be at their headquarters Thursday evening, at 8 o'clock, prompt. Let all be on duty. The R. T is Friday. B. K. L. O. P.
OLCOTT B. PARKE, C. P.
CHAUNCEY MILLER, T. L.

WEST CHICAGO GRAND MASS MEETING AT THE

[1840.] Anti-Slavery Almanac. 11

BRANDING SLAVES.

"TWENTY DOLLARS REWARD. Ranaway from the subscriber, a negro woman and two children; the woman is tall and black, and *a few days before she went off, I BURNT HER WITH A HOT IRON ON THE LEFT SIDE OF HER FACE;* I tried to make the letter M, *and she kept a cloth over her head and face, and a fly bonnet over her head, so as to cover the burn;* her children are both boys, the oldest is in his seventh year; he is a *mulatto* and has blue eyes; the youngest is a black and is in his fifth year. [N. C. Standard, July 18, 1838.] MICAJAH RICKS, Nash County.

One hundred dollars reward for Pompey, 40 years old, he is *branded on the left jaw.*—Mr. R. P. Carney, in the Mobile Register, Dec. 22, 1838.

"Ranaway a negro girl called Mary, has the letter A *branded on her cheek and forehead.*"—Mr. J. P. Ashford, Natchez Courier, August 24, 1838.

"Ranaway, Bill, has a burn *in his buttock, from a piece of hot iron in shape of a T.*"—Mr. J. N. Dilahunty, Woodville, N. O. Com. Bulletin, July 21, 1837.

"TWENTY DOLLARS REWARD.—Ranaway from the subscriber a negro girl named Molly. The said girl was sold by Messrs. Wm. Payne & Sons, and purchased by a Mr. Mosca, and sold by him to Thos. Frisley, of Edgefield District, of whom I bought her. She is 16 or 17 years of age, LATELY BRANDED ON THE LEFT CHEEK, THUS, R, AND A PIECE TAKEN OFF HER EAR ON THE SAME SIDE; THE SAME LETTER ON THE INSIDE OF BOTH HER LEGS. [Charleston, S. C. Courier, 1825.]" ABNER ROSS, Fairfield District.

"Was committed to jail a negro man, says his name is Josiah, *branded on the thigh and hips in three or four places, thus* (J. M.)—J. L. Jolley, Sheriff of Clinton, Co. M., in the Clinton Gazette, July 23, 1836.

About a year since I knew a slave, who had deserted his master, to be caught, and fastened to the stocks. On the next morning he was *chained in an immovable posture, and BRANDED IN BOTH CHEEKS WITH RED HOT STAMPS of iron.*—Letter from a clergyman written in Natchez, (Mi.) in 1833.

"Fifty dollars reward for my fellow Edward, he has *the letter E on his arm.*"—Mr. Thos. Ledwith, Jacksonville, East Florida, in the Charleston, S. C. Courier, Sept. 1, 1838.

"Ranaway a negro boy Harper, *has a scar on one of his hips in the form of a G.*"—Mr. W. Bissewll, Pinkeville, Ala., in the Huntsville Dem. Aug 22, 1837.

The masters seldom, if ever, try to govern their slaves by moral influence, but by whipping, kicking, beating, starving, *branding, ear-hauling, scalding with irons, imprisoning,* or by some other cruel mode of torture. They often boast of having invented some new mode of torture, by which they have "tamed the rascals."—Rev. Horace Moulton, of the M. E. Church, Marlborough, Mass., who spent five years in Georgia, between 1817 and 1824.

SLAVERY AND THE SLAVE TRADE AT THE NATION'S CAPITAL.
HAIL, COLUMBIA!!

View of the Capitol at Washington.

One would think that slavery and the slave trade were the last things to have a legal and protected existence in the capital of a boasted free nation. But there they are—unpaid toil, whips, chains, dungeons, separations, murders, and all! That slave coffle marching by the capitol is not fancy, but a fact not unfrequently occurring. Dr. Torrey (Portraiture of Domestic Slavery, p. 64), states, on the authority of Mr. Aldgate, a member of the House of Representatives, that "during the last session of Congress (1815–16), as several members were standing in the street near the new capitol, a drove of manacled colored people were passing by, and when just opposite, one of them elevating his manacles as high as he could reach, commenced singing the favorite national song, "Hail Columbia! happy land," &c.

So late as the session of 1838–9, a similar scene was enacted. The House, in base subserviency to the slaveholders, had passed resolutions declaring that Congress had no constitutional power to abolish slavery in the District of Columbia, and excluding all petitions on the subject of slavery from being read or referred. "Nine days after the adoption of these resolutions," says Hon. J. R. Giddings (Rights of the Free States subverted, p. 13) "a coffle of thirty slaves chained together, and followed by about the same number of females, who were permitted to travel unchained, were driven past the capitol, on their way to a southern market."

Slavery and the Slave Trade no Right at the Nation's Capital.

When the people of this country rose in resistance to British oppression, they declared to the world (Dec. Am. Ind.)—"We hold these truths to be self-evident: That all men are created equal: that they are endowed by their Creator with certain inalienable rights: that among these are life, liberty and the pursuit of happiness."

When the same people adopted the present Constitution of Government, they also declared, in the preamble, that its object was "to form a more perfect union, establish justice, insure domestic tranquility, provide for the common defence, promote the general welfare, and secure the blessings of liberty to ourselves and

1840.] Anti-Slavery Almanac. 15

SELLING A MOTHER FROM HER CHILD.

"'Do you often buy the wife without the husband?' 'Yes, very often;' and *frequently,* too, they sell the mother while they keep her children. I have often known them take away the infant from its mother's breast, and keep it, while they sold her.'"—Prof. Andrews, late of the University of N. C., in his recent work on Slavery and the Slave-Trade, p. 147, relates *the foregoing conversation with a slave-trader on the Potomac.*

Hon. James K. Paulding, the Secretary of the Navy of the U. States, in his "Letters from the South," published in 1817, says he heard a slave-trader say—"Many is the time I have separated wives from husbands, and husbands from wives, and parents from children; but then I made them amends by marrying them again as soon as I had a chance; that is to say, I made them call each other man and wife, and sleep together, which is quite enough for negroes. I made one bad purchase, though," continued he. 'I bought a young mulatto girl, a lively creature, a great bargain. She had been the favorite of her master, who had lately married. The difficulty was to get her to go, for the poor creature loved her master. However, I swore most bitterly I was only going to take her to her mother's at——, and she went with me, though she seemed to doubt me very much. But when she discovered, at last, that we were out of the state, I thought she would go mad; and, in fact, the next night she drowned herself in the river close by. I lost a good five hundred dollars by this foolish trick.'"—Vol. I. p. 121.

"One of my neighbors sold to a speculator a negro boy, about 14 years old. It was more than his poor mother could bear. Her reason fled, and she became a perfect maniac, and had to be kept in close confinement. She would occasionally get out and run off to the neighbors. On one of these occasions she came to my house. With tears rolling down her cheeks, and her frame shaking with agony, she would cry out, '*don't you hear him—they are whipping him now, and he is calling for me.*' This neighbor of mine, who tore the boy away from his poor mother, and thus broke her heart, was a *member of the Presbyterian church.*"—Rev. Francis Hawley, Baptist Minister, Colebrook, Ct.

"Absconded from the subscriber, a negro man, by the name of Wilson. He was born in the county of New Kent, and raised by a gentleman named Ratliffe, and by him sold to a gentleman named Taylor, on whose farm he had a wife and several children. Taylor sold him to Mr. Slater, who, in consequence of removing to Alabama, Wilson left; and when retaken was sold, and afterwards purchased, by his present owner, from T. McCargo & Co., of Richmond."—Richmond Whig, July 25, 1837.

1840.] Anti-Slavery Almanac. 7

HOW SLAVERY IMPROVES THE CONDITION OF WOMEN.

"John Ruffner, a slaveholder, had one slave named Pincy, whom he, as well as Mrs. Ruffner, would often flog very severely. I frequently saw Mrs. Ruffner flog her with the broom, shovel, or anything she could seize in her rage. She would knock her down and then kick and stamp her most unmercifully, until she would be apparently so lifeless, that I more than once thought she would never recover. The cause of Pincy's flogging was not working enough, or making some mistake in baking, &c. &c."—Mrs. N. Lowry, a native of Ky., now member of a Church, in Osnaburg, Stark co. Ohio.

"My uncle used to tie his "house wench" to a peach tree in the yard, and whip her till there was no sound place to lay another stroke, and repeat it so often that her back was continually sore. Whipping the females around the legs, was a favorite mode of punishment with him. They must stand and hold up their clothes while he plied his hickory."—Wm. Leftwich, a native of Virginia, and son of a slaveholder, now member of the Presbyterian Church, Delhi, Ohio.

"In the winter of 1828-29, I put up for a night at Frost Town, on the national road. Soon after there came in a slaver with a drove of slaves. I then left the room, and shortly afterwards heard a scream, and when the landlady inquired the cause, the slaver coolly told her not to trouble herself, he was only chastising one of his women.—It appeared that three days previously her child had died on the road, and been thrown into a crevice in the mountain, and a few stones thrown over it; and the mother weeping for her child was chastised by her master, and told by him, she should have something to cry for."—Colonel T. Rogers, a native of Kentucky, a Presbyterian elder at New Petersburg, Highland co. Ohio.

"Benjamin Lewis, an elder in the Presbyterian church, engaged a carpenter to repair his house. Kyle, the builder, was awakened very early in the morning by a most piteous moaning and shrieking. He arose, and following the sound, discovered a colored woman, nearly naked, tied to a fence, while Lewis was lacerating her. A second and a third scene of the same kind occurred, and on the third occasion the altercation almost produced a battle between the elder and the carpenter."—Rev. George Bourne, of New York, who was a preacher seven years in Virginia.

James T. De Jarnett, Vernon, Autauga co. Alabama, thus advertises a woman in the Pensacola Gazette, July 14, 1838. "Celia is a *bright copper-colored negress, fine figure and very smart. On examining her back, you will find marks caused by the whip.*"

P. Abella, advertises a woman in the N. O. Bee, of Jan. 29, 1833, "having marks of the whip behind her neck, and *several others on her rump.*"

236

NEW YORK ILLUSTRATED NEWS.

JOHN ANDERSON, THE FUGITIVE SLAVE

JOHN ANDERSON, THE FUGITIVE SLAVE IN CANADA.

The Anderson Fugitive Slave case has caused much excitement, both in England and in this country. Anderson's history is a very brief one. He was a negro slave with apparently a mixture of white blood in his veins, was brought up in the State of Missouri, and married a slave girl, by whom he had one child sharing the lot of his master's other live stock, he was sold into a part of the country many miles away from his wife. In the year 1853 he fled from the plantation to which he was transferred, and appeared in the quarter where his wife was located. Here he was descried by a planter named Seneca Digges, who had no claim over him, but who, in the common interest of slaveholding, gave chace with four slaves, whom he placed on the track of the fugitive. They ran down Anderson, and Digges closed with him. Anderson, thus brought to bay, stabbed Digges mortally. He then made his way to Canada. His wife and child are still in bondage in Missouri.

The United States Government claimed him of the Canadian authorities at Toronto, as a murderer, and on the 9th of February he was brought before the Court of Common Pleas, on a writ of *habeas corpus* issued by Chief Justice Draper. The points urged on behalf of the prisoner were these. First, that the prisoner was entitled to the writ on which he was brought before the Court, and upon the return to that writ to have inquired into the matters charged against him. Second, that the evidence was not sufficient to put him upon his trial for the crime of murder, assuming that he was entitled to the protection of British law.

Third, that the treaty requires that a charge under it should be first laid in the States, and that the evidence did not show that any charge had been laid against the prisoner. Fourth, that even if the Canadians were bound to administer this law of Missouri, the evidence did not show that this State of Missouri had any power to pass such a law, and it cannot be presumed that she had that power, inasmuch as she is but a municipality in relation to other governments, and the law is against natural justice. Fifth, that the word "murder" mentioned in the treaty means murder according to the laws of both countries ; and, if not, that by the treaty itself and British statute the crime charged is to be determined by the laws of Canada—that it is the criminality that is to be determined by the laws of Canada.

After hearing the evidence, Chief Justice Draper said that the Court desired to dispose of this case as quickly as possible, so that Anderson might not be kept in custody any longer than was necessary, if the decision went in his favor ; but it was questionable whether, if judgment was to be given on all the points involved, the case would be decided during the present term. At all events they would give the prisoner the benefit of a speedy discharge if they came to an opinion in his favor on the technical point as to the insufficiency of the commitment. On this question they would probably be able to give a decision that day week—the last day of term. An order would be made for the prisoner to be brought up next Saturday, and in the meantime he would be committed to the custody of the Sheriffs of the united counties of York and Peel.

On Saturday, the 16th ult., the Court of Common Pleas, as was generally anticipated, discharged Anderson, on the grounds that the warrant of commitment was not issued in conformity with the statute, because—1st. It did not contain a charge of murder, but merely of felonious homicide ; whereas the treaty and the British statute do not authorize a surrender, and, consequently, not a committal for the purpose of surrender, for any homicide not expressed to be murder. 2nd. That it was not expressed to be for the purpose of surrender, but only until the prisoner should be discharged by due course of law—whereas the statute requires both. Upon the merits of the question itself no judgment was given.

237

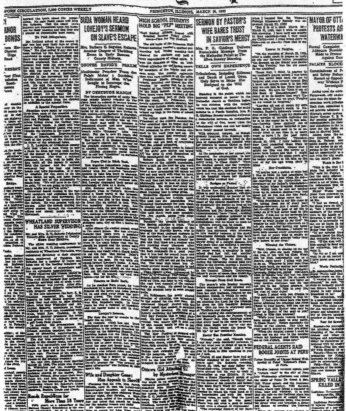

The Case of Jim Gray.

1823-1914

The famous case of Jim Gray, a fugitive slave, had its start about this time. On September 4, 1859, three negroes escaped from their master, Richard Phillips, near New Madrid, Missouri. One of them, Jim Gray, was caught in Union county, Illinois, and lodged in jail by the state authorities. A man named Root applied for a writ of habeas corpus, but the judge of the court would not grant it. Root then came to this city and applied to Judge Caton of the Supreme Court. The writ was granted and Root went back to Union county to serve it on the Sheriff. That official, being in sympathy with the slave owners, at first refused to obey, but finally concluded that inasmuch as the Supreme Court had issued the order he had best take notice.

Jailor Albright started north with the negro, but on the way to Ottawa he was overtaken by the negro's master, who demanded Gray on a writ issued by the United States Commissioner at Springfield. Albright did not want to resist the Government, still he wanted to obey the Supreme Court of Illinois. He was helped out of his difficulty by a United States Marshal, who deputized him, and thus he held the negro under both writs.

Judge Caton freed Gray from arrest by the state, but he still remained a prisoner of the government. The little spark that had been kindled by the Berkley case had by this time grown into a flame. The ablest lawyers in the city—E. S. Leland, Burton C. Cook, O. C. Gray and J. O. Glover—volunteered their services to defend the negro. Julius Avery was prosecutor. But the law was all on one side, and Judge Caton ordered the negro to be taken before the United States Commissioner at Springfield. It is believed that the Judge feared an uprising of the people, for he took occasion to remark that he hoped he lived in a law abiding community. So believing, he had had the negro brought to Ottawa for trial, but should any attempt be made to set the law at defiance he would never again try a similar case in this city.

While the case was being tried the anti-slavery people on the outside were not idle. They formed plans to rescue Gray. When the Judge announced his decision James Stout, a lawyer and an ardent Abolitionist, sprang up on a bench and shouted: "Gentlemen, I move that this meeting resolve itself into a committee to carry out the law." The marshal started for the door, holding the negro by the arm. The people who purposely filled the aisle stood back on each side, making a clear passage to the door. Several men seized the marshal and the negro was released. He was grabbed by John Hossack and dragged down the aisle and out of the building, the crowd inside having surrounded the marshal in order to prevent pursuit.

Outside the court house a carriage was in waiting. Gray jumped the fence and entered the carriage. Charles Campbell was in the driver's seat and applied the whip. About this time Peter Meyer sought to block the game and by seizing the bridle on one of the horses nearly upset the carriage. Then John Hossack stepped up, with fists clenched. Meyer released his hold and the carriage sped away, up La Salle street, into Superior street, and across the aqueduct bridge. Four miles from the city another vehicle with horses was in waiting; and thus Jim Gray landed safely in Canada.

Arrests Follow.

Of course the men who engineered this daring rescue of Gray got into trouble. Eight persons were indicted by the United States grand jury. Two left for parts unknown; six were taken into custody. They were John Hossack, Dr. Joseph Stout, Claudius B. King, James Stout, Hervey King and E. W. Chamberlin. While waiting for a train to Chicago a large crowd assembled at the depot and speeches were made by Burton C. Cook, Brunson Murray and Rev. G. W. Bassett.

Feeling themselves martyrs the prisoners refused bail. They were confined in the debtors' department of the Cook county jail. Then came the trials. Judge Drummond was on the bench, attorneys Burton C. Cook, Isaac N. Arnold, Jo Knox and Messrs. Larned and Goodwin appeared for the defense. District Attorney Fitch and Judge Arrington represented the government.

John Hossack was fined $100 and sentenced to ten days in jail; Dr. Joseph Stout at his second trial (the jury disagreed in his first trial) received a similar punishment; James Stout was acquitted and Claudius B. King pleaded guilty and was fined $10 and given one day in jail.

John Hossack's Speech.

When asked by Judge Drummond whether he had anything to say as to why he should not be sentenced Mr. Hossack delivered one of the most remarkable addresses ever heard in a court-house. Following is the full text of his address:

I have a few words to say why sentence should not be pronounced against me. I am found guilty of a violation of the fugitive slave law, and it may appear strange to your Honor that I have no sense of guilt. I came, sir, from the tyranny of the Old World when but a lad, landed upon the American shores, having left my kindred and native land in pursuit of some place where men of toil would not be crushed by the property-holding class. Commencing the struggle of life at the tender age of twelve years, a stranger in a strange land, having to earn my bread by the sweat of my brow, you Honor will bear with me, unaccustomed as I am to appear in courts, much less to address them. I have feared that I might fail in bearing myself on this occasion worthy of the place and the position I occupy and the great principles involved in the case before you. I say to your Honor, therefore, if I fail in observing the usual forms of the place it will be from a want of judgment and error of the head and not of the heart. Therefore, I do not think I shall fare worse at the hands of your Honor if I state plainly my views and feelings on the great question of the age—the rights of man. I feel that it is a case that will be referred to long after you and I have gone to meet the great Judge of all the earth.

It has been argued by the prosecution that I, a foreigner, protected by the laws of my adopted country, should be the last to disobey those laws; but in this I find nothing should destroy any sympathy for the crushed, struggling children of toil in all lands.

Surely, I have been protected. The fish in the rivers, the quail in the stubble, the deer in the forest have been protected. Shall I join hands with those who make wicked laws in crushing out the poor black man,

MR. AND MRS. JOHN HOSSACK.

for whom there is no protection but in the grave, where the wicked cease from troubling and the weary are at rest?

It is true, sir, I am a foreigner. I first saw the light among the rugged and free hills of Scotland; a land, sir, that never was conquered, and where a slave never breathed. Let a slave set foot on that shore and his chains fall off forever, and he becomes what God made him—a man. In that far off land I heard of your free institutions, your prairie lands, your projected canals and your growing towns. Twenty-two years ago I landed in this city. I immediately engaged on the public works, on the canal then building that connects this city with the great river of the West. In the process of time the state failed to procure money to carry on the public works. I then opened a prairie farm to get bread for my family, and I am one of the men that made Chicago what it is to-day, having shipped some of the first grain that was exported from this city. I am, sir, one of the pioneers of Illinois who have gone through the hardships of the settlement of a new country. I have spent my best days, the strength of my manhood. I have eleven children who are natives of this my adopted country. No living man, sir, has greater interest in its welfare; and it is because I am opposed to carrying out wicked and ungodly laws, and love the freedom of my country, that I stand before you to-day.

Again, sir, I ought not to be sentenced because, as has been argued by the prosecution, I am an Abolitionist. I have no apologies to make for being an Abolitionist.

Discovery and Conquests

OF THE

NORTHWEST

WITH THE

HISTORY OF CHICAGO

IN TWO VOLUMES
VOL. I.

BY

Rufus Blanchard.

CHICAGO:
R. BLANCHARD AND COMPANY
164 RANDOLPH ST.
1898

The first effort to gather all the children of the village emerges in 1830. Mr. J.B. Beaubien and Lieutenant Hunter (in the Secession War, Major-General David held in a house belonging to Beaubien, where Randolph Street meets Michigan Avenue. At one corner of that crossing now stands Chicago's grand Public Library Building. That school house was a low and gloomy but large log building, which could boast of five rooms. The Forbes family gave up a room to the school of twenty-five pupils, in which Mr. Forbes assisted. The dark and rough walls were later enlivened by a tapestry of white cotton sheeting. Mr. Foot carried on he school the next year.

In the fall of 1833, Miss Eliza Chappel, afterward the wife of Rev. Jeremiah Porter, opened "an infant school," plainly, a school for the smaller children, on the south side of the river and near the fort. She had about twenty pupils. From Mr. Wells we learn that in the same autumn Mr. Granville T. Sproat from Boston opened an "English and Classical School" n a Baptist Church on South Water Street, near Franklin: and in the following March, he had as an assistant Miss Sarah L. Warren (Mrs. Abel E. Carpenter). Relating her experiences in one of her letters she says: "I boarded at Elder Freeman's. His house must have been situated four or five blocks southeast of the school, near Mr. Snow's, with scarce a house between. What few buildings there were then were mostly on Water Street. I used to go across without regard to streets. it was not uncommon, in going to and from school, to see prairie wolves, and we could hear them howl at any time in the day. But the great difficulty we had to encounter was mud. Rubbers were of no account, and I was obliged t have a pair of men's boots.

Of the work of the ladies before the city charter in 1837 gave the e schools into the hands of the corporation, we say that Miss Chappel called to her assistance Miss Elizabeth Beach and Miss Mary Burrows, and herself retired in the winter of 1834 to 1835, giving her place to Miss Ruth Leavenworth. Mr. John S. Wright, then a young man of but twenty years of age, at his mother's wish and at her expense erected a building for Miss Leavenworth's school. When she ceased teaching in 1836, Miss Frances Langdon Willard opened a school for the instruction of young ladies in the higher branches of education. She taught many years in at least six sates, and kept a private record of her pupils in each place: this interesting book, which enrolls many of the matrons f Chicago, has passed into the hands of her grand niece, Mary Frances Willard, now of John Marshall High School in the same city. Miss Louisa Gifford (Mrs. Dr. Dyer) became Miss F.L. Willard's successor; and the school became a public school, while Miss Willard opened another school on her original lines.

We should not pass te name of John S. Wright without testimony to his work for education in Chicago, Illinois and the West. Coming from Massachusetts to Chicago in 1832 at the age of seventeen, he entered quickly into all public interests: he was not a teacher, but his educational influence surpassed that of may teachers: he was not an agriculturist, but founded and edited the Prairie Farmer, and excellent and powerful farmers' paper: that was a great educational agency, because his educational articles, which began with its first number were addressed to the great class of cultivators of the soil, and not to teachers. Where anything was to be said or done for common or normal schools John S. Wright was never lacking.

GET ON BOARD FOR MORE ADVENTURE

A Selected Annotated Bibliography of African American Children's Literature on the Underground Railroad

Every subject touched on in this study of the Underground Railroad lends itself to further inquiry. Consult libraries, The Internet, historical societies, museums, and resource people (some of whom may be your very own relatives). Check into books, magazines, kits, games, CD roms, films, videos, maps, and audiotapes. You'll discover information that helps you feel as if you can see, hear, touch, taste and smell life in those days when the Underground Railroad was operating.

On the following pages you'll find materials that will enable you to vicariously meet, hear, suffer and rejoice with passengers, conductors, station operators, and their descendants. *Photo courtesy Chicago & Northwestern Railroad*

Underground Railroad books are too numerous to list completely. The annotated bibliography in this chapter begins with the very earliest books on the subject. It was developed by Dr. Gary Smith, Associate Professor of English, DePaul University; Donyell Gray, Research Assistant; Kathleen Bethel, African American Studies Librarian, Northwestern University; Agnes Miller, African American Images Bookstore; and Glennette Tilley Turner, author of the Underground Railroad in Illinois.

So much has been written on this topic in the meantime, the reader should also refer to Books in Print, *Illinois Libraries*, (Vol. 80, No. 4) and other library and on-line resources such as:

~ http://www.cr.nps.gov/ugrr

~ http://www.ugrr.org/ugrr/learn/jp-bib.html

~ www.nationalgeographic.com/features/99/railroad/randl.html, and

~ http://www.ugrr.org/books/biblio.htm The bibliography, which was printed in *Illinois Libraries*, can be accessed online. Go to http://www.sos.state.il.us/ and click on Illinois State Library's web page.

~ For more information on the multi-state UGRR operations, consult the National Park Service Underground Railroad Special Resource Study and the first web site listed above.

~ Visit http://sunsite.unc.edu/docsouth and http://vi.uh.edu/pages/mintz/primary.htm. for slave narratives. See Born in Bondage by Marie Jenkins Schwartz (Harvard University Press) to learn about the lives of enslaved children.

~ Refer to these periodicals: *National Georgraphic*. July 1984; the *Sunday Magazine* of the *Chicago Tribune,* Summer 2000; and the magazine of the National Parks and Conservation Association, July/August 1998.

~ View the following videos:

• "The Underground Railroad: Connections to Freedom and Science" video produced by Classroom for the Future in cooperation with NASA Headquarters (http://core.nasa.gov);

• "The Underground Railroad in Illinois" and "Trail Through DuPage County" (JMDoggett@aol.com); keyword "Underground Railroad";

• "The Underground Railroad" produced by and available from The History Channel

~ Play games such as "Escape" (www.UGRR-Illinois.com).

~ Sing along with audiotapes of "Songs of the Underground Railroad."

~ Take historical tours such as those conducted by Black Coutours, (773) 233-8907 in order to vicariously experience what it was like to travel the Underground Railroad to freedom.

In addition to information on the Underground Railroad you'll find that libraries, museums, bookstores, and the Internet also have a wealth of materials on such related subjects as:

~ Climate

~ Rivers and canals

~ Indians of Illinois

~ Population growth

~ Flora and Fauna of Illinois

~ Religion

~ Treaties

~ Politics

~ Northwest Territory

~ Lincoln-Douglas Debates

~ Fur trade

~ Early modes of transportation

~ Illinois Constitution

~ Inn, taverns, and housing in general

~ Early trails

~ Education

~ Salt and lead mining

~ Mills

~ Occupations

~ Historic court cases

Mary Richardson Jones was a pioneer in the suffrage movement and was hostess to Susan B. Anthony, Carrie Chatman Catt, Emma Chandler and Mrs. John Brown. She and her husband, John Jones operated an Underground Railroad station. They also entertained John Brown, Allan Pinkerton, Frederick Douglass and Nathan Freer. *Courtesy of the Vivian G. Harsh Collection, Chicago Public Library*

Bibliography

1850
Vidi. MR. FRANK, THE UNDERGROUND MAIL-AGENT Philadelphia: Lippincott, Grambo & Co, 1853.

1860
Mitchell, William H. THE UNDERGROUND RAILROAD: FROM SLAVERY TO FREEDOM. London: W. Tweedie 1860. (Reprint 1970)

1870
Pettit, Eber M. SKETCHES IN THE HISTORY OF TEE UNDERGROUND RAILROAD, COMPRISING MANY THRILLING INCIDENTS OF THE ESCAPE OF FUGITIVES FROM SLAVERY, AND THE PERILS OF THOSE WHO AIDED THEM. Fredonia, NY: W. McKinstry & Son, 1879.

1880
Haviland, Laura S. A WOMAN'S LIFE WORK: LABORS AND EXPERIENCES OF LAURA S. HAVILAND. Salem, NH: 1881. (Reprint 1984)

Smedley, Robert Clemens. HISTORY OF THE UNDERGROUND RAILROAD IN CHESTER AND THE NEIGHBORING COUNTIES OF PENNSYLVANIA. Lancaster, PA: Office of the Journal, 1883.

1890
Haviland, Laura Smith. A WOMAN'S LIFE WORK: INCLUDING THIRTY YEARS' SERVICE ON THE UNDERGROUND RAILROAD AND IN THE WAR. Grand Rapids, MI: S. B. Shaw Publishers, 1897.

Johnson, Homer Uri. FROM DIXIE TO CANADA: ROMANCE AND REALITY OF THE UNDERGROUND RAILROAD. Orwell, OH: H. U. Johnson, 1896. (Reprint in 1970)

Siebert, Wilbur Henry. THE UNDERGROUND RAILROAD FROM SLAVERY TO FREEDOM. New York: MacMillan, 1898. (Reprint in 1968) Contains accounts of operations and a detailed map of routes.

William, James. LIFE AND ADVENTURE OF JAMES WILLIAMS, A FUGITIVE SLAVE, WITH A FULL DESCRIPTION OF THE UNDERGROUND RAILROAD. Philadelphia: Sickler, 1893.

1900
Severance, Frank Hayward. OLD TRAILS ON THE NIAGARA FRONTIER. Cleveland, OH: Burrows Brothers, 1903.

1910
Butler, Marvin Benjamin. MY STORY OF THE CIVIL WAR AND THE UNDERGROUND RAILROAD. Huntington. IN: The United Brethren Publishing Establishment, 1914. An account of service in the 44th regiment Indiana volunteers.

Cockrum, William Monroe. HISTORY OF THE UNDERGROUND RAILROAD AS IT WAS CON-

John Jones. In addition to his work for the Underground Railroad and repeal of the Black Codes, he was active in the Negro convention movement for many years after the Civil War. He worked with inventors S.R. Scottron and Lewis Howard Latimer, and with Richard T. Greener, former U.S. consul to Vladivostok, Russia, to gain equal rights. *Courtesy of the Viviian G. Harsh Collection, Chicago Public Library*

DUCTED BY THE ANTI-SLAVERY LEAGUE; INCLUDING MANY THRILLING ENCOUNTERS BETWEEN THOSE AIDING THE SLAVES TO ESCAPE AND THOSE TRYING TO RECAPTURE THEM. Oakland City, IN: J W. Cockrum, 1915.

1920

Allee, Marjorie Hill. SUSANNA AND TRISTRAM. New York: Houghton Mifflin Co., 1929.

Fauset, Arthur Huff. SOJOURNER TRUTH: GOD'S FAITHFUL PILGRIM. North Carolina: University of North Carolina Press, 1938. Biography of the slave woman who became a famous abolitionist (Reprint 1944, 1971)

Long, Laura. HANNAH COURAGEOUS. New York: Longman, 1939.

Siebert, Wilbur. THE UNDERGROUND RAILROAD IN MASSACHUSETTS. Worcester, MA: American Antiquarian Society, 1936.

Swift, Hildegarde Hoyt. THE RAILROAD TO FREEDOM: A STORY OF THE CIVIL WAR. New York: Harcourt, Brace, & Co., 1932. A fictionalized account of the life of Harriet Tubman. Contains reproductions of the dialect of the period.

Washington, Booker T. UP FROM SLAVERY, AN AUTOBIOGRAPHY. Garden City, NY: Doubleday, 1933.

1930

Jones, Ruth Forsdick. ESCAPE TO FREEDOM. New York: Random House, 1958. A story about two boys who join the work of running a "station" on the Underground Railroad. Based on the true adventures of the author's grandparents.

Levy, Mimi Cooper. CORRIE AND THE YANKEE. New York: Viking, 1959. The story of Corrie, a ten-year-old slave girl who hides a wounded Yankee soldier in her playhouse during the Civil War. She bravely guides him to the Union forces and is rewarded by finding her father a scout in the northern army.

Person, Tom. NEW DREAMS FOR OLD. New York: Longmans, 1957. The struggles of the new South to shake off the bonds of old custom - economic and racial - vividly told in this story of Mississippi cotton country.

Petry, Ann Lane. HARRIET TUBMAN: CONDUCTOR ON THE UNDERGROUND RAILROAD. New York: Crowell, 1955. Biography emphasizing the character and personality of Harriet Tubman, whose unshakable faith led her to guide hundreds of slaves to freedom by the Underground Railroad.

Riley, Louise. TRAIN FOR TIGER LILY. New York: Viking, 1954. Tiger Lily is a magical place where a chain of fantastic events is set off by the arrival of a train on which there are four children two animals, and a magician train porter.

Siebert, Wilbur Henry. THE MYSTERIES OF OHIO'S UNDERGROUND RAILROADS. Columbus: Long's College Book Co. 1951.

Philo Carpenter operated Underground Railroad stations in his home and in the First Baptist Congregational Church. His home in Chicago was the UGRR station where Israel Blodgett of Downers Grove and John Coe of Hinsdale took passengers. Carpenter's brother was married to the sister of Julius Warren, founder of Warrenville.

Steinman, Beatrice. THIS RAILROAD DISAPPEARS. New York: F. Watts, 1958. Thirteen -year-old Seth convinces his parents and neighborhood abolitionists that he can be trusted as a conductor on the Underground Railroad.

Sterling, Dorothy. CAPTAIN OF THE PLANTER: THE STORY OF ROBERT SMALLS. Garden City, NY: Doubleday, 1958. Biography of Robert Smalls, who was born a slave, and during the Civil War piloted a captured Confederate boat past the guns of Fort Sumter and delivered it to the Union forces. Later he became a leader of his people and was sent to Congress. He suffered humiliation during Reconstruction because he refused to compromise his principles.

FREEDOM TRAIN: THE STORY OF HARRIET TUBMAN. New York: Scholastic Book Services, 1954. A biography of Harriet Tubman as a conductor on the Underground Railroad.

Wriston, Hildreth Tyler. SUSAN'S SECRET. New York: Farrar, Straus & Giroux, 1957.

Yates, Elizabeth. AMOS FORTUNE, FREE MAN. New York Puffin Books, 1950. (Reprints 1963, 1989) A biography of Amos Fortune, an eighteenth-century African prince. After being captured by slave traders, he was brought to Massachusetts where he remained a slave until he was able to buy his freedom at sixty years old.

1940

Allen, Merritt Parmelee. BATTLE LANTERNS. New York: Longmans, 1949. About a series of adventures which befall a young man during the Revolutionary War. (Reprint 1967)

Buckmaster, Henrietta. LET MY PEOPLE GO: THE STORY OF THE UNDERGROUND RAILROAD AND THE GROWTH OF THE ABOLITION MOVEMENT. New York: Harper, 1941.

Curtis, Anna Louis. STORIES OF THE UNDERGROUND RAILROAD. New York: The Island Workshop Press Co-op, 1941.

DeAngeli, Marguerite. THEE, HANNAH! Garden City, NY: Doubleday, 1946. Nine year-old Hannah, a Quaker in Philadelphia just before the Civil War wants to have some fashionable dresses like other little girls. But she comes to appreciate her heritage and its plain dressing when her family saves the life of a runaway slave.

Graham, Shirley. THERE ONCE WAS A SLAVE: THE HEROIC STORY OF FREDERICK DOUGLASS. New York: Messner, 1947.

Hayes, Florence. SKID. Boston: Houghton, 1948. Skid moves from Georgia to Connecticut where he faces problems which he eventually solves.

Howard, Elizabeth. NORTH WINDS BLOW FREE. New York: W. Morrow, 1949.

Meadowcroft, Enid La Monte. BY SECRET RAILWAY. New York: T. Y. Crowell Co., 1948. Jim a freed slave boy fled in 1860 to the home of David Morgan in Chicago He is betrayed by a boarder who kidnaps Jim for the reward David, the white boy, finds Jim and helps him on his way to Canada by way of the Underground Railroad.

L.C. Paine Freerer was a prominent lawyer who settled in Chicago in 1836 and died in Wheaton in 1878. He made Underground Railroad passengers and touring black antislavery speakers welcome in his home. He encountered personal danger when he served armed court officials with legal warrants. On one occasion he and a party on horseback chased a party of slave catchers nearly across the state of Illinois in an attempt to free an enslaved man, but without success.

McMeekin, Isabella. JOURNEY CAKE. New York: Messner, 1942. In 1794 Juba, a free woman of color takes six motherless white children into Kentucky where their father has gone to settle.

Nolen, Eleanor Weakley. A JOB FOR JEREMIAH. London; New York: Oxford University Press, 1940. A little slave boy tries many jobs while selecting his future trade.

1950
Bontemps, Arna. FREDERICK DOUGLASS: SLAVE, FIGHTERS, FREEMAN. New York: Knopf, 1959. A biography of the runaway slave who devoted his life to the abolition of slavery and the fight for Black rights.

Breyfogle, William x. MAKE FREE: THE STORY OF THE UNDERGROUND RAILROAD. Philadelphia: Lippincott, 1958.

Buckmaster, Henrietta. FLIGHT TO FREEDOM: THE STORY OF THE UNDERGROUND RAILROAD. New York: Crowell, 1958. A history of the founding and operation of the Underground Railroad with background material on slavery, the growth of the abolition movement in spite of opposition in the North. The leaders of both races and the role of the African American after the Civil War includes many accounts of the experiences of escap-

249

ing slaves.

Douglass, Marjory Stoneman. FREEDOM RIVER. Old Tappan, NJ: Scribner, 1953. A tale of three boys - one white one black and one a Seminole Indian - who find their separate freedoms.

Fisher, Aileen Lucia. A LANTERN IN THE WINDOW. New York: T. Nelson, 1957. Twelve-year-old Peter goes to live with his Quaker uncle whose farm on the bank of the Ohio River gives him a view of the steamboats he loves and a role in the Underground Railroad.

Hagler, Margaret. LARRY AND THE FREEDOM MAN. New York: Lothrop, 1959. A twelve-year-old white boy and his uncle, The Freedom Man, help Daniel a slave boy and his family obtain their freedom when they meet on a journey to Kansas.

1960

Bacmeister, Rhoda. W. VOICES EN THE NIGHT. Indianapolis, IN: Bobbs, 1965. New England and an Underground Railroad station are the background for this story. When Jeanie's widowed mother is forced to break up her family because she cannot take care of them, Jeanie is sent to live with the Aldens, who secretly operate a station.

Bradford, Sarah. HARRIET TUBMAN: THE MOSES OF HER PEOPLE. Secaucus, NJ: Citadel, 1961. A story of Harriet Tubman, the illiterate escaped slave who made nineteen journeys deep into the South to escort over 300 slaves to freedom. The book deals mostly with the exciting details of her pilgrimages, but also stresses her fervent religious motivation.

Joseph Henry Hudlun, Sr. was a member of the Chicago Board of Trade for forty years. During the Great Chicago Fire he rescued many valuable docments. His oil portrait hangs in the Board's Hall of Celebrities. The home he and Anna Hudlun built near Dearborn Station was one of the first built in Chicago by black owners. They operated an Underground Railroad station there. *Courtesy of the Vivian G. Harsh Collection, Chicago Public Library*

Browin, Frances Williams. LOOKING FOR ORLANDO. New York: Criterion Books, 1961.

Carrighar, Sally. THE GLASS DOVE. Garden City, NY: Doubleday, 1962.
Clark, Margaret Gogg. FREEDOM CROSSING. New York: Funk & Wagnalls, 1969. After spending four years with relatives in the South, a fifteen-year-old girl accepts the idea that slaves are property and is horrified to learn when she returns North that her home is a station on Underground Railroad.

Danforth, Mildred E. A QUAKER PIONEER: LAURA HAVILAND, SUPERINTENDENT OF THE UNDERGROUND RAILROAD. New York: Exposition Press, 1961.

Douglass, Frederick. LIFE AND TIMES OF FREDERICK DOUGLASS. Ed by Barbara Rirchie. New York: Crowell, 1966. An adaptation of the last revision (1892) by the author of a book first published in 1842. It is a story of Douglass' escape from slavery and his rise to prominence.

Epstein, S. HARRIET TUBMAN: GUIDE TO FREEDOM. Champaign, IL: Garrard Publishing Co., 1968. Born a slave but determined to be free, Harriet Tubman ran away from slavery and returned many times to free her enslaved people.

Falls, Thomas. CANALBOAT TO FREEDOM. New York: Dial Press, 1966. This book describes a friendship between two boys one a white teenage orphan bound out on a canalboat and the other a Black deckhand. The deckhand protects the orphan from the cruelty of the captain, and the boy in turn joins the deckhand in his Underground Railroad activities.

Foster, G. Allen. THE EYES AND EARS OF THE CIVIL WAR. New York: Criterion Books, 1963. Black barbers bartenders, and waiters listened and reported to northern generals or copied maps from tablecloths. Generals such as McClellan refused to believe in their intelligence; but Pinkerton discovered the freed slave, John Scobell, who became ostensibly an entertainer but actually a spy in the Confederate camp. Old Ben was sent by Sheridan to sell vegetables to Rebecca Wright, a Quaker, and carried messages back and forth, wrapped in foil in a decayed tooth.

Fritz, Jean. BRADY. New York: Coward, McCann & Geoghegan, 1960. A story set in Pennsylvania in 1836. Although Brady Minton feels some embarrassment at his father's fervent feelings about slavery, he is sympathetic to the abolitionist position. As he gains enough responsibility to be trusted with information about the Underground Railroad, Brady finds that his opinions have been strengthened.

Gara, Larry. THE LIBERTY LINE: THE LEGEND OF THE UNDERGROUND RAILROAD. Lexington: University of Kentucky Press, 1961. The author questions and attempts to determine the extent to which the Underground Railroad accounts are factual.

Herschler, Mildred Barger. FREDERICK DOUGLASS. Chicago: Follett Publishing Co., 1969. As a young child, little Frederick was determined not to remain enslaved for all of his life.

Kraus, Joanna Halpert. MEAN TO BE FREE: A FLIGHT NORTH ON THE UNDERGROUND RAILROAD: A DRAMA IN TWO ACTS FOR YOUNG PEOPLE 8-12. Rowayton, CT: New Plays for Children, 1967.

Kristof, Jane. STEAL AWAY HOME. Indianapolis: Bobbs-Merrill, 1969. Two slave boys run away from their South Carolina plantation in an attempt to reach their freed father five hundred miles to the North.

Ladenburg, Thomas J. and William S. McFeely. THE BLACK MAN IN THE LAND OF EQUALITY. New York: Hayden Book Co., 1969. Traces the history of the black man in America through the Reconstruction of the 1870's and the desegregation of the 1950's to the riots of the 1960's.

251

Lawrence, Jacob. HARRIET AND THE PROMISED LAND. New York: Simon & Schuster, 1968. (Reprint 1993) A brief biography in verse about Harriet Tubman and her dedicated efforts to lead her fellow slaves to freedom.

Lester, Julius, ed. TO BE A SLAVE. New York: Dial Press, 1968. A compilation selected from various sources and arranged chronologically of the reminiscences of slaves and ex-slaves about the experiences from the leaving of Africa through the Civil War and into the early twentieth century.

Loguen, Jermain Wesley. THE REV. J. W. LOGUEN, AS A SLAVE AND AS A FREEMAN; A NARRATIVE OF REAL LIFE. New York: Negro Universities Press, 1968. (Reprint 1859)

McGovern, Ann. RUNAWAY SLAVE: THE STORY OF HARRIET TUBMAN. New York: Four Winds Press (Scholastic), 1965. A simply told biography of Harriet Tubman which gives a vivid account of her role as a conductor on the Underground Railroad.

WANTED—DEAD OR ALIVE: THE TRUE STORY OF HARRIET TUBMAN. New York: Four Winds Press, 1965. A biography of the slave who escaped to freedom, then returned and led three hundred other slaves to the North by way of the Underground Railroad.

McPherson, James M. THE NEGRO'S CIVIL WAR: HOW NEGROES FELT AND ACTED DURING THE WAR FOR THE UNION. New York: Pantheon, 1965. The author presents documentary evidence from Black and abolitionist newspapers, pamphlets, letters, speeches and official records to show that Blacks actively participated and many became leaders in the emancipation of the slaves from 1860 to 1865.

Patterson, Lillie. FREDERICK DOUGLASS. Champaign, IL: Garrard Publishing Co., 1965. The reader follows Frederick through his increasing hatred of slavery and his escape. His home in New York became one of the Underground Railroad stations for fleeing slaves.

Sterling, Dorothy. FOREVER FREE: THE STORY OF THE EMANCIPATION PROCLAMATION. Garden City, NY: Doubleday, 1963. Describes the events leading up to the signing of the Emancipation Proclamation that freed over four million slaves in the United States.

Sterling, Philip and Logan Rayford. FOUR TOOK FREEDOM: THE LIVES OF HARRIET TUBMAN, FREDERICK DOUGLASS, ROBERT SMALLS, AND BLANCHE K. BRUCE. Garden City. NY: Doubleday, 1967. Biographical portraits of four famous African Americans who escaped the slavery into which they had been born to further the fight for freedom and equality.

Sterne, Emma Gelders. THE LONG BLACK SCHOONER: THE VOYAGE OF THE AMISTAD. Chicago: Follett Pub Co., 1968. A fictional account of the 1839 revolt of Africans aboard the slave ship Amistad and the subsequent Amistad Case argued by John Quincy Adams before the United States Supreme Court.

Still, William. THE UNDERGROUND RAILROAD. New York: Arno Press, 1968. William Still,

Anna Elizabeth Lewis Hudlun was known as the "Fire Angel" because of the hospitality she extended to fire victims during the Chicago fires. In 1871 she and Joseph Hudlun opened their five room home to five families—some black and some white. Their home was a mecca of social and civic activity. It was an Underground Railroad station before and during the Civil War. *Courtesy of the Vivian G. Harsh Collection, Chicago Public Library*

black Quaker member of the Pennsylvania Anti-Slavery Society, secretary of the Philadelphia Vigilance Committees active abolitionist, and son of two slaves, worked as an agent on the Underground Railroad. He interviewed "passengers" in order to gain information that would enable family members to locate loved ones in Canada. This book is a compilation of those interviews he recorded in narrative form, as well as letters and newspaper clippings about slavery and the runaways.

Strother, Horatio T. THE UNDERGROUND RAILROAD IN CONNECTICUT. Middletown, CT: Wesleyan University Press, 1962.

Williams, James. LIFE AND ADVENTURES OF JAMES WILLIAMS, A FUGITIVE SLAVE, WITH A FULL DESCRIPTION OF THE UNDERGROUND RAILROAD. Saratoga, CA: R. & E Research Associates, 1969.

Williamson, Joanne. AND FOREVER FREE. New York: Knopf, 1966. The social and political scene in New York City during the years leading up to the Emancipation Proclamation is shown through the story of an eighteen-year-old German immigrant who befriends a runaway slave.

1970

Cavanah, Frances. THE TRUTH ABOUT THE MAN BEHIND THE BOOK THAT SPARKED THE WAR BETWEEN THE STATES. Philadelphia: Westminster, 1975. Story of Josiah Henson the role model for Harriet Beecher Stowe's "Uncle Tom," who helped many slaves escape to freedom and founded a settlement for Blacks in Canada.

Childress, Alice. WHEN THE RATTLESNAKE SOUNDS: A PLAY. New York: Coward McCann & Geoghegan, 1975. One day in the life of Harriet Tubman when she worked as a hotel laundress and gave courage and inspiration to two co-workers.

Chittenden, Elizabeth F. PROFILES IN BLACK AND WHITE: STORIES OF MEN AND WOMEN WHO FOUGHT AGAINST SLAVERY. New York: Scribner, 1973.

Davis, Ossie. ESCAPE TO FREEDOM: A PLAY ABOUT YOUNG FREDERICK DOUGLASS. New York: Trumpet Club, 1976. A drama with songs, dialogue, and dance. Born a slave, young Frederick Douglass endures many years of cruelty before escaping to the North to claim his freedom.

Dunne, Mary Collins. THE SECRET OF CAPTIVES' CAVE. New York: Putnam, 1976. When he moves back to his dead father's birthplace, Dennis tries to uncover the mystery surrounding

Captives Cave which is linked to his ancestors.

Forman, James. SONG OF JUBILEE. New York: Farrar, Straus & Giroux, 1971. This expose of slavery reveals the ambivalent feelings among slaves in one household, particularly after freedom is granted.

Fox, Paula. THE SLAVE DANCER New York: Dell, 1973. A stark view of slavery as seen through the eyes of a young white boy who is shanghaied on a slaver and forced to make music for its human cargo.

Freedman, Florence B. TWO TICKETS TO FREEDOM: THE TRUE STORY OF ELLEN AND WILLIAM CRAFT, FUGITIVE SLAVES. New York: Simon and Schuster, 1971. Contemporary sources such as newspaper articles, journals, and the published story of William Craft help reconstruct this interesting account.

Grant, Matthew G. HARRIET TUBMAN, BLACK LIBERATOR. Mankato, MN: Creative Education, 1974 A biography of the famous conductor on the Underground Railroad who worked to free her people before, during, and after the Civil War.

Gray, Genevieve. THE YELLOW BONE RING. New York: Lothrop, 1971. The pride and responsibility of freedom are explored in this dramatic story of a young ex-slave in the First South Carolina Volunteers, the first Black Union Army regiment.

Greenfield, Eloise. HONEY, I LOVE. New York: Thomas T. Crowell Co, 1978. A picture book collection of poems about various subjects including a poem about Harriet Tubman and her escape from slavery.

Heidish, Marcy. A WOMAN CALLED MOSES. New York: Houghton Mifflin Company, 1976. Harriet Tubman looks back over her life and tells her own story. The reader sees her as a seven-year-old enslaved African her heartaches and griefs on through her escape by way of the Underground Railroad.

Henderson, Nancy. WALK TOGETHER: FIVE PLAYS ON HUMAN RIGHTS. New York: Messner, 1972. One of the plays is the story of slaves risking their lives for freedom in the Underground Railroad.

Jacob, Helen Pierce. THE DIARY OF STRAWBRIDGE PLACE. New York: Atheneum, 1978. A family of Quakers operating a station on the Underground Railroad spirits slaves from Ashtabula Ohio across Lake Erie to freedom.

Johnson, Ann Donegan. THE VALUE OF HELPING: THE STORY OF HARRIET TUBMAN. La Jolla, CA: Value Communications, 1979. Describes the helpful work of Harriet Tubman in aiding slaves to flee the South in assisting the Union army during the Civil War and in establishing homes for the old and needy after the war.

Harrison, Lowell Hayes. THE ANTISLAVERY MOVEMENT IN KENTUCKY. Lexington, KY: University Press of Kentucky, 1978.

254

Katz, Bernard and Jonathan Katz. BLACK WOMAN: A FICTIONALIZED BIOGRAPHY OF LUCY TERRY PRINCE. New York: Pantheon Books, 1973. The story of the young New England slave girl who grew up to win her freedom and fight for her rights as a woman a property owner, and a free person.

Khan, Lurey. ONE DAY LEVIN...HE BE FREE: WILLIAM STILL AND THE UNDERGROUND RAILROAD. New York: E P. Dutton, 1972. Chronicles the efforts of William Still son of an escaped slave, to help his people through his work with Philadelphia's Anti-slavery Society and the Underground Railroad.

Lester, Julius. LONG JOURNEY HOME: STORIES FROM BLACK HISTORY. New York: Dial Press, 1972. Six stories about slaves and ex-slaves.

Calvin DeWolf was a self-taught man. He did manual labor at Grand River Institute, in Ohio, in exchange for the opportunity to study Greek and Latin. He settled in Chicago in 1837. He taught two years then went to work in a law office so that he could study law. He was a practicing lawyer until he was elected Justice of the Peace. He was one of the founders of the anti-slavery society in 1859 and helped establish the *Western Citizen* which was edited by Zebina Eastman.

Ludwig, Charles. LEVI COFFIN AND THE UNDERGROUND RAILROAD. Scottdale, PA: Herald Press, 1975.

Mathews, Marcia M. THE FREEDOM STAR. New York: Coward, McCann & Geoghegan, 1971. Pencil drawings and simple text follow a young runaway slave's adventures in pursuing the North Star which will guide him to freedom in Canada.

May, Charles Paul. STRANGER IN THE STORM. New York: Schuman, 1972. A runaway slave helps two little girls survive in a blizzard, and they in turn help him hide from his pursuers.

McGowan, James A. A STATION MASTER ON l THE UNDERGROUND RAILROAD: THE LIFE AND LETTERS OF THOMAS GARRETT. Moylan, PA: Whimsie Press, 1977.

McNeer, May. STRANGER IN THE PINES. Boston: Houghton Mifflin, 1971. A bound boy finds a new life in a Quaker community and through a freedman, learns the healing power of herbs.

McQuilkin, Frank. THINK BLACK: AN INTRODUCTION TO BLACK POLITICAL POWER. New York: Bruce Pub Co., 1970. Traces the history of Blacks in America from their arrival as slaves in the seventeenth century to the present-day struggle for civil rights.

Meltzer, Milton. UNDERGROUND MAN. Scarsdale, NY: Bradbury, 1972. The difficult life of a white abolitionist who worked actively in the Underground Railroad.

Smucker, Barbara Claassen. RUNAWAY TO FREEDOM: A STORY OF THE UNDERGROUND RAILWAY. New York: Harper & Row, 1978. Two young slave girls escape from a plan-

255

Allan Pinkerton

Allan Pinkerton solved his first crime quite by chance. While he was a cooper, or barrel maker, in Dundee, he went to gather reeds with which to bind the barrels. He rowed his boat to an island in the Fox River where the reeds grew. There, he discovered the hiding place of counterfeiters whom the local sheriff had been unable to locate. Pinkerton instantly gained a reputation as a detective.

tation in Mississippi and wind a hazardous route toward freedom in Canada via the Underground Railroad.

Talmudge, Marian and Iris Gilmore. BARNEY FORD: BLACK BARON. New York: Dodd, 1973. An indomitable man who escaped from slavery and became a wealthy leader in the political, social, and business life of Denver, Colorado.

Turner, Glennette. THE UNDERGROUND RAILROAD IN DuPAGE. Wheaton, IL: Newman, 1978.

Warner, Lucille Schulberg. FROM SLAVE TO ABOLITIONIST: THE LIFE OF WILLIAM WELLS BROWN. New York: Dial Press, 1976. The memoirs of a fugitive slave a man important in the abolitionist movements in England and America. (Adaptation)

White, Anne Terry. NORTH TO LIBERTY: THE STORY OF THE UNDERGROUND RAILROAD. Champaign, IL: Garrard Pub Co., 1972. Describes the operation, stations, and famous conductors on the Underground Railroad, a network that helped many slaves escape from bondage.

Williams, Jeanne. FREEDOM TRAIL. New York: Putnam, 1973. Jared continues his stand against slavery in pre-Civil War Kansas even though his father is killed by proslavers.

Winslow, Eugene. AFRO-AMERICANS '76: BLACK AMERICANS IN THE FOUNDING OF OUR NATION. Chicago: Afro-Am Pub Co., 1975. Provides biographical sketches of Afro-Americans who contributed to the exploration, Revolution, and growth of the United States.

1980

Anderson, Joan A. WILLIAMSBURG HOUSEHOLD. New York: Clarion Books, 1988. Focuses on events in the household of d white family and its black slaves in Colonial Williamsburg in the eighteenth century.

Avi. SOMETHING UPSTAIRS. New York: Avon Books, 1988. When he moves from Los Angeles to Providence, Rhode Island, Kenny discovers that his new home is haunted by the spirit of a black slave boy who asks Kenny to return with him to the early nineteenth century and prevent his murder by slave traders.

Bains, Rae. HARRIET TUBMAN: THE ROAD TO FREEDOM (Braille) Livonia, MI: Seedlings

REVEREND ABRAHAM HALL
Rev. Hall was not only a leader in the African Methodist Episcopal Church. He was the grandfather of Lloyd Augustus Hall, the holder of many patents. Lloyd Hall specialized in perfecting methods of preserving foods. His work was essential to te development of dehydrated Army rations during World War II. *Courtesy of Vivian G. Harsh Collection, Chicago Public Library*

Braille Books for Children, 1983. The biography of a slave whose flight to freedom was the first step in her becoming a "conductor" on the Underground Railroad.

Bledsoe, Lucy Jane. HARRIET TUBMAN. Englewood Cliffs, NJ: Quercus, 1989.

Blockson, Charles L. THE UNDERGROUND RAILROAD. New York: Berkley, 1989. A comprehensive study of the Underground Railroad arranged by the geographic regions in which it operated Based on many primary sources.

Bradley, David. THE CHANEYSVILLE INCIDENT. New York: Harper & Row, 1981.

Carlson, J. HARRIET TUBMAN: CALL TO FREEDOM. New York: Fawcett Columbine, 1989. Traces Harriet Tubman's life, experience, and efforts to aid slaves in escaping to the North, as well as her assistance to the Union cause during the Civil War.

Collier, Christopher and James Lincoln Collier. WAR COMES TO WILLY FREEMAN. New York: Delacorte Press, 1983. Historical novel that portrays the plight of Black people during the American Revolution.

Collier, James Lincoln. WHO IS CARRIE? New York: Dell Pub Co., 1987. A young Black girl living in New York City in the late eighteenth century observes the historic events taking place around her and at the same time solves the mystery of her own identity.

Ferris, Jeri. GO FREE OR DIE: A STORY ABOUT HARRIET TUBMAN. Minneapolis: First Avenue Editions, 1988. A biography of the Black woman whose cruel experiences as a slave in the South led her to seek freedom in the North for herself and for others through the Underground Railroad.

Haley, Alex. A DIFFERENT KIND OF CHRISTMAS. New York: Doubleday, 1988. This adventure, set in 1855, tells the story of a young white Southerner who helps in the Underground Railroad and in an enslaved African's Christmas Eve escape attempt.

Hamilton, Virginia. ANTHONY BURNS: THE DEFEAT AND TRIUMPH OF A FUGITIVE SLAVE. New York: A A Knopf, 1988. A biography of the slave who escaped to Boston in 1854, was arrested at the instigation of his owner, and whose trial caused a furor between abolitionists and those determined to enforce the Fugitive Slave Acts.

THE HOUSE OF DIES DREAR. New York: Collier Books, 1984. A black family moves into an enormous house once used as a hiding place for runaway slaves Mysterious sounds and events as well as the discovery of secret passageways make the family believe they are in grave danger.

THE MYSTERY OF DREAR HOUSE: THE CONCLUSION OF THE DIES DREAR CHRONICLE. New York: Greenwillow Books, 1987. A black family living in the house of long-dead abolitionist Dies Drear must decide what to do with his stupendous treasure hidden for one hundred years in a cavern near their home.

Hurmence, Belinda. A GIRL CALLED BOY. New York: Clarion, 1982. Mysteriously transported in time to the 1850's, a young girl learns to respect the courage of her slave forebears.

Johnson, Georgia. A TOWPATH TO FREEDOM. East Lansing: G. A Johnson Publishing, 1989.

Klingel, Cynthia Fitterer. HARRIET TUBMAN. Mankato, MN: Creative Education, 1987. A biography of the runaway slave who risked her life to help other slaves escape to freedom.

Larrie, Reginald. MAKIN' FREE: AFRICAN-AMERICANS IN THE NORTHWEST TERRITORY. Detroit: B. Ethridge Books, 1981. A book which traces the early arrival and exploits of a number of lesser known African Americans who explored the Northwest regions of the United States and Upper Canada.

Lester, Julius. THIS STRANGE NEW FEELING. New York: Scholastic, Inc. 1985. The impact of slavery on the human spirit is presented in three love stories based on true events.

McKissack, Patricia and Frederick McKissack. FREDERICK DOUGLASS: THE BLACK LION. Chicago: Children's Press, 1987. Frederick Douglass becomes a spokesperson in the antislavery movement.

Meyer, Linda D. HARRIET TUBMAN: THEY CALLED ME MOSES. Seattle: Parenting Press, 1988. Biography of the Black woman who lived as a slave, free woman, conductor of the Underground Railroad and benefactor to the needy.

Miller, Douglas T. FREDERICK DOUGLASS AND THE FIGHT FOR FREEDOM. New York: Facts on File, 1988. Traces the life of the black abolitionist, from his early years in slavery to his later success as a persuasive editor orator and writer.

Phelan, Helen C. AND WHY NOT EVERY MAN? AN ACCOUNT OF SLAVERY, THE UNDER-GROUND RAILROAD, AND THE ROAD TO FREEDOM IN NEW YORK'S SOUTHERN TIER. Interlake, NY: Heart of the Lakes Pub, 1987.

Polcovar, Jane. HARRIET TUBMAN. Danbury, CT: Childrens Press Choice, 1988.

Sabin, Francene. HARRIET TUBMAN. Mahwah, NJ: Troll Associates, 1985. A biography of the

258

Black woman who escaped from slavery and became a well-known figure in the Underground Railroad as she led scores of slaves north to freedom.

Scott, John Anthony and Robert Alan Scott. JOHN BROWN'S OF HARPER'S FERRY: WITH CONTEMPORARY PRINTS, PHOTOGRAPHY PRINTS, PHOTOGRAPHS, AND MAPS. New York: Facts on File Publications, 1988. Describes the life of the abolitionist whose struggle to free American slaves resulted in the raid on Harpers Ferry.

Sears, Richard D. THE DAY OF SMALL THINGS: ABOLITIONISM IN MIDST SLAVERY, BEREA, KENTUCKY, 1854-1864. Lanham, MD: University Press of America, 1986.

Smith, Kathie Billingslea. HARRIET TUBMAN. New York: J Messner, 1988. Traces the life of the woman who, once a slave herself, came to be called Moses by the slaves she led North to freedom out of the pre-Civil War South.

Rev. Richard DeBaptiste is associated with Olivet Baptist Church in Chicago. He and many members of his church worked with members of Quinn Chapel A.M.E. Church in antislavery activities. He also took the personal risk of loaning his freedom papers to Underground Railroad passengers. After his years as pastor of Olivet he provided outstanding leadership to Second Baptist Church in Elgin. *Courtesy of the Vivian G. Harsh Collection, Chicago Public Library*

Stadelhofen, Marcie Miller. LAST CHANCE FOR FREEDOM. Syracuse, NY: New Readers Press, 1983.

Stein, R. Conrad. THE STORY OF THE UNDERGROUND RAILROAD. Chicago: Childrens Press, 1981. Discusses the network of groups and individuals throughout Ohio and the New England states who aided slaves escaping from their captivity during the nineteenth century.

Turner, Ann Warren. NETTIE'S TRIP SOUTH. New York: Macmillan, 1987. A ten year-old northern girl encounters the ugly realities of slavery when she visits Richmond, Virginia, and sees a slave auction.

Turner, Glennette Tilley. TAKE A WALK IN THEIR SHOES. New York: Cobblehill Books, 1989. (Reprint in 1992, Puffin Books) Presents biographical sketches of fourteen notable African Americans, including Martin Luther King, Jr., Rosa Parks, and "Satchel" Paige, accompanied by brief skits in which readers can act out imagined scenes from their lives.

Walker, Juliet. E K FREE FRANK: A BLACK PIONEER ON THE ANTEBELLUM FRONTIER. Lexington: University Press of Kentucky, 1983.

Walker, Robert Wayne. DANIEL WEBSTER JACKSON AND THE WRONGWAY RAILWAY. San Diego: Oak Tree Publications, 1982. A teenage boy decides to leave his foster home in Missouri rather than become involved in Judge Hatcher's scheme to break up the Underground Railroad

David and Sarah West and their five children loaded their household goods into a wagon and left Erie County, New York, in the fall of 1843. After 23 days of travel, resting on Sundays, they arrived in Sycamore. Their house became the stopping place for visiting Congregational ministers and it was an Underground Railroad station. In 1840 David West voted (only Caucasian men had the franchise) for the Liberty Party's presidential candidate, James G. Birney.

that is operating in the territory.

Wells, Marian. THE SILVER HIGHWAY. Minneapolis: Bethany House Publishers, 1989.

1990

Adler, David A. A PICTURE BOOK OF HARRIET TUBMAN. New York: Holiday House, 1994. Biography of the Black woman who escaped from slavery to become famous as a conductor on the Underground Railroad.

Adler, David A. A PICTURE BOOK OF SOJOURNER TRUTH. New York: Holiday House, 1994. An introduction to the life of the woman born into slavery who became a well-known abolitionist and crusader for the rights of African Americans.

Allen, Danice. ARMS OF A STRANGER. New York: Avon Books, 1995.

Armstrong, Jennifer. STEAL AWAY. New York: Orchard Books, 1992. In 1855 two thirteen year-old girls, one white and one black, run away from a southern farm and make the difficult journey north to freedom, living to recount their story forty-one years later to two young girls.

Beatty, Patricia. JAYHAWKER. New York: Beech Tree, 1995. In the early years of the Civil War, teenage Kansas farm boy Lije Tulley becomes a Jayhawker, an abolitionist raider freeing slaves from the neighboring state of Missouri, and then goes undercover there as a spy.

Unknown Author. WHO COMES WITH CANNONS? New York: Morrow Junior Books, 1992. In 1861 twelve-year-old Truth, a Quaker girl from Indiana, is staying with relatives who run a North Carolina station of the Underground Railroad when her world is changed by the beginning of the Civil War.

Becvar, Patsy. A PLACE CALLED MOTHER HUBBARD CUPBOARD. Chicago: Nystrom, 1991. This book is used to introduce the concepts of slavery and the Underground Railroad.

Benjamin, Anne. YOUNG HARRIET TUBMAN: FREEDOM FIGHTER. Mahwah, NJ: Troll Associates, 1992. A simple biography of the Black woman who was never caught as she helped over 300 slaves escape through the Underground Railroad.

Bentley, Judith. HARRIET TUBMAN. New York: F. Watts, 1990. Details Harriet Tubman's life, experiences, and efforts to aid slaves in escaping to the North, as well as her assistance to the Union cause during the Civil War.

Bial, Raymond. THE UNDERGROUND RAILROAD. Boston: Houghton Mifflin, 1995. Text and photo-illustrations are combined to provide young readers with general and specific details about the Underground Railroad.

Bisson, Terry. HARRIET TUBMAN: ANTISLAVERY ACTIVIST. New York: Chelsea House Publishers, 1990. Describes the life of the abolitionist, including her origins as a slave in Maryland, her role as a "conductor" for the Underground Railroad, her service to the Union during the Civil War, and her role in establishing an old-age home for Afro-Americans.

Blockson, Charles L. HIPPOCRENE GUIDE TO THE UNDERGROUND RAILROAD. New York: Hippocrene Books, 1994.

Bond, James O. CHICKAMAUGA AND THE UNDERGROUND RAILROAD: A TALE OF TWO GRANDFATHERS. Baltimore, MD: Gateway Press, Inc. 1993.

Braithwaite, Diana. MARTHA AND ELVIRA: A ONE ACT PLAY. Toronto: Sister Vision, 1993.

Brandt, Nat. THE TOWN THAT STARTED THE CIVIL WAR. Syracuse, NY: Syracuse University Press, 1990.

Burns, Bree. HARRIET TUBMAN. New York: Chelsea Juniors, 1992. A biography of the Afro-American woman best known for her work with the Underground Railroad, describing her childhood as a slave her escape to the North, her work during the Civil War, and more.

Caccamo, James F. HUDSON, OHIO AND THE UNDERGROUND RAILROAD. Hudson, OH: The Friends of the Hudson Library, Inc. 1992.

Carter, Polly. HARRIET TUBMAN AND BLACK HISTORY MONTH. Englewood Cliffs, NJ: Silver Press, 1990. Examines the experiences of the runaway slave who risked her life to help others through the Underground Railroad.

Coffin, Levi. REMINISCENCES OF LEVI COFFIN. Salem, NH: Ayer Company, 1992. Narrative of escaped slave Levi Coffin, the reputed president of the Underground Railroad. (Reprint)

College Hill Historical Society MY EYES HAVE SEEN THE GLORY: A COLLEGE HILL SOURCE-BOOK OF BLACK HISTORY. Cincinnati: The Society, 1993.

Connell, Kate. TALES FROM THE UNDERGROUND RAILROAD. Austin: Raintree Steck-Vaughn, 1993. Describes the efforts of the vast secret network of sympathetic people who helped Blacks escape slavery in the South via the Underground Railroad.

Cosner, Shaaron. THE UNDERGROUND RAILROAD. New York: Franklin Watts, 1991. Describes the Underground Railroad which helped slaves escape to freedom.
Craft, William. RUNNING A THOUSAND MILES FOR FREEDOM, OR THE ESCAPE OF WILLIAM AND ELLEN CRAFT FROM SLAVERY. Salem, NH: Ayer Co., 1991.

Crews, Donald. BIGMAMA'S. New York : Greenwillow Books, 1991. Visiting Bigmama's house in the country, young Donald Crews finds his relatives full of news and the old place and its surroundings just the same as the year before.

Douglas, Marjory Stoneman. FREEDOM RIVER. Miami: Valiant Press, 1994. In the 1840s, as Florida prepares to become a state, an Indian boy, black slave, and white settler become friends and explore their differences and common bonds.

Douglass, Frederick. ESCAPE FROM SLAVERY: THE BOYHOOD OF FREDERICK DOUGLASS IN HIS OWN WORDS. Ed and illus. by Michael McCurdy New York: Knopf, 1994. A revised and shortened edition of THE NARRATIVE OF THE LIFE OF FREDERICK DOUGLASS, AN AMERICAN SLAVE. This version of Douglass' autobiography presents the early life of the slave who became an abolitionist, journalist, and statesman.

Elisha, Dan. HARRIET TUBMAN AND THE UNDERGROUND RAILROAD. Brookfield, CT: Millbrook Press, 1993. A biography of the African American woman who escaped from slavery, led slaves to freedom on the Underground Railroad, aided Northern troops during the Civil War, and worked for women's suffrage.

Forrester, Sandra. SOUND THE JUBILEE. New York: Lodestar Books, 1995. A slave and her family find refuge on Roanoke Island, North Carolina during the Civil War.

Gaines, Edith M. FREEDOM LIGHT. Cleveland: New Day Press, 1991. The story of the antislavery heroes of Ripley, Ohio, based on eyewitness accounts of two of their leaders John Rankin and John Parker.

Guccione, Leslie D. COME MORNING. Minneapolis: Carolrhoda Books, 1995. Twelve-year-old Freedom the son of a freed slave living in Delaware in the early 1850s, takes his father's work in the Underground Railroad when his father disappears.

Hamilton, Virginia. MANY THOUSAND GONE: AFRICAN AMERICANS FROM SLAVERY TO FREEDOM. New York: Knopf, 1993 Recounts the journey of Black slaves to freedom via the Underground Railroad, an extended group of people who helped fugitive slaves in many ways.

—— THE PEOPLE COULD FLY: AMERICAN BLACK FOLKTALES. New York: Knopf, 1993. Retold Afro-American folktales of animals, fantasy, the supernatural and desire for freedom born of the sorrow of the slaves, but passed on in hope.

Haskins, James. GET ON BOARD: THE STORY OF THE UNDERGROUND RAILROAD. New York:

Scholastic, 1993. Discusses the Underground Railroad, the secret, loosely organized network of people and places that helped many slaves escape north to freedom.

Hoobler, Dorothy. NEXT STOP, FREEDOM: THE STORY OF A SLAVE GIRL. Englewood Cliffs, NJ: Silver Burdett Press, 1991. Emily, a slave girl who longs to read, escapes from slavery with the help of Harriet Tubman.

Hopkinson, Deborah. SWEET CLARA AND THE FREEDOM QUILT. New York: Knopf, 1993. A young slave stitches a quilt with a map pattern which guides her to freedom in the North.

Johnson, LaVerne C. KUMI AND CHANTI TELL THE STORY OF HARRIET TUBMAN. Chicago: Empak Enterprises, 1992. Two African children following their mission of exploring African-American history record the story of Harriet Tubman, who escaped from slavery and led over 300 of her people to freedom along the Underground Railroad.

Kinard, Lee. HARRIET TUBMAN'S FAMOUS CHRISTMAS EVE RAID. Nashville: James C Winston Publishers, 1995.

Lawrence, Jacob. THE GREAT MIGRATION: AN AMERICAN STORY. New York: HarperCollins, 1993. A series of paintings chronicles the journey of African Americans who, like the artist's family, left the rural South in the early twentieth century to find a better life in the industrial North.

The portrait of the John Wagner family of Aurora was painted by artist Sheldon Peck. It was unusual in that Peck usually painted portraits of individuals. His making an exception to this practice may have had something to do with the fact that the Wagners operated an Underground Railroad station in Aurora and Peck operated one in Lombard. *Courtesy of the Aurora Historical Society*

Levine, Ellen. IF YOU TRAVELED ON THE UNDERGROUND RAILROAD. New York: Scholastic, 1993. Describes the Underground Railroad which helped slaves escape to freedom.

Marcey, Sally. THE UNDERGROUND RAILROAD. Wheaton, IL: Tyndale House Publishers, 1991. A plot-your-own story about the Underground Railroad Follow the Ringers as they find a hidden tunnel under the old church in town and discover it may have been used to hide slaves The reader's choices will determine which of fifteen endings will happen.

McCay, Willie. YOUNG INDIANA JONES AND THE PLANTATION TREASURE. NY: Random House, 1990.

McClard, Megan. HARRIET TUBMAN: SLAVERY AND THE UNDERGROUND RAILROAD. Englewood Cliffs, NJ: Silver Burdett Press, 1990. A biography of the courageous woman who rose from slave beginnings to become a heroic figure in the Underground Railroad.

McKissack, Patricia C. CHRISTMAS IN THE BIG

HOUSE, CHRISTMAS IN THE QUARTERS. New York: Scholastic, 1994. Describes the customs, recipes, poems, and songs used to celebrate Christmas in the big plantation houses and in the slave quarters just before the Civil War.

SOJOURNER TRUTH: AIN'T I A WOMAN? New York: Scholastic, 1992. A biography of the former slave who became well-known as a abolitionist and advocate of women's rights.

McMullan, Kate. THE STORY OF HARRIET TUBMAN: CONDUCTOR OF THE UNDERGROUND RAILROAD. New York: Dell, 1991.

Monfredo, Miriam Grace. NORTH STAR CONSPIRACY. New York: St. Martin's Press, 1993.

Monjo, F. N. THE DRINKING GOURD: A STORY OF TIDE UNDERGROUND RAILROAD. New York: HarperCollins, 1993. When he is sent home alone for misbehaving in church, Tommy discovers that his house is a station on the Underground Railroad.

Pfeifer, Kathryn Browne. HENRY O. FLIPPER. New York: Twenty-First Century Books, 1993. Examines the life of the first African American graduate of West Point, including his dishonorable discharge from the Army which was reversed nearly 100 years later.

Phillips, Raelene. FREEDOM'S TREMENDOUS COST. Elkhart, IN: Bethel Pub Co, 1993. The Stivers family tradition continues Hannah and her children struggle for freedom, this time for southern slaves escaping to the North with the help of abolitionists and the Underground Railroad.

Polacco, Patricia. PINK AND SAY. New York: Philomel Books, 1994. Say Curtis describes his meeting with Pinkus Alee, a black soldier, during the Civil War, and their capture by Southern troops.

The author confers with Fulton County historian Curtis Strode who wrote a newspaper series based on the UGRR activiies of his great grandfather, Francis Overton and fellow abolitionists. The Overton Farm was on the route between Quincy and Galesburg.

Porter, Connie Rose. MEET ADDY: AN AMERICAN GIRL. Middleton, WI: Pleasant Co., 1993. Nine-year-old Addy Walker escapes from a cruel life of slavery to freedom during the Civil War.

ADDY LEARNS A LESSON: A SCHOOL STORY. Middleton, WI: Pleasant Co., 1993. After escaping from a plantation in North Carolina, Addy and her mother arrive in Philadelphia where Addy goes to school and learns a lesson in true friendship.

Rappaport, Doreen. ESCAPE FROM SLAVERY: FIVE JOURNEYS TO FREEDOM. New York: HarperCollins, 1991. Five accounts of slaves who managed to escape to freedom during the period preceding the Civil War.

Ringgold, Faith. AUNT HARRIET'S UNDERGROUND RAILROAD IN TIDE SKY. New York: Crown, 1992. With Harriet Tubman as her guide,

Cassie retraces the steps escaping slaves took on the Underground Railroad in order to reunite with her younger brother.

Robinet, Harriette. IF YOU PLEASE, PRESIDENT LINCOLN. New York: Atheneum Books for Young Readers, 1995. Shortly after the Christmas of 1863, fourteen-year-old Moses thinks he is beginning a new free life when he becomes part of a group of other former slaves headed for a small island off the coast of Haiti.

Rosen, Michael J. A SCHOOL FOR POMPEY WALKER. San Diego: Harcourt Brace Children's Books, 1995. At the dedication of a school named after him, an old former slave tells the story of his life and how his white friend helped him earn the money for the school by repeatedly selling him into slavery, after which he always escaped.

Ruby, Lois. STEAL AWAY HOME. New York: Macmillan, 1994. In two parallel stories, a Quaker family in Kansas in the late 1850s operates a station on the Underground Railroad, while almost 150 years later twelve-year-old Dana moves into the same house and finds the skeleton of a black woman who helped the Quakers.

Stadelhofen, Marcie Miller. ERIE FREEDOM SIDE. Syracuse, NY: New Readers Press, 1990.

Stepto, Michele, ed. AFRICAN-AMERICAN VOICES. Brookfield, CT: Millbrook Press, 1995. A collection of writings by such authors as W.E.B. DuBois, Toni Morrison, Rita Dove, Richard Wright, and Ralph Ellison, exploring the connections of circle, veil water, and song that link past and present African American cultures.

Stolz, Mary. CEZANNE PINTO: A MEMOIR. New York: A. A. Knopf, 1994. In his old age, Cezanne Pinto recalls his youth as a slave on a Virginia plantation and his escape to a new life in the North.

Sullivan, Charles, ed. CHILDREN OF PROMISE: AFRICAN-AMERICAN LITERATURE AND ART FOR YOUNG PEOPLE. New York: Harry N. Abrams, 1991. Poems, prose, photographs, and paintings explore the African-American experience as seen through art and literature by black or about black subjects.

Targ-Brill, Marlene. ALLEN JAY AND THE UNDERGROUND RAILROAD. Minneapolis: Carolrhoda Books, 1993. Recounts how Allen Jay, a young Quaker boy living in Ohio during the 1840s, helped a fleeing slave escape his master and make it to freedom through the Underground Railroad.

Taylor, Marian W. HARRIET TUBMAN. Danbury, CT: Grolier, 1990.

Turner, Glennette Tilley. RUNNING FOR OUR LIVES. New York: Holiday House, 1994. A family of fugitive slaves becomes separated while traveling to freedom aboard the Underground Railroad.

Washington, Booker T. UP FROM SLAVERY. Ed. by William L. Andrews. Oxford: Oxford University Press, 1995.

Weinberg, Larry. GHOST HOTEL. Mahwah, NJ: Troll, 1994. Mysteriously drawn to an Indiana museum, a twelve-year-old paralyzed girl encounters ghosts who return her to a former life, where she attempts to save the son of a freed slave traveling by Underground Railroad in Kentucky.

Winter, Jeanette. FOLLOW THE DRINKING GOURD. New York: Dragonfly Books, 1992. By following the directions in a song, "The Drinking Gourd," taught to them by an old sailor named Peg Leg Joe, runaway slaves journey north along the Underground Railroad to freedom in Canada.

Wright, Courtni Crump. JOURNEY TO FREEDOM: A STORY OF THE UNDERGROUND RAIL-ROAD. New York: Holiday House, 1994. Joshua and his family, runaway slaves from a tobacco plantation in Kentucky, follow the Underground Railroad to freedom.

"During all my slave life I never lost sight of freedom. It was always on my heart; it came to me like a solemn thought, and often circumstances much stimulated the desire to be free and raised great expectation of it"— *Ambrose Headen, born 1822, enslaved in North Carolina and Alabama.*

Index

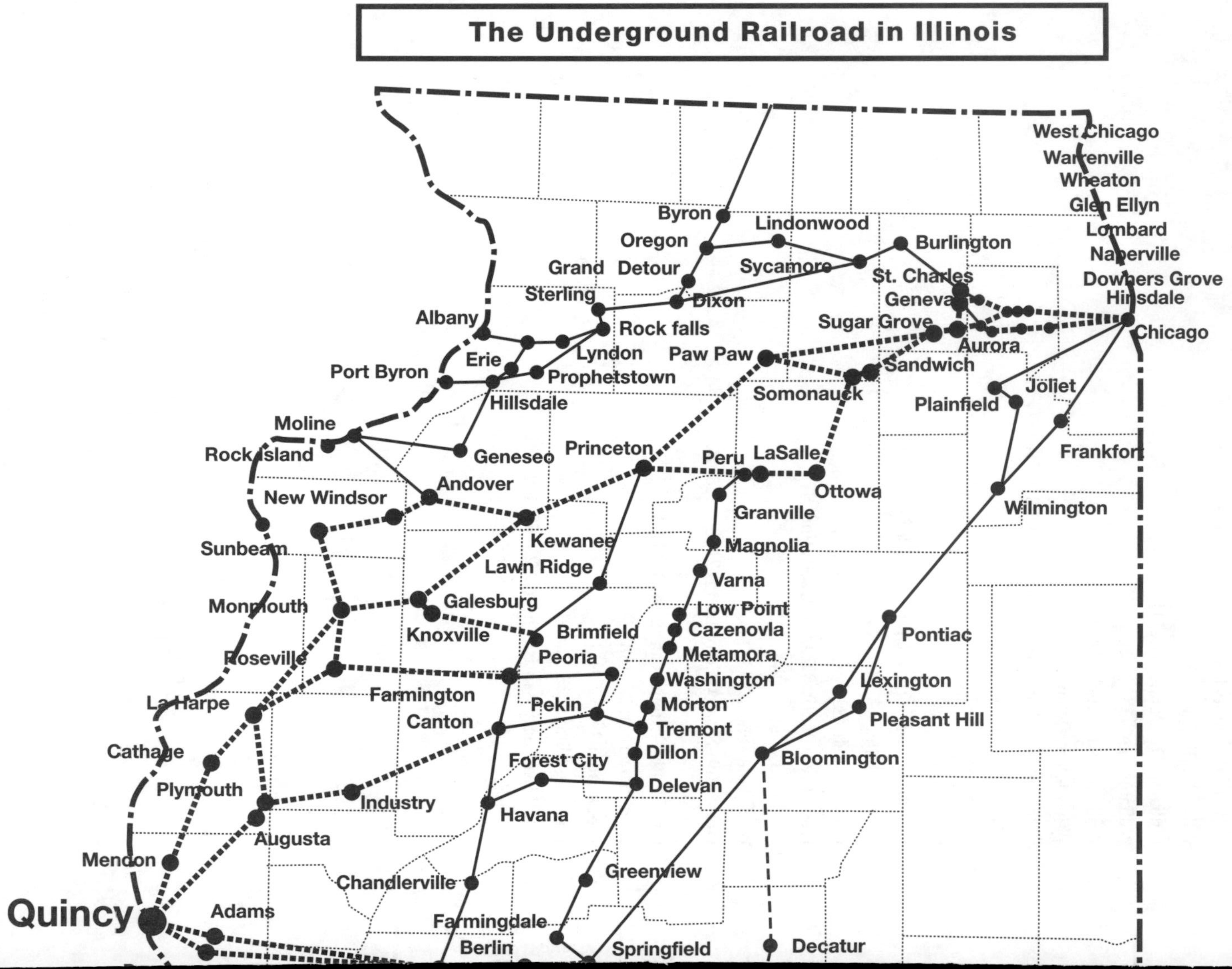
The Underground Railroad in Illinois
West Chicago
Warrenville
Wheaton
Glen Ellyn
Lombard
Naperville
Downers Grove
Hinsdale
Chicago
Byron
Lindonwood
Oregon
Burlington
Grand Detour
Sycamore
St. Charles
Sterling
Dixon
Geneva
Albany
Rock falls
Sugar Grove
Lyndon
Paw Paw
Aurora
Erie
Sandwich
Port Byron
Prophetstown
Somonauck
Jöliet
Hillsdale
Plainfield
Moline
Rock Island
Geneseo
Princeton
Peru
LaSalle
Frankfort
Andover
Ottowa
New Windsor
Wilmington
Granville
Sunbeam
Kewanee
Magnolia
Lawn Ridge
Varna
Monmouth
Galesburg
Low Point
Cazenovla
Knoxville
Brimfield
Pontiac
Metamora
Roseville
Peoria
Washington
Farmington
Lexington
La Harpe
Pekin
Morton
Canton
Tremont
Pleasant Hill
Cathage
Dillon
Bloomington
Forest City
Plymouth
Delevan
Industry
Havana
Augusta
Mendon
Greenview
Chandlerville
Quincy
Adams
Farmingdale
Berlin
Springfield
Decatur

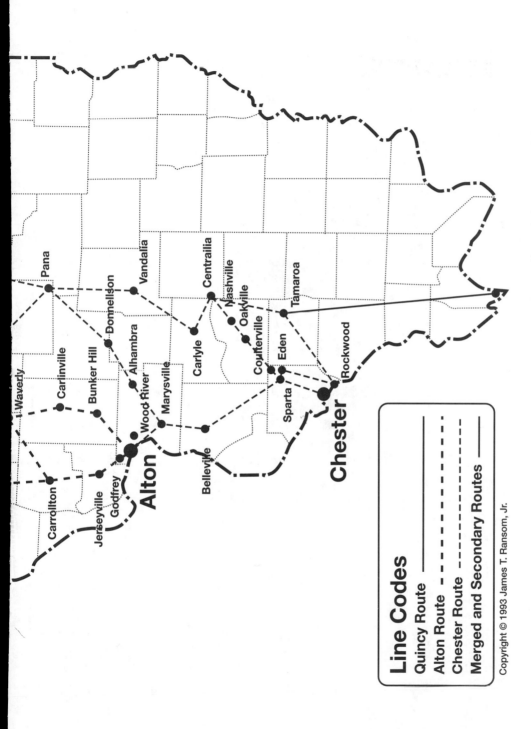

Waverly
Pana
Carlinville
Donnellson
Bunker Hill
Vandalia
Alhambra
Centrailia
Wood River
Marysville
Nashville
Carlyle
Oakville
Coulterville
Carrollton
Jerseyville
Godfrey
Alton
Eden
Sparta
Tamaroa
Belleville
Rockwood
Chester

Line Codes
Quincy Route ——————
Alton Route – – – – – –
Chester Route –·–·–·–·
Merged and Secondary Routes ——————

Copyright © 1993 James T. Ransom, Jr.

SAMUEL HARPER AND WIFE,

OF WINDSOR, ONTARIO,

the two survivors of the company of slaves abducted by John
Brown from Missouri in the winter of 1858–1859.

(From a recent photograph.)

*Courtesy of the DuSable Museum of
African American History*

Glennette Turner's book, THE UNDERGROUND RAILROAD IN ILLINOIS, is a wonderful resource tool for teachers that could be useful in a variety of ways. This book will enhance literature studies related to the Underground Railroad, Civil War history, as well as women's rights.

Barbara Campbell, Fourth Grade Teacher
Pleasant Hill, Wheaton

Glennette Turner's THE UNDERGROUND RAILROAD IN ILLINOIS is more conclusive evidence that she is one of America's foremost teachers and historians of the Underground Railroad. Indeed, more than other writers on the topic, she thoroughly understands the Underground Railroad's deeper meanings for the American story, especially its heroic dimensions, and she has dedicated her literary life to making the Underground Railroad a familiar part of our collective past.

Dr. Gary Smith, Department of English
DePaul University

THE UNDERGROUND RAILROAD IN ILLINOIS is a significant addition to the body of work available on this research topic. Mrs. Turner's style makes the reader feel like an eyewitness to this important story.

Marti Guarin, Charter Librarian
Illinois Math and Science Academy

Mrs. Turner has gathered and included related materials from a wide range of sources. Her book is indispensable and an invaluable contribution to current research on this most important subject. I strongly recommend, THE UNDERGROUND RAILROAD IN ILLINOIS, to any and all who seek to expand their knowledge on this subject.

Margaret Goss Burroughs, Founder, Director Emeritus
DuSable Museum of African-American History, Chicago

Glennette Turner has written a superb book. This resource not only tells the story of people and places on the Underground Railroad, it will give anyone — teacher, student or interested reader — a thorough map for the journey along the trail of this important history.

Julia Pferdehirt, Author
FREEDOM TRAIN NORTH: Stories of the Underground Railroad in Wisconsin